D0238902

Performing Violence in Contemporary Ireland

Performing Violence in Contemporary Ireland

Edited by Lisa Fitzpatrick

Carysfort Press

A Carysfort Press Book

Performing Violence in Contemporary Ireland
Edited by Lisa Fitzpatrick

First published as a paperback in Ireland in 2010 by
Carysfort Press Ltd
58 Woodfield
Scholarstown Road
Dublin 16
Ireland

ISBN 978-1-904505-44-0

Typeset by Carysfort Press Ltd

Printed and bound by eprint limited
Unit 35
Coolmine Industrial Estate
Dublin 15
Ireland

Cover design by Alan Bennis

This book is published with the financial assistance of
The Arts Council (An Chomhairle Ealaíon) Dublin, Ireland

Contents

Acknowledgements

This book emerged from a symposium on the performance of violence on the contemporary Irish stage that was convened by Drama at the School of Creative Arts at the University of Ulster in Derry, in November 2006, and generously supported by the University's Humanities Research Institute. The symposium raised and discussed issues that ranged from the significance of silence in the performance of violence to the representation of violence in music and registers of speech, to technical problems of performing the work of 'in-yer-face' playwrights like Martin McDonagh, and I would like to thank all the speakers for their thought-provoking contributions to this project. I would also like to thank my colleagues, Carole-Anne Upton, Tom Maguire, and Paul Devlin, all of whom have contributed in various ways.

As editor I would like to offer my sincere thanks to the contributors for their valuable interventions into this important topic. My thanks to the publishers, particularly to Eamonn Jordan for his support throughout the process: Alan Bennis: Chris McCallion: and the colleagues and students at the School of Creative Arts whose input and critiques were invaluable.

1 | Introduction:
Performing Violence in Contemporary Ireland

Lisa Fitzpatrick

The performance of violence on stage has concerned theatre practitioners and theorists since Aristotle, with the concept of decorum,
borrowed from his *Poetics* and developed by Horace and by
Renaissance scholars like Castelvetro, Scaliger and Robortello, still
often referenced in contemporary scholarship. Yet stage decorum is
more often honoured in the breach than in the observance,
particularly in the Anglophone theatre tradition to which Irish
theatre largely belongs. Scenes of violence are commonplace from
the enactments of the scourging and crucifixion in the medieval
Mystery Cycles to the In-Yer-Face movement, and more or less
graphic representations of murder, rape and torture can be found, in
both comedies and tragedies, throughout theatre history. This
tradition gives contemporary playwrights like Martin McDonagh,
Conor McPherson, Gary Mitchell, and Martin Lynch, amongst
others whose work is discussed here, a long and rich theatrical
genealogy. Yet the problems of performing and witnessing violence
are rarely explored. How are acts of violence represented
mimetically and diegetically on the Irish stage, and in what ways
and why are those representations limited? What are the ethical
issues involved in representing violence? How is it received?

'Performance' as defined here, though, is not limited to the
theatrical, but is based instead on Richard Schechner's 'Seven
Functions of Performance'. Schechner lists, 'to entertain: to make
something that is beautiful: to mark or change identity: to make or
foster community: to heal: to teach, persuade, or convince: to deal
with the sacred and/or the demonic' (46). He visualizes

performance as both a fan and a web, composed of and incorporating a variety of human activity including, crucially, the 'eruption and resolution of crisis', 'ritualization', and 'rites, ceremonies' (2005, xvi). This book is divided into two main sections, the first of which deals primarily with theatrical performance, the second with place and space. This structure is not intended to be restrictive, however: the essays speak to each other across both parts of the collection. In different ways, they explore a range of aspects of performance in relation to violence, asking, what is the role of space and place? And where do public street performances such as processions, parades, and commemorative rituals fit into the Irish Republic as it nears the centenary of 1916, and the emerging post-Ceasefire society in Northern Ireland?

Danine Farquharson's essay *Pity vs Fear*, which opens this collection, identifies three main discourses of violence: Arendt, who argues that violence is arbitrary, and vastly under-examined: Deleuze, arguing that it is unfathomable and 'does not speak', and Bowman, who defines it as that which disturbs the sacred by breaking into 'an integral space'. This ripping of the sacred into the open is what connects Arendt's conception of violence as arbitrary and Deleuze's as unfathomable: we cannot predict the outcome: the results of violence are tangible but the violence itself is not. For Farquharson, *The Oresteia* is a performative theorizing of violence, and that trilogy, together with Carr's intertextual *Ariel*, forms the primary material for her discussion.

Also, returning to Greek tragedy, but this time to Heaney's translations, Eugene O'Brien explores the intimate relationship between violence and justice, quoting Derrida's argument that the founding moment of law is a 'performative and interpretative violence':

> how to distinguish between the force of law [loi] of a legitimate power and the allegedly originary violence that must have established this authority and that could not itself have authorized itself by an anterior legitimacy so that, in this initial moment, it is neither legal nor illegal, just nor unjust (234).

Analyzing Heaney's *The Burial at Thebes* (based on *Antigone*) and *The Cure at Troy* (based on *Philoctetes*), O'Brien's essay examines the poet-playwright's aesthetic, ethical, and political engagement with the violence in Northern Ireland.

It is not surprising that a number of essays address recent and historical political and cultural developments in Northern Ireland, post-Ceasefire. Paul Devlin's essay *Restaging Violence* provocatively suggests a revisioning of Martin Lynch's *The Interrogation of Ambrose Fogarty* to address a contemporary iconography of terrorism and human rights abuses, as the work nears its thirtieth anniversary. Using Foucault's and Soja's concepts of heterotopia and 'Thirdspace', he examines the dramaturgical implications of dislocating *Fogarty* from its original socio-political and spatial context to restage it as an essentially new theatrical event. Devlin argues that such productions or revivals may 'create sites to stage heterotopic crises', to situate the spectatorship in new, panoptic relationships to contemporary crises. Lisa Fitzpatrick's essay considers three recent productions as examples of the utopian performative, in which the audience affectively experience moments of intersubjective connectedness, that allow glimpses of other possibilities. The productions under discussion are all rooted in sites or landscapes of cultural and historical significance, their 'haunted' status contributing to the experience of shared history and memory among the spectators. The essay considers ways in which theatre in Northern Ireland has been engaging with experiences of trauma, violence and grief as the post-Ceasefire society continues to take shape.

Alongside Devlin's and Fitzpatrick's address to spectatorship, essays by Tom Maguire, Paul Moore, and Cormac Newark all address another element of the reception process: the aural. Moore's paper proposes that the auditory is at least as important as the visual in his exploration of the work of 1950s comedian James Young, whose radio performances engaged with the 'sonic ecology' of Belfast and Northern Ireland to conjure a range of characters, both male and female. Young's denunciation of sectarianism is problematized by Moore in his analysis, as it both issues a demand to 'stap fightin' while, in performance, representing Catholics as 'Other' to normative Northern Irish Protestant identity. Cormac Newark explores the representation of violence in music. Ian Wilson's opera *Hamelin*, staged by Opera Theatre Company in Dublin in 2003, tells the story of the *Pied Piper*, but with dark intimations that the violent trauma of the story is more domestic and intimate than the tale of the Piper suggests. Newark analyzes the musical score and libretto to identify the methods by which 'the repressed violence of Hamelin's recent history' is represented to the audience. Tom Maguire's essay on speaking violence in Conor McPherson's monodramas also addresses the issue of what is heard.

Both *Rum and Vodka* and *The Good Thief* contain scenes of extraordinary violence, but these are spoken by the solo performer rather than enacted under the spectator's gaze. Maguire explores the role of silence in the ethical representation of diegetic violence, noting that silence can mark the unsayable, the inexpressible: and its importance in allowing the audience time to reflect. These moments of reflection allow the audience to engage imaginatively with the horrors that they do not directly witness.

This question of the ethical dimensions of representing violence recurs in a number of essays in various forms. In addition to Maguire's exploration of the role of silence, and Devlin's evocation of the irruption of the 'Real' in the form of images of Abu Ghraib and of the War on Terror, Catherine Rees raises the problem of laughter as a method of confusing 'the audience's normative and conventional ethical standards', and Tim Miles looks at the work of Gary Mitchell as counter-narrative to the hegemonic metanarrative of the Peace Process. Defining counter-narrative with reference to Molly Andrews' critical writing, Miles recognizes it as an unstable category in which the categories of dominant and resistant are multi-layered and constantly shifting. He considers Mitchell's writing as counter-hegemonic in the light of a post-colonial narrative of the movement from war to peace, and in relation to the dominant images of Loyalism in the contemporary mass media. Also addressing images of the Northern Irish troubles, Rees's essay examines the notion of the 'conceivable but not representable' in Martin McDonagh's *Lieutenant of Inishmore*. It traces the processes involved in creating terror and fear of violence in the audience, and the extent to which the realization of the violence alters the dynamic amongst the spectators and can give rise to the comedic. Kyna Hamill's essay also draws upon *Lieutenant*, this time to address representations of urban and rural violence in Irish theatre, culture and film. Hamill argues that violence has been manifested using a limited number of contrasting representations: namely, the stylized, urban depictions of violence in the struggle for independence, and brutal rural brawls. Citing Synge, Behan, Keane and McCaffrey in support of her argument, she explores the reception of violence and the limits of representation.

David Grant's essay, like Paul Devlin's, invokes the panopticon. This case study in prison theatre also draws on Boal's 'Rainbow of Desire' technique to explore the experience of the prisoner-participants and the visiting practitioners in the rehearsal and performance of Frank McGuinness's *Observe the Sons of Ulster* at Hydebank Young Offenders' Centre. Considering the framing of the performance within the prison community, the life experiences of the prisoners, and their family relationships, Grant examines the transformative possibilities that prevent this kind of work from being more than a 'public performance of punishment'.

The final three essays in the collection – by Jonathan Harden, Holly Maples, and Kris Brown and Elisabetta Viggiani – address public performances in the form of protest marches, commemorations and parades. Harden's essay engages with the concept of space as victim, in a substitution of Brook's space of performance for Riches' second performer. Arguing from Riches, Certeau, and Foucault, it reads the Civil Rights marches in Derry and Belfast as symbolic representations of violence, stating, 'all acts of procession ... have the potential to be redrafted as violence ... Civil Rights marches represent symbolically other forms of violence being visited upon the protestors and those they represent.' Holly Maples' essay also examines processions and parades, but this time in their commemorative function, using the memorial celebrations of the Easter Rising and of the Battle of the Somme in Dublin in 2006. Maples reads these commemorations against Roach's notion of surrogation and Anderson's work on community formation, arguing that their original function is displaced as they are read instead as celebrations of the economic prosperity of the time and Ireland's European identity: 'as performative acts of both collective cultural identity and pastness'. Finally, Brown and Viggiani explore the performance of Provisional IRA identity through the deliberate use of public ritual, which is ironically but consciously shaped by British commemorative practice. The essay offers two case studies: Tom Williams, and the 25th anniversary of the Hunger Strikes. The paper argues that memorials 'function as theatrical backdrops for ritual performance, defining its spatial boundaries and agencies'.

There are, of course, gaps in the collection. Tellingly, there is no sustained engagement with representations of domestic violence and rape. While such acts of violence are not absent from the stage, they tend not to be the main focus of the dramatic action. In addition, they are often framed so that they communicate metaphorically: thus, the domestic violence in Daragh Carville's *Family Plot* refers to the sectarian violence in Northern Ireland: it functions primarily on that level, and the woman's subjective experience is not heard. Conor McPherson's play *The Good Thief* suggests the rape of the kidnapped woman and her child, in a brief though chilling moment. Even Marina Carr, whose work is known for its representation of family violence, creates characters that signify on the level of the mythic rather than as politicized engagements with domestic abuse as a social or gender issue. Other further areas for research include the reflections of directors, choreographers, and performers on their experiences of engagement through practice with the topic. However, this collection is intended as an early intervention into a key aspect of contemporary performance in Ireland: it aims to raise questions and open debates for further scholarship.

Bibliography

Derrida, J., 'The Force of Law' in *Acts of Religion* ed. Gil Anidjar (London: Routledge, 2002)

Schechner, R., *Performance Studies* (New York: Routledge, 2002)

---, *Performance Theory* (New York: Routledge, 2005)

Part I: The Spoken Word, Music, and Spectacle

2 | Pity vs. Fear: Performing Violence in Aeschylus' *Oresteia* and Contemporary Irish Drama

Danine Farquharson

> Human beings suffer.
> They torture one another.
> They get hurt and get hard.
> No poem or play or song
> Can fully right a wrong
> Inflicted and endured (Seamus Heaney, *Voices from Lemnos*).

There is no doubt that Irish writers have engaged, adapted, played with and embodied the characters, themes and plots of great texts of ancient Greece and Rome. Stephen Dedalus wonders which of Aristotle or Plato 'would have me banished from his commonwealth' (Joyce 238). Jimmy Jack entertains a fantasy life with the goddess Athene – 'them flashing eyes would fair keep a man jigged up constant!' (Friel 5). Cassandra speaks anew and newly Irish in 'Mycenae Lookout' – 'in she went / to the knife, / to the killer wife' (Heaney, 390). However, as distinguished Heaney critic Helen Vendler points out, Seamus Heaney's 'unsettling and surprising transformation' of Aeschylus' *Oresteia* into the five-poem sequence 'Mycenae Lookout' is 'a totally unexpected move ... of unprecedented linguistic violence' (181). Vendler's wonder results from what she rightly sees as Seamus Heaney's ability to take 'seriously the violence of Aeschylus' own language, in which words of sexual violation and words of bloodshed interchange so rapidly that the two categories are shaken into a single dark emulsion' (187). But more relevant to the discussion of this essay, Vendler also sees a particular moment in contemporary Irish history as allowing Heaney the chance to unleash his 'hitherto pent-up historical anger'

(183). Following the 1994 cease-fire in Northern Ireland, Heaney begins to express, 'for the first time, a full-voiced anger against the prolonged carnage that took away from him, as from others in Northern Ireland, the possibility of a normal life' (186). The rage and suffering of the artist finds partial voice in the linguistic articulation of violence. What is striking for me, in a consideration of violence on the stage, is that of all the Greek tragedies and mythic paradigms available to Irish authors it is only Seamus Heaney and, more recently, playwright Marina Carr who look closely to Aeschylus' *Oresteia*. Both Heaney and Carr come to the *Oresteia* sideways – approaching the bloodletting of the house of Atreus and the culminating system of justice from oblique angles. Rejecting the primacy of the chorus and Clytemnestra in Aeschylus's tragedy, Heaney uses the watchman and Cassandra (who dies in the first play of the trilogy) as key voices. Carr's *Ariel* is a mixture of Euripides' *Electra* and the *Oresteia*. Neither artist employs the same adaptive gestures as Tom Paulin's *The Riot Act*, Aiden Carl Mathews' *Antigone* or Brendan Kennelly's *Antigone*. Why? Because Aeschylus's plays are about violence itself – its motivations, effects, causes, and ramifications.

This essay will begin with the question of why the *Oresteia*, compared to *Antigone* for example, is relatively ignored by Irish playwrights when they turn to the classics for adaptation. Following a brief discussion of adaptations of Greek plays that do exist and the themes and issues that draw Irish artists to the classics, the following discussion will offer a way of theorizing violence, then an analysis of how Aeschylus' trilogy performs violence with comparative notes toward Marina Carr's *Ariel*. My theory has something to do with performing violence in the classical tradition as well as what I see as Aeschylus' treatment of violence itself – a treatment that makes his trilogy not immediately or obviously applicable to the history of 'prolonged carnage' in Ireland.

In *Dying Acts: Death in Ancient Greek Tragedy and Modern Irish Tragic Drama*, Fiona Macintosh makes a point worth repeating: 'there are many points of contact between ancient Greece and modern Ireland and these have been highlighted and debated from at least the Middle Ages onwards' (xvii). Indeed, Declan Kiberd opens his introduction to an excellent collection on just this topic, *Amid Our Troubles: Irish Versions of Greek Tragedy*, with the same idea: 'As early as the twelfth century, the first Irish-language translation of Virgil, *Imtheachta Aeniasa*, made its appearance: and thereafter texts abounded with comparisons between local heroes and Aeneas, local beauties and Helen, local scholars and Ennius' (vii). While it doesn't take much imagination to suggest why any person, community, or culture would want to use the ancients as paradigmatic ancestors, it is more interesting to consider which of the ancient texts bear the most frequent adaptation or translation. In the case of contemporary Irish theatre, it seems the Antigones and Medeas and Iphigenias far outweigh the Agamemnons.

Colin Teevan and J. Michael Walton have done admirable work on tracking and assessing recent translations of Greek tragedies onto the Irish stage,[1] and reach astute conclusions that are relevant to this discussion. Working with previous studies by Marianne McDonald and Anthony Roche,[2] Teevan reads the 'veritable explosion' of Irish versions of Greek tragedies in Northern Ireland in 1984 primarily through the lens of identity politics, concentrating on the role of female protagonists (78-79). Teevan argues that binaries such as Britain/Ireland, authority/victim, colonizer/colonized are not enough to 'do justice to the intricacies' of debates over identity, and that gender must be included in discourse (78). Thus, Teevan correctly characterizes certain Greek plays as appealing to the dramatic potential of the 'woman-in-opposition-to-authority' (81). *The Trojan Women*, *Medea*, and *Antigone* all make for obviously fruitful source texts. He ends his article on a note that is germane to my discussion of violence and Aeschylus:

> When the Abbey Theatre first approached me to translate a Greek tragedy I was sorely tempted to suggest *The Oresteia* – what translator of Greek would not? To the best of my knowledge it has never received a main stage production in Ireland, while it is regularly produced in Britain. Somehow, however, I could not get a handle on it. It seemed inappropriate to the Irelands I was living in, being ultimately an assertion of a society's unity and shared values. (86)

---

[1] Teevan's article, 'Northern Ireland: Our Troy? Recent Versions of Greek Tragedies by Irish Writers' and Walton's 'Hit or Myth: the Greeks and Irish Drama' in *Amid Our Troubles* not only track various recent Irish translations (with Teevan concentrating on Northern Ireland) but they also offer insights into the possible political and cultural reasons as to why. Both works are essential reading for this topic.

[2] Marianne McDonald, 'When Despair and History Rhyme,' *New Hibernia Review* 1.2 (1997): 57-70 and Anthony Roche, 'Ireland's *Antigones*: Tragedy North and South,' *Cultural Contexts and Literary Idioms in Contemporary Irish Literature*, ed. Michael Kenneally (Gerrard's Cross, 1988): 221-50.

J. Michael Walton may come close to articulating the difficulty of getting a 'handle on' the *Oresteia* that prevented Teevan from translating the plays to the Irish stage. Walton writes that although 'issues of loyalty and betrayal, the conflicts of order and anarchy, the imperatives of duty and instinct ... still live and breathe' through Aeschylus' trilogy, there remains the paradox of 'the resolution of the unresolvable' (13)[3]. Walton sees the irresolvable problem in the Oresteia as 'should you punish or applaud a man who avenges his father by killing his mother?' (13) – and that question is undeniably vexed. However, as I will argue later in this paper, Aeschylus does resolve that problem through the intervention of the gods and, as Walton also notes, the introduction of a democratic system. Therefore, what I see as the source of the difficulty in the *Oresteia*, that problem of resolving the irresolvable, is actually the difficulty and problem of understanding and performing violence.

Theorizing Violence

In 1969 Hannah Arendt published a special supplement for *The New York Review of Books* titled 'Reflections on Violence' in which she claims that 'no one concerned with history and politics can remain unaware of the enormous role violence has always played in human affairs: and it is at first glance rather surprising that violence is so seldom singled out for special consideration ... no one questions or examines what is obvious to all' (2). Arendt's essay, a version of which would later be published in book form as *On Violence*, is timely: she speaks to the May 1968 uprisings, the assassination of Bobby Kennedy and the war in Vietnam. And while the driving force behind the article is to show the wrong-headedness of the 'new left's' embrace of violence as both an end in itself and as a means toward change, she is convincing in her assertion that theorists of the political right and left are wrong in equating violence with power. Under Arendt's analysis, violence is always instrumental in the service of power, violence can destroy power, but it cannot create power (11). For all her provocative beginnings ('no one has done this before'), Arendt is more concerned with reconceptualizing power in a nuclear age than with violence *per se*.

---

3 In 'The Irish and Greek Tragedy' Marianne McDonald writes that 'Aeschylus' Oresteia appealed to [poet Louis] MacNeice for its acceptance of authority, reverence for the gods, and respect for the state' (44).

However, her most useful observation about violence is its unpredictability: 'all violence harbours within itself an element of arbitrariness.' What is striking about Arendt's essay for the purposes of the discussion to follow is twofold: firstly, that there is something 'obvious' about violence that often leaves it unexamined: and secondly, that violence is also uncontrollable, erratic, even chaotic. Unexamined, destructive, arbitrary: such are the elements of violence that profoundly resonate with arguably the greatest contemplation of violence, bloodletting and justice in the canon of Western Literature.

'The matter is too big for any mortal man who thinks he can judge it' (470-71).[4] So wrote the Greek tragedian Aeschylus in the final play of his *Oresteia* trilogy, *The Eumenides*. The 'matter' is a violence so powerful as to destroy the balance of the cosmos and require the intervention of the gods to not only restore order but to establish a new legal system. The great chain of bloodletting and retribution that begins with the murder of Agamemnon (perhaps with the sacrifice of Iphigenia) unleashes the chthonic power of the Erinyes (or the Furies), who represent the ravished primordial scream of horror at the violent rending. A brief summary of the trilogy's plot is helpful at this stage. The first play, *Agamemnon*, depicts the victorious return of King Agamemnon to Argos following the battles at Troy, and his murder by estranged wife Clytemnestra (who cannot forgive Agamemnon for sacrificing their daughter Iphigenia to the gods to get the winds to sail to Troy) and her lover Aegisthus. The second play, *The Libation Bearers* (also referred to as *The Chorephoroi*) takes place several years later when Clytemnestra and Aegisthus have secured in their power in Argos. Clytemnestra and Agamemnon's son, Orestes, returns from exile and, disguised as a traveller, gains entrance into the palace and murders both Aegisthus and his mother. The avenging spirits of his mother, the Furies or the Erinyes, begin to haunt Orestes and 'even before the play is over, the assassin knows that his act was not the final but has created more suffering' (Lattimore 26). In the final play, *The Eumenides*, Orestes is cleared of guilt by Apollo but is still pursued by the Erinyes. One divine verdict clashes with another over guilt and retribution. The fate of Orestes thus falls into the hands of Athene and, by her will, a jury of mortal men. The jury's vote is even

---

4 All quotations from Aeschylus's *Oresteia* are from Richmond Lattimore's translation and cited by line number.

and Athene casts the decision in favour of Orestes but not before the wrathful Erinyes are invited by Athene to become new goddesses of protection over Athens – the Eumenides (the kindly ones). They accept Athene's accommodation and thus quell their wrath in favour of guardianship of the *polis*. The retributive cycle of violence that cursed the House of Atreus is thus concluded.

Aeschylus might have been the earliest but he is not the last writer to consider violence as an open wound or radical rending of the universe. There is a large and diverse literature on war and warfare from von Clausewitz to Marx and Engels to John Keegan (in the last two centuries alone), but as Arendt notes, such discussions deal with the implements of violence and not with violence as such. Here, I will argue that Aeschylus's *Oresteia* trilogy of plays – *Agamemnon, The Libation Bearers, The Eumenides* – sets out to perform what René Girard sees as the vital translation of reciprocal violence into ritualized violence. In *Violence and the Sacred*, Girard contends that the destructive nature of violence is tamed and becomes 'creative and protective in nature' when it is ritualized (144). And what is ritualized in Ancient Greece if not the performance of tragedy? Aeschylus's masterpiece, which culminates in a celebration of Athenian justice, does more than discipline the cyclical bloodletting of violent murder in the myth of the House of Atreus. His trilogy articulates what I have come to understand as the three main discourses of violence or approaches to understanding violence.[5] In this way, the *Oresteia* is definitive and fundamental to the performance of violence.

If Hannah Arendt asserts that violence is vastly under-examined, then Giles Deleuze goes one step further by claiming that violence is near unfathomable in its openness and, as such, results in silence. In his 1989 essay 'The Language of Sade and Masoch' Deleuze writes that 'in principle, violence is something that does not speak' (518). Violence may not speak, but it is profoundly spoken about, acted upon, and rendered material in its effects. In 'The Violence in Identity', Glenn Bowman succinctly outlines the etymological

---

5 The portion of this article devoted to the discourses of violence in contemporary scholarship is an expanded version of my work with Dr. Sean Farrell on *Shadows of the Gunmen: Violence and Culture in Modern Ireland*. I would like to acknowledge and thank Dr. Farrell for his contribution to these approaches to violence in historical and literary discourse. I would also like to thank Dr. George Robertson for his advice and direction in my research on Aeschylus (and his help with Ancient Greek verb tenses).

origins of the word violence to reveal that all uses of the word violence – to break, to ravish, to desecrate, to corrupt, to treat roughly, to break in upon – contain 'the concept of an integral space broken into and, through that breaking, desecrated' (25). Violence is a tearing, a rending open into the absolute. Violence is a radical space of openness that destroys the sacred and creates an imbalance and disorder. The ripping of the sacred into an open space is what Arendt sees as the element of arbitrariness, what Deleuze sees as unfathomable: we cannot predict what will happen once the violation has occurred. Because violence is an opening and is also unpredictable, then the vast majority of thinkers who seek to understand violence must deal with the tangible results of violence because those results can be, to some degree, measured, assessed and analyzed.

Approaches to understanding violence can therefore be categorized into three groups. The first approach is the philosophical, which attempts to comprehend and explain the phenomenology of violence. Several questions emerge from such an approach: does violence have meaning? What is the manifestation of violence? What is the unique structure of the existence of violence? The philosophical approach illuminates the concept of violence but does not necessarily address its materiality. Hannah Arendt is an obviously crucial thinker in this arena, but more recent contributions also exist.[6] Beatrice Hanssen's *Critique of Violence: Between Poststructuralism and Critical Theory* weaves philosophy with political theory and comparative literature to see how these discourses can address the idea of violence and the language of violence. Significantly, hers is a cross-disciplinary approach. Hanssen is one among many contemporary thinkers who recognize that no single discursive mode will adequately answer any of the questions relating to violence. In a similar way, it is only by taking all three plays of the *Oresteia* together that an understanding of Aeschylus's philosophy of violence can be understood. As I shall articulate later, it is in his depiction of the Erinyes that Aeschylus makes material the concept of violence and he only does so in relation to justice.

---

[6] However, in 'Philosophy and its Other – Violence: A Survey of Philosophical Repression from Plato to Girard', Tobin Siebers argues that not only does the phenomenon of violence remain 'virtually untouched as a philosophical subject' but that philosophy actually represses violence (1-2).

The second approach is the ethical or judicial. This discourse is concerned with questions of the legitimacy and necessity of violence: under what circumstances is violence acceptable? What are the legal and social consequences of unacceptable violence? The modern library on the legitimacy of violence arguably begins with Walter Benjamin's 1921 'Critique of Violence' and his questioning of whether violence can be a just or unjust means to an end. Other contemporary contributors to this discussion include Michel Foucault's study of power and the modern prison in *Discipline and Punish* and legal theorist Cass Sunstein's analysis in 'Is Violent Speech a Right?' of the political ramifications of violence in relation to freedom of speech. Such considerations are concerned with the state and with authority – how bodies of law and order structure a community that must deal with violence in relation to the good. The essential problem for thinkers such as Benjamin and Sunstein is not violence so much as justice: what mechanisms can be used to protect the community from the amplification of bloodshed? The ethical/judicial approach to understanding violence acknowledges that any concept of justice or communal good must address violence in individuals, groups, and nations. *The Eumenides* is, according to more than one critic, consumed with exactly these questions of justice.

The third and final category encompasses the vast array of works that examine social or cultural aspects of violence. The ethical/legal approach can be interpreted as broadly sociological, but underpinning that approach is a philosophical concern for the good and the just. Scholars interested in the social/cultural dynamics of violence tend to engage the ways in which violence relates to other concerns: gender, class, race, and nation. By far the most diverse and widely used category of analysis in the last century, this social/cultural approach tends to narrow into particular places, times and/or events in order to tease out the various ramifications of violence for individuals and communities. In his analysis of religion and violence and the role of the sacrifice and scapegoat, René Girard is a principal twentieth century theorist in this regard. The social/cultural can also be comparative, as in Göran Aijmer and Jon Abbink's *Meanings of Violence: A Cross-Cultural Perspective*. Aijmer and Abbink believe that while 'each discipline has its own distinct contribution to make to the study of violence – the challenge, however, is to integrate some of them into a larger whole and to reshape our perception of the nature and causes or relevant

factors of violent behaviour' (7). The Ancient Greek fear of pollution
– *miasma* – as enacted in the *Oresteia* is evidence that the
social/cultural approach to violence is also at work in Aeschylus's
trilogy. As I shall discuss later, Clytemnestra's 'sacrifice' speech in
Agamemnon succinctly articulates these three approaches to
understanding violence, in particular the violent slaying of another
human being.

What connects all three modes is their discursive nature: these
are all ways of talking about and writing about violence. All these
approaches exist in the realm of the representational, but not
necessarily the performative. To return to the *Oresteia*, Aeschylus
brings the difficulties of theorizing and performing violence to bear
on the House of Atreus. When the goddess Athene is called upon to
'render final judgment' in the blood for blood catastrophe of Atreus,
she not only casts a vote in support of Orestes – thereby facing the
wrath of the Erinyes, to be euphemistically renamed the Eumenides
– but she also establishes the tribunal and system of justice whereby
future decisions can be made. That a god must come down into the
realm of human beings in order to re-establish order makes clear
Aeschylus's belief that the violence of the human world will never be
abolished by human deeds. Only the absolute (as personified by the
gods) can address the absolute (the opening up that is violence).
Before the farewell to Athene, the final words of the chorus are
'Much wrong in the world is thereby healed' (987). 'Much' but by no
means all of the wrong is healed. So it is that even in this early
Western literary representation of familial, communal and national
violence, the language of violence remains open, ambivalent, and
unfinished. Violence remains at odds with order in the Aeschylean
universe and while violence cannot be eliminated or avoided, it can
be transmuted and tamed into the structures of the community.

Playing Violence in the Oresteia

The Ancient Greeks did not depict murder or bloodshed on the
stage. Because 'Greek plays dealt with the limits of human ability to
control the world, from the security of their seats, [the audience]
contemplated a world where nothing was secure' (Wiles 113).
Violence – which dramatically disturbs the 'secure' world – is not
absent from Greek theatre. Clear forms of emotional, psychological
and verbal violence are evident in Hellenistic plays. However, in the
surviving literary texts, bloody murder is notably absent and

'religious taboos may explain why in plays the act of killing is never accomplished in front of the audience, though non-violent death may occur' (Wiles 115). The standard view of why the Greeks did not perform physical violence on stage is a fear of pollution.

In his book *Miasma*, Robert Parker assesses the idea of pollution in Ancient Greece as an element of the irrational: a defilement or impairment of a thing's form or integrity that affects the killer, the victim, and the community (4). In the idea of impairment of integrity, Parker's definition of pollution is strikingly similar to the idea that violence is a violation, a crossing of a threshold or the transgression of a boundary. To defile one's integrity is violence. According to Parker, 'the unifying factor' of the violation or act of violence 'is the polluting act, which sets up a chain of abnormal relations between humans – victim, killer, associates of killer – the connecting links in which are supernatural powers' (Parker 109). 'Pollution, therefore, is not so much a rationalization as a vehicle through which social disruption is expressed ... little or none of it results from killings that are felt to be quite appropriate' (Parker 121, 124). What is important to note is that pollution, disruption and violence are interrelated. Pollution affects the murderer and the victim and the community of both in such a way as to contaminate or defile that which is sacred or healthy. In another striking similarity between pollution and violence, one act tends to lead to another: 'Orestes in the *Oresteia*, although he is driven to matricide by the fear of one pollution, is seized by another after performing [murder]' (Parker 1). Both violence and the pollution it engenders are uncontrollable and compulsively repetitive, and it is little wonder that such forces provoke fear and loathing in the Greek world.

Marina Carr's 2002 play, *Ariel*, is constructed to provoke fear and horror: the *Oresteia* is constructed to provoke pity and wonder from the process of attending a tragic spectacle. This difference is vitally important in light of the performance of violence. Using Aristotle's *Poetics*, Fiona Macintosh writes '*Pathos*, in Aristotle's definition, is a destructive or painful action, examples of which are deaths on the stage. ... Aristotle claims that pity and fear may be evoked by spectacle (*opsis*), but insists that this is an inferior dramaturgical device ... to resort to visual manifestations of suffering alone is to run the risk of providing cheap thrills' (126). I am not suggesting that Carr's play is 'cheap', but I am arguing that her use of violence in *Ariel* is for radically different reasons than

Aeschylus' desire to avoid purely fearful reactions to his tragedy. Carr translates *Agamemnon* into a contemporary family drama, and so the killing of the 'king' on stage has a performative logic. Aeschylus was struggling with the paradox of the unending nature of violence and the thrust of society toward law and order. Bloodshed on his stage would defeat his purpose. Bloodshed on her stage is part of her purpose.

Interestingly, there are exceptions to the apparent rule in Greek theatre that violence is not to be performed on stage, the most notable being Ajax's suicide in Sophocles' eponymous play. As Easterling notes in 'Form and Performance' there are only four stage deaths in the surviving plays of ancient Greece: Ajax's suicide, the non-violent deaths of Alcestis and Hippolytus in *Suppliant Women* and the 'mysterious suicide of Evadne in *Suppliant Women*' (154). Further, these deaths are in 'stark contrast to the many offstage bloody deaths' and so Easterling asks: 'Was this because dramatists were under constraint, inhibited by religious scruples, or consideration of taste from showing what they would have liked to show, or aware, perhaps, that a brilliantly told (and mimed?) narrative might be more easily 'read' in a large open-air theatre than a piece of realistic stage business?' (154). Easterling goes on to assert that violent deaths, while not acted upon stage, are in fact narrated in great detail. Peter Burian supplements this idea in his 'Myth into *muthos*: the shaping of tragic plot' by noting the importance of how confrontations in Greek tragedy are verbal: 'the threat of physical violence is one of tragedy's important verbal tools, and in general what we may call verbal violence is a regular feature of tragic discourse ... Words are tools of power ... The power of such words is not easily controlled, and it should come as no surprise that their effects are often dramatically opposed to what the speaker intended or the hearer understood' (Burian 199-200). Here again is the element of the uncontrollable. Violence, pollution, and now confrontational (violent) language all have an arbitrariness that – in these critic's reconstruction of the Ancient Greek mind at least – is not only terrifying but also in need of structure. In a paradoxical way, Aeschylus uses one of these uncontrollable elements in order to control the other two. Language becomes the domain of violence and pollution. It is in the spoken word that violence is performed and thus contained.

One example of what Easterling refers to as a 'brilliantly told narrative' of violence is in *Agamemnon*, where the king's death is actually 'played' three times. Easterling notes 'the intricacy with which the violent events are thus "orchestrated" suggests that in avoiding direct presentation of the moment of killing or violent wounding the dramatists were making creative choices for positive reasons' (154). This sentiment echoes that of René Girard – the ritualization of violence gives it potentially positive and constructive qualities. The first 1000 lines of the play are devoted to anxious and foreboding language worrying about the violence to come. However, the first 'orchestration of violence' is in the language of Cassandra's visions:

> What is this new and huge
> stroke of atrocity she plans within the house
> to beat down the beloved beyond hope of healing? (1101-1104)

Anticipating the 'stroke' of death as well as the wound which will be difficult, if not impossible, to heal, Cassandra's prophesy is quickly realized. About 300 lines later, the audience hears the second telling of violence in Agamemnon's offstage cries of agony, not once but twice: 'Ah, I am struck a deadly blow and deep within!' (1343) and 'I am wounded twice' (1345). Clytemnestra herself speaks the third narration of the king's murder in her 'sacrifice speech.' In this verbal description of the killings (of both Agamemnon and his lover-prophetess Cassandra) the bloodied bodies of the victims would be displayed on stage, but not the deadly blows (Easterling 155). Clytemnestra's speech is worth quoting at length:

> I stand now where I struck him down. The thing is done.
> Thus have I wrought, and I will not deny it now.
> That he might not escape nor beat aside his death,
> as fishermen cast their huge circling nets, I spread
> deadly abundance of rich robes, and caught him fast.
> I struck him twice. In two great cries of agony
> he buckled at the knees and fell. When he was down
> I struck him of the third blow, in thanks and reverence
> to Zeus the lord of dead men underneath the ground.
> Thus he went down, and the life struggled out of him: and
> as he died he spattered me with the dark red
> and violent driven rain of bitter savored blood
> to make me glad, as gardens stand among the showers
> of God in glory at the birthtime of the buds.
> These being the facts, elders of Argos assembled here,
> be glad, if it be your pleasure: but for me, I glory (1379-1394).

The chorus responds: 'We stand here stunned' (1399). Who could blame them? Of course they are stunned. Clytemnestra has killed the king. She is arrogantly bragging about it and claiming allegiance with Zeus in her actions. The relish with which she describes the deed – 'violent driven rain of bitter savored blood' – is important in that she clearly expresses Parker's idea that the violent act pollutes both the victim and the perpetrator. Clytemnestra savours the blood of Agamemnon because it is her bitterness over his sacrifice of Iphigenia that motivates her crime. Clytemnestra's descriptive language is potent in its use of imagery and it is impossible to quarrel with Easterling that such verbal representations of violence have as much if not more power than a realistic action.

The vividness of Clytemnestra's speech is not merely articulated through metaphor and imagery but also through Aeschylus's use of verb tenses. In the original Greek, Clytemnestra's telling of the murder mixes the past and present tenses. 'I struck' and 'have I wrought' in lines 1379 and 1380 are in the past tense, as to be expected in her telling of her past actions. But in 1382-83 'I spread' and 'I struck' are in fact in the present tense in the Greek. In line 1385 'he buckled' is in the past, but the next 'I struck' is in the present tense as are 'the life struggled out' and 'he splattered'. This presentation of the strokes and the victim's struggle for his life suggests that the violence does not terminate with the action. Rather, the violence continues to be performed in the present. Further, the life is still struggling out of the kin, and the blood splatter now has a presence or life of its own. As Clytemnestra tells it, the violent actions are still occurring in the here and now. Thus, the blood becomes the polluting force to be feared and to be cleansed.[7]

The Chorus is not only stunned by the arrogance and intensity of Clytemnestra's language of violence, they are shocked by her *hybris*, which is also linked to violence. According to N. R. E. Fisher, '*hybris* is essentially the serious assault on the honour of another, which is likely to cause shame, and lead to anger and attempts at revenge. *Hybris* is often, but by no means necessarily, an act of violence: it is essentially deliberate activity' (1). In this formulation, *hybris* may or may not be an 'act' of violence, but it is always an 'assault.' Fisher is

---

[7] I also agree with the way in which Fiona Macintosh reads Clytemnestra's speech 'Couched in the language of fertility ritual – a travesty of striking proportions – her account of Agamemnon's murder exudes a sexual energy worthy of the Marquis de Sade' (84).

arguing against the traditional view that *hybris* is more a personality trait that speaks of a mortal who forgets the limitations of mortality and seeks to be godlike or to compete with the gods. That traditional view is presented by Douglas L. Cairns's rebuttal of Fisher: '*hybris* must be defined in terms of an intention to insult a specific victim' (2). Whatever the case, for my purposes Clytemnestra's *hybris* is clearly a violation. Her actions are an act of violence in three ways: she violates honour with her intention to kill, she violates the King's bodily integrity and she violates the King's social and political position. Thus, Clytemnestra's murder of Agamemnon is necessarily complicated and should not be read as a single act. She has polluted the palace and by extension the entire state of Argos: she has played the murder with amazing clarity and vividity in the shifting of verb tenses: and she violates again in her language of *hybris* and invocation of Zeus as her ally. I agree with Easterling that the reason Aeschylus 'plays' Agamemnon's death three times in this one performance is to 'draw attention to the problematic nature of violent deeds' (155). Violence is far too complex to be performed with a simple sword blow.

And yet, Marina Carr does not hold any blows in her depiction of Frances' killing of Fermoy (her Clytemnestra and Agamemnon) in *Ariel*. In the final scene of Act Two, Fermoy offers an explanation to Frances for why he killed their daughter years ago (power and ambition), Frances wails in grief ('*weeping like we've never seen, stands there heaving and choking and wailing*' the stage directions tell us) and then the murder:

> **FRANCES**. ... Where is she? (*Stabs him*)
> **FERMOY**. (*Reels*) Frances.
> **FRANCES**. (*Another stab*) Where is she?
> **FERMOY**. You think you can do away wud me ... Gimme thah.
> *A struggle. FRANCES stabs him again.*
> **FRANCES**. And you thought I was afraid a the knife. (*Another stab*) Where is she?
> **FERMOY**. (*Falls to the ground. She gets on top of him*) No ... Frances ... no ... Stop ... stop ...
> **FRANCES**. And did you stop when Ariel cried ouh for mercy? Did ya?
> Tell me where she is.
> **FERMOY**. This wasn't ... this ... Sweet God in your ...
> **FRANCES**. Tell me. Where is she?
> **FERMOY**. (*Whispers as he dies*) Cuura Lake.
> **FRANCES**. Cuura Lake.

She throws down the knife. 'Mors et Vita' music, and blackout
(59-60).

Unlike Clytemnestra, who has nearly a decade to plan her murder with precision, Frances slays her husband in the fury and heat of the moment upon learning their daughter has been killed by the father. Carr has four fatal blows struck at Fermoy, not Aeschylus' ritualized three strikes, and Frances desperately seeks knowledge of the daughter's location whereas Clytemnestra seeks vengeance and power.

In her review of the Abbey Theatre's 2002 production of *Ariel*, Marianne McDonald makes clear that Carr is drawing on several Greek tragedies, in addition to Shakespeare, for her play and not solely the *Oresteia* (www.didaskalia.net). McDonald also notes the affinities that do exist between *Ariel* and the *Oresteia* (red carpets, cycles of bloodletting) as well as divergences, such as the portrayal of Electra. In McDonald's opinion, *Ariel* fails to live up to its theatrical ancestors and, while my assessment is from the published text alone, I agree. In particular, McDonald's critique concerning violence parallels with my own belief that Carr wanted to inspire fear and loathing and not pity or sympathy in her audience:

> the greatest difference between the Greek tragedies which seem to have inspired this play, is that even in Euripides' darkest vision, he creates some audience identification with or sympathy for the characters. There was also some underlying sense of ethics involved and a sense of hope at the end by virtue of the characters of human beings who survive the worst that the gods send to them. One is at a loss to find that in Carr's play ... I left Ariel not renewed as I do after Greek tragedy, but disgusted at the gratuitous violence, pretentiousness, the banal dialogue ... It is a pity when Greek tragedy that showed violence offstage is flouted to pander to a modern taste for violence. (www.didaskalia.net)

Such a scathing review, with which I concur, begs the question of why bother comparing Carr's play to Aeschylus? The point is to highlight not only the complexity of issues with which the *Oresteia* deals, but also to emphasize that the performance of violence – in the best of representations – cannot be divorced from that complexity. Because Aeschylus is working through a paradox, his three plays are more adequate to the task of performing violence than, arguably, any single play could hope to achieve.

If homicide, not to mention regicide, is one of the most appalling acts in Greek tragedy, then the second play of Aeschylus' trilogy, The

Libation Bearers, compounds the problem. One of Orestes' opening questions herein is 'Can I be right?' referring to his desire to avenge his father's murder with another murder (15). This play is a mood piece on madness and guilt and the Chorus absorbs (or is contaminated by) the language of pollution seen in Clytemnestra's sacrifice speech to introduce the action:

> Through too much glut of blood by our fostering ground
> the vengeful gore is caked and hard, will not drain through.
> The deep-run ruin carries away
> the man of guilt. Swarming infection boils within (66-70).

Aeschylus maintains the idea of pollution being alive with infectious behaviour (it is 'vengeful' and it can carry a man away). If the action of *Agamemnon* wounds and violates the sacred space and opens the philosophical question of violence, then *The Libation Bearers* enacts the chaotic effect of violence, rendered here as revenge.

Before killing his mother, Orestes asserts, 'You killed, and it was wrong. Now suffer wrong' (930). An eye for an eye, or reciprocal violence, does not end violence but perpetuates the bloodshed and thus creates further difficulties and continuing disorder. Following the matricide, Orestes is beset with doubt: 'What shall I call it but right? ... Did she do it or did she not? ... the smear of blood conspires' (997-1010). Spilled blood conspires to drive Orestes mad with guilt and shame. Orestes is, however, fully aware that his deed carries no honour and is stained with its own *hybris*: 'my victory is soiled, and has no pride' (1017). The middle play appropriately ends with more questions and no answers. The final lines of the text spoken by the Chorus are: 'Where is the end? Where shall fury of fate be stilled to sleep, be done with?' (1077). At the moment of vengeance and the appearance of the Erinyes in Orestes' mind ('they come like gorgons, they wear robes of black, and they are wreathed in a tangle of snakes' 1048), none of the questions about justice, righteousness and order can be answered. And so it must be in *The Eumenides* that Aeschylus brings all the difficulties of performing violence to the feet of the goddess Athene.

The Open Question of Violence

The final play of the *Oresteia* is ultimately concerned with a *polis* that 'has a right and obligation to ensure the safety of its citizens against private acts of violence' (Podlecki 50). The trilogy as a whole enacts the translation of reciprocal violence into ritual violence so that violence itself can be transmuted into justice. The wound, the opening, or the pollution is to be healed, closed, or cleansed and such is done through the actions of men in a tribunal. In *Agamemnon* there is the unleashing of the horror, in *The Libation Bearers* there is the accumulation of violence and in *The Eumenides* there is the closing of the wound. Aeschylus's brilliant representation of the cleansing of the House of Atreus is particularly striking for what Sommerstein calls a 'sublime paradox' (284): just as the trilogy employs the arbitrariness of language to control the chaos of violence, so too does Aeschylus transform the very goddesses of revenge into the guardians of justice.

In the *Oresteia* Aeschylus depicted for the first time in human form the earth spirits known as the Erinyes or the Furies. These ugly creatures ('gorgons' according to Orestes) are considered either a personification of the clinging filth that stems from murder (Wiles 42), or a personification of the oppressed victim's cry for vengeance (Podlecki 8). The third play gives full expression to the third mode of representing violence: questions of justice in the face of continuing bloodshed. Significantly, the scene of *The Eumenides* shifts from Argos to Athens as if Aeschylus knows that any deliberation over questions of justice for a violent wrong must be distanced – in time and in space – from the crime. The need for distance in judicial matters is not only articulated in the shift of location, but also in the descent of Athene into the realm of mortals to act as final arbiter. But the answer to all the questions that end *The Libation Bearers* cannot come solely from a god: rather, the gods and the mortals must together bind the wound of the murderous House of Atreus.

Athene is all too aware of the dilemma she faces: either she allows the Furies to condemn Orestes to madness and death or she absolves Orestes and allows the Furies to continue in their damaging wrath – this time against the innocents of the community:

> Even I have not the right to analyse the cases of murder where wrath's edge
> is sharp. And all the more since you [the Furies] have come, and clung
> a clean and innocent supplicant, against my doors.
> You bring no harm to my city. I respect your rights.
> Yet these, too, have their work. We cannot brush them aside,
> and if this action so runs that they fail to win,
> the venom of their resolution will return

to infect the soil, and sicken all my land to death.
Here is the dilemma. Whether I let them stay or drive
them off, it is a hard course and will hurt. Then, since
the burden of the case is here, and rests on me,
I shall select judges of manslaughter, and swear
them in, establish a court for all time to come (470-484).

Athene then asks that both parties call witnesses, argue their case, and that the jury cast votes one way or another.

With this legal system, according to Sommerstein, *The Eumenides* exhibits a 'shift from violence to persuasion' (67) and the 'personification of wrathful *talio*' – or the Erinyes –is transmuted into the workers of justice (67). This is not to say that justice – or *dike* – did not exist before Orestes' trial at the hands of Athene's court. Rather, Aeschylus is suggesting that the single-minded justice of Zeus and the Erinyes was flawed: theirs was an older form of justice that 'strikes at the innocent almost as much as the guilty' (Sommerstein 275) and it must be adapted. So it is that the 'curse-goddesses' are transmuted into the 'kindly ones' – a euphemistically altered trio of goddesses who remain 'supernatural agents whose efficacy could be invoked to come to the assistance of an oppressed party' (Podlecki 7). They are a 'cosmic and almost mystical' element called upon to restore order. The reason the Erinyes must be transformed into the Eumenides is because the Erinyes are invoked by Clytemnestra to avenge her murder – she demands justice for her violent death, which is itself a revenge of a violent death. Neither Orestes' nor Clytemnestra's status as victim is obvious. Aeschylus has brilliantly taken the myth of the House of Atreus and used the culminating scenes of Orestes' trial to demonstrate the need to move from reciprocal violence to ritualized violence in the form of a trial and legal systems. The 'older' justice of Zeus seems to lead to more violence and thus 'in his final masterpiece Aeschylus grappled with – we might almost say, was consumed by – the notion of 'justice': what it is, how it is to be realized in the sphere of human activity, and (most difficult of all), what part the gods play in helping men achieve it' (Podlecki 40).

The 'sublime paradox' of the last play of the trilogy is that 'those deities who most vehemently protested the new form of justice are made to be themselves its ultimate guardians' (Sommerstein 284). After a tie vote from the Athenian jury, Athene casts the deciding ballot in favour of Orestes. Then, Athene painstakingly convinces the wrathful deities to take a place of honour in Athens: 'do not render it barren of fruit, nor spill the dripping rain of death in fierce and jagged lines to eat the seeds ... Put to sleep the bitter strength in the black wave and live with me and share my pride of worship' (801, 832). Echoing but altering Clytemnestra's metaphor of bitter rain to describe the pain of violence, Athene offers the Erinyes honour and they eventually accept. Hence their name changes from Erinyes to Eumenides. The translation of wrath into justice is performed on stage as the black chthonic robes the goddesses wear at the beginning of the play are exchanged for 'the investiture of purple stained robes' (1028) – a colour of majesty but also of the blood stained robes of Agamemnon described by Clytemnestra as a 'deadly abundance.' The English language use of 'address a wrong' or 'redress a crime' or 'dress a wound' is obviously not relevant to Aeschylus's Greek: however, the idea of covering the opening of violence is interesting in light of any performances of costume. A wound needs to be dressed to begin healing, but a scar remains on the skin.

Thus, violence is not eradicated: it is rather redressed into a system of justice and law. It is not as though the violent rending of the cosmos is completely healed in the transformation of the Erinyes, but rather the scar of healing remains in the colour of the Eumenides' robes. By bringing the forces of pollution and vengeance to life, Aeschylus laid the foundations for a new concept of democratic justice whereby the life of the *polis* is altered (Wiles 42). But Aeschylus is too shrewd to believe that Athene's court of law will end all violence. Instead, it can only be one possible answer to the problem of violent actions. The final prayer of the Chorus in *The Eumenides* acknowledges this partial solution of justice against violence:

> Let not the dry dust that drinks
> the black blood of citizens
> through passion for revenge
> and bloodshed for bloodshed
> be given our state to prey upon.
> Let them render grace for grace.
> Let love be their common will:
> let them hate with single heart.
> Much wrong in the world is thereby healed (978-987).

The balanced rhythm and syntax of the prayer ('bloodshed for bloodshed' and 'grace for grace') does not negate either side of the dilemma but instead holds both in an uneasy equilibrium. Their final line, as I noted earlier, leaves the question of violence open. 'Much wrong' might be healed, but not all wrongs. Violent actions, violent *hybris*, pollution, and bloodshed are quelled by rhetoric, order, persuasion and structure – all called into existence through Athene and the legal courts of Athens. As Athene says, 'Persuasion has her sacred place of worship' (885). But the forces of destruction are by no means eliminated.

Bloody, vengeful, ruthless killing may occur off-stage in the *Oresteia*, but through the entire trilogy there is no doubt that violence – in all its theoretical and representational modes from violation to revenge to justice – is performed. This essay is obviously mostly concerned with thinking through the performance of violence in the *Oresteia*: however, if Helen Vendler is correct – and I believe she is – that Irish artists are just now beginning to consider the applicability of these issues in relation to contemporary Irish life, then the great Irish translations of the *Oresteia* cannot be far from the stage.

Bibliography

Aijmer, Göran and Jon Abbink, eds. *Meanings of Violence: A Cross Cultural Perspective* (Oxford and New York: Berg Publishers, 2000).

Arendt, Hannah, 'A Special Supplement: Reflections on Violence.' *The New York Review of Books* 12. 4 (27 Feb 1969).

Benjamin, Walter, 'Critique of Violence.' *Reflections: Essays, Aphorisms, Autobiographical Writings.* Ed. Peter Demetz (New York: Harcourt Brace Jovanovich, 1978).

Bowman, Glenn, 'The Violence of Identity.' *Anthropology of Violence and Conflict.* Ed. Bettina E. Schmidt (London: Routledge, 2001): 25-46.

Burian, Peter, 'From Myth into *muthos*: the shaping of tragic plot.' *The Cambridge Companion to Greek Tragedy.* Ed. P. E. Easterling (Cambridge: Cambridge University Press, 1997): 178-210.

Cairns, Douglas L., 'Hybris, Dishonour, and Thinking Big.' *The Journal of Hellenic Studies* 116 (1996): 1-32.

Carr, Marina, *Ariel* (Loughcrew: The Gallery Press, 2002).

Clausewitz, Carl von, *On War.* Ed. and Trans. Michael Eliot Howard (Princeton, NJ: Princeton University Press, 1976).

Deleuze, Gilles, 'The Language of Sade and Masoch.' *Everyday Theory: A Contemporary Reader.* Eds. Becky McLaughlin and Bob Coleman (New York: Pearson 2005): 518-522.

Easterling, P. E., 'Form and Performance.' *The Cambridge Companion to Greek Tragedy.* Ed. P. E. Easterling (Cambridge: Cambridge University Press, 1997): 151-177.

---, 'From Repertoire to canon.' *The Cambridge Companion to Greek Tragedy.* Ed. P. E. Easterling (Cambridge: Cambridge University Press, 1997): 211-227.

Farquharson, Danine and Sean Farrell, ed. and intro. *Shadows of the Gunmen: Violence and Culture in Modern Ireland* (Cork: Cork University Press, 2007).

Fisher, N. R. E., *Hybris: A Study in the Values of Honour and Shame in Ancient Greece* (Warminster, England: Aris & Phillips Ltd., 1992).

Foucault, Michel, *Discipline and Punish: the Birth of the Prison*. Trans. Alan Sheridan (New York: Pantheon, 1977).

Friel, Brian, *Translations* (London: Faber, 1981).

Girard, René, *Violence and the Sacred* (Baltimore: Johns Hopkins UP, 1977).

Hanssen, Beatrice, *Critique of Violence: Between Poststructuralism and Critical Theory* (London: Routledge, 2000).

Heaney, Seamus, 'Mycenae Lookout.' *Opened Ground: Selected Poems, 1966-1996* (New York: Farrar, Straus and Giroux, 1998): 387-394.

---, 'Voices from Lemnos.' *Opened Ground*: 305.

Joyce, James, *Ulysses*, Annotated Student Edition (London: Penguin, 1992).

Keegan, John, *The First World War* (London: Hutchinson, 1998).

Kiberd, Declan, 'Introduction.' *Amid Our Troubles: Irish Versions of Greek Tragedy*. Eds. Marianne McDonald and J. Michael Walton (London: Methuen, 2002): vii-xiii.

Lattimore, Richmond, trans. Aeschylus: *Oresteia* (Chicago: U of Chicago P, 1953).

Macintosh, Fiona, *Dying Acts: Death in Ancient Greek and Modern Irish Tragic Drama* (Cork: Cork University Press, 1994).

McDonald, Marianne, 'The Irish and Greek Tragedy.' *Amid Our Troubles: Irish Versions of Greek Tragedy*,eds M. McDonald and J. M. Walton (London: Methuen, 2002): 37-86.

---, 'When Despair and History Rhyme.' *New Hibernia Review* 1.2 (1997): 57-70.

---, 'Review of Marina Carr's Ariel.' *Didaskalia* 6.1 (Spring 2004): www.didaskalia.net/reviews/2002_10_02_01.html

McDonald, Marianne and J. Michael Walton, eds. *Amid Our Troubles: Irish Versions of Greek Tragedy* (London: Methuen, 2002).

Parker, Robert, *Miasma* (Oxford: Clarendon Press, 1983).

Podlecki, Anthony J., ed., Trans., Commentary. *Aeschylus: Eumenides* (Warminster, England: Aris & Phillips Ltd., 1989).

Roche, Anthony, 'Ireland's *Antigones*: Tragedy North and South.' *Cultural Contexts and Literary Idioms in Contemporary Irish Literature*. Ed. Michael Kenneally (Gerrard's Cross, Bucks.: Colin Smythe, 1988): 221-50.

Siebers, Tobin, 'Philosophy and its Other – Violence: A Survey of Philosophical Repression from Plato to Girard.' *Anthopoetics* 1.2 (Dec 1995): 1-10.

Sommerstein, Alan H., *Aeschylean Tragedy* (Bari: Levante Editori, 1996).

Sunstein, Cass R., 'Is Violent Speech a Right?' *American Prospect* 22 (Summer 1995): 34-37.

Teevan, Colin, 'Northern Ireland: Our Troy? Recent Versions of Greek Tragedies by Irish Writers.' *Modern Drama* 41 (1998): 77-89.

Vendler, Helen, 'Seamus Heaney and the Oresteia: 'Mycenae Lookout' and the Usefulness of Tradition.' *Amid Our Troubles: Irish Versions of Greek Tragedy*, eds M. McDonald and J. M. Walton (London: Methuen, 2002): 181-197.

Walton, J. Michael, 'Hit or Myth: the Greeks and Irish Drama.' *Amid Our Troubles: Irish Versions of Greek Tragedy*, eds M. McDonald and J. M. Walton (London: Methuen, 2002): 3-36.

Wiles, David, *Greek Theatre Performance: An Introduction* (Cambridge: Cambridge University Press, 2000).

3 | The Force of Law in Seamus Heaney's Greek Translations

Eugene O'Brien

The writing career of Seamus Heaney has been coterminous with the thirty years of violence that have characterized the politics of Northern Ireland. Now given the Northern Irish context of that work, one would expect that some form of critique of his aesthetic in terms of the notions of nationalist politics, and of the identificatory stance contained therein, would be a major strand of critical discourse. One would, however, be wrong. Of the few studies which deal with this area, the diversity of perspective instantiates the lack of epistemological clarity in these approaches to date. Eoghan Harris is typical in seeing Heaney's work as having not much to say to modern Ireland, coming, as he sees it 'from haunts of coot and fern' (1995), while Desmond Fennell sees his writing as a published form of 'private musing,' something which he sees as far removed from any political stance (33).

In contrast to these views of his work as avoiding political engagement, Edna Longley, Ciarán Carson and Conor Cruise O'Brien have all, to some degree, seen Heaney as an aestheticizer of political violence, as someone who is sanctifying the violence of his tribe. As Blake Morrison summarizes, speaking of some of the poems in the opening section of *North*, it seems as if he is having these poems 'written for him' by his nationalist, Catholic psyche (67). To Fennell, on the other hand, Heaney is placed in the dock for being a political quietest, unsure of his allegiance, and unwilling to speak for his own people, as exemplified by his 'silence' during the hunger strike in the Maze prison from March to October in 1981 (38). Finally, David Lloyd sees Heaney as reducing history to myth, and privileging aesthetics over ethics (13-40).

Clearly the issue of violence in Heaney's writing is a problematic one, and the poet himself has probed his own symbolic approach to violence and art. Writing about the role of the artist in the face of the political confrontation in Belfast in 1971, Heaney says that he is 'fatigued by a continuous adjudication between agony and injustice, swung at one moment by the long tail of race and resentment, at another by the more acceptable feelings of pity and terror' (Heaney 1980, 30). Perhaps the most important words in this passage are 'continuous adjudication'. The interaction of active and passive voices in this passage outlines the complexity of the struggle that is ongoing within the culture, and within the poet. Heaney's metaphor of being 'swung' by the 'long tail' represents the atavistic, visceral emotions that were rife in Belfast at this time. Members of Heaney's own community were slaughtering for the 'common good' (Heaney 1975, 45), even as he was writing, and this internecine violence, itself both caused by, and creative of, a binary opposition, foregrounded questions about the nature and function of art.

The etymology of 'adjudicate' helps to clarify the issue at this point. Stemming from the Latin '*judicare*,' the original composite was '*jus*' (law) and '*dicere*' (to say). The word highlights Heaney's difficulty in continually attempting to 'say the law' of proper aesthetic, ethical and political action in a violent contemporary context, and his own attempt to do this involves a 'search for images and symbols adequate to our predicament' (Heaney, 1980, 56). Interestingly, there is a connection between violence and the law that has been pointed out, in a parallel context, by the French theorist Jacques Derrida. In 'The Force of Law', Derrida offers his most probing analysis of the concept of the law and how it operates. Tracing his thoughts through a *pensée* of Blaise Pascal and the work of Montaigne, he stresses the aporetic relationship between the law and justice, using the Kantian dictum of 'no law without force' to syncretize these positions (Derrida 233).

The general view is that Pascal wrote this passage with the work of Montaigne in mind. Montaigne made the point that laws are 'not in themselves just but are rather just only because they are laws', and he goes on to speak about 'the mystical foundation of the authority of laws' as being simply custom (Derrida 2002, 239). Clearly, part of the signification of the title of this essay for Derrida is that law as societal construct, deriving from this mystical foundation of authority, can only be law through its enforcement: there is 'no law without force as Immanuel Kant recalled with the greatest rigour' (Derrida 233). Here the force is the threat of punishment if the law is violated – the mailed fist held within the velvet glove.

Derrida points to the aporia that most laws must have been created through an act of violence (another example of the force of law) whereby control and power were won:

> How to distinguish between the force of law [loi] of a legitimate power and the allegedly originary violence that must have established this authority and that could not itself have authorized itself by any anterior legitimacy so that, in this initial moment, it is neither legal nor illegal, just or unjust (234).

Here the irony is that an act which may have been foundational in terms of setting up a law, the taking of a country, or a province by war, will later be seen as illegal when referred to the law which was enacted after the original act of violence. In other words, when one group uses violence to overthrow another, it then, on achieving power, invariably makes such actions illegal.

In Irish history for example, in 1916, a number of members of the political party Sinn Fein, without any democratic mandate or ethical warrant, undertook an armed rebellion against the British government. Under the invocation of martial law, the British authorities executed sixteen of the rebel leaders for treason. Six years later, some of those same insurgents, now members of the first native Irish government, executed former comrades in a bitter civil war over the future of the country, using the self-same martial law which executed their former leaders in 1916.

Derrida goes on to probe how the very emergence of justice and law, the 'instituting, founding and justifying moment of law implies a performative force, that is to say always an interpretive force and a call to faith': not in the sense, this time, that law would be in the service of force or the prevailing ideology but that instead it would maintain a 'more complex relation to what one calls force, power or violence' (241). For Derrida, the founding moment of law, in a society or culture, is never a moment 'inscribed' in the history of that culture since it 'rips it apart with one decision', a decision which he sees as a 'coup de force', a 'performative and interpretative violence' which is in itself 'neither just nor unjust' (241).

In Heaney's quest for adjudication, for saying the law, he looks at the performative nature of violence in originary contexts and finds the symbols adequate to his society's predicament in the translations of two plays from ancient Greece: Sophocles *Antigone*, translated as *The Burial at Thebes*, and *The Cure at Troy*, his translation of Sophocles's *Philoctetes*. At the beginning of *The Cure at Troy*, the chorus speaks about the connection between the voice of the aesthetic and the forces of violence:

> Poetry
> Allowed the god to speak. It was the voice
> Of reality and justice. The voice of Hercules
> That Philoctetes is going to have to hear
> When the stone cracks open and the lava flows. (2)

The imagery of stones and lava in this extract is, in my opinion, thematic of a central concern in Heaney's work, namely the role of visceral emotions, atavisms and prejudices within the mindsets of those engaged in violence in Northern Ireland, and the *locus* of such emotions is to be found in the relationship between the different traditions and notions of territory and home. However, the violence here will be verbal.

In an essay appropriately entitled *The Place of Writing*, Heaney makes the point that 'the poetic imagination in its strongest manifestation imposes its vision upon a place rather than accepts a vision from it' (1989, 20), and goes on to add that 'we are more and more aware of writing as a place in itself, a destination in art arrived at by way of art' (1989, 19). In terms of *The Cure at Troy*, the writer can either become captivated by cracking 'stones' and flowing 'lava,' or he can listen for the voice of 'reality and justice.' Here the force of law will be the voice of justice and the reality is that this justice will be imagined as outside of the socio-political binary of Greeks versus Trojans. Here the speaking of the law is enunciated by the god, and poetry, the vehicle of the images and symbols adequate to our predicament, will allow this to happen. In *The Cure at Troy* the conflicts between politics and ethics, between loyalty to one's tribe and loyalty to a higher sense of humanity and truth, between values which are the products of a particular ideology and those which aspire to some form of transcendent position, are set out.

In this play, Philoctetes has been left by the Greeks on the island of Lemnos because a foul-smelling suppurating wound caused by a 'snake-bite he got at a shrine', has left him 'rotting like a leper' (17). A Trojan soothsayer, Helenus, one of King Priam's sons, had prophesied that Troy would only be captured if Philoctetes and his bow were present, so Odysseus and the hero of the play, Neoptolemus (the son of Achilles), are sent to obtain the bow. From the beginning, the stage is set in terms of a conflict between tribal loyalty and some transcendental notion of ethical and legal value and responsibility: in other words between law as tribal act of force and some higher concept of a broader intersubjective justice.

The opening lines of the chorus set out the connection between the island of Lemnos and the island of Ireland, as well as between the siege of Troy and notions of siege in Northern Ireland:

> People so staunch and true, they're fixated,
> Shining with self-regard like polished stones (1).

Here, the difference between hero and victim is elided, as the tribal certainties and loyalties of Greeks and Trojans are superimposed onto the contemporary situation of Northern Ireland. This becomes unequivocal near the end of the play when the chorus sums up the developments with an interpolation that speaks of a 'hunger-striker's father' standing in a graveyard, and a 'police widow in veils' fainting at 'the funeral home' (77). Hence, the dilemma of the Greeks obeying orders, and taking the bow of Philoctetes against his wishes, can set up resonances with contemporary Irish communal and sectarian loyalties, but can also avoid succumbing to any gravitational entrapment through the creative use of translation.

Consequently, the chorus can see that a loyalty to the tribe which is not counterweighted by some sense of a greater force of law causes people who are convinced that they are 'in the right' to 'repeat themselves … no matter what.' This parallel of the Freudian repetition complex (*Wiederholungszwang*), can also be seen as a constitutive factor in the replication of the violence in Northern Ireland, as generation after generation becomes involved (or is interpellated, in Althusserian terms), in sectarian violence in the defence of the ideological certainties of a particular community, be that nationalist or unionist (Althusser 1977). The modal cause of this repetitive, trans-generational involvement is a sense of communal grievance, the 'self-pity' that 'buoys them up,' which is developed and fed by pondering upon past injustices.

Philoctetes, as symbolic of this tendency, identifies again and again with his wound: 'I managed to come through/but I never healed' (18): 'this ruins everything./I'm being cut open' (40): 'has the bad smell left me?' (57): 'Some animals in a trap/Eat off their own legs' (53): 'All I've left is a wound' (61). His subjectivity is intrinsically bound up with his wound: symbolically, he is unable to face the future because of his adhesion to the past: his wound interpellates him as a particular type of ideological subject. Having already spoken of 'self-pity,' the chorus goes on to point out the self-fulfilling prophecy that such an attitude can bring about:

> And their whole life spent admiring themselves
> For their own long-suffering.
> Licking their wounds
> And flashing them around like decorations (2).

This veneration of the wounds of the past is exactly how sectarian ideology seduces new subjectivities into existing moulds. Philoctetes embodies the siege mentality that has been rife in Northern Ireland in his cry: 'No matter how I'm besieged./I'll be my own Troy. The Greeks will never take me' (63).

Another aspect of such entrapment is the sense of immanence within a culture, which sees value only in those areas wherein the existing legal and political imperatives are validated. In *The Cure at Troy*, it is Odysseus who symbolizes this voice of political pragmatism. He defines himself and Neoptolemus as 'Greeks with a job to do' (Heaney 1995, 3), and makes similar matter of fact pronouncements as the play proceeds, informing the younger man that 'you're here to serve our cause' (Heaney 1995, 6). In the service of his cause, Odysseus can rationalize almost anything, telling Philoctetes that his 'aim has always been to get things done/By being adaptable' (Heaney 1995, 57), and this adaptability is grounded in his tribal loyalty. He can gloss over the sufferings of Philoctetes by invoking his own sense of the law: 'We were Greeks with a job to do, and we did it,' and in answer to the ethical question about the lies that have been told, he gives the classic response of political pragmatism: 'But it worked! It worked, so what about it?' (Heaney 1995, 65). In a sense this is his version of 'we were only obeying orders', a phrase which has an unfortunate history in our culture.

For Derrida, one of the key points about the law is that it changes over time and can itself then be an agent of broader societal change. His discussion of justice is similarly contextualized. He immediately distinguishes between justice and the law, and makes the point that the law can be deconstructed. In an argument that follows logically from his view of inauguration as both a break with, and a con-tinuation of, a tradition, he goes on to speak of the legal system as a history of transformations of different laws:

> You can improve the law. You can replace one law by another one. There are constitutions and institutions. There is a history,

and a history as such can be deconstructed. Each time you replace one legal system by another one, one law by another one, or you improve the law, that is a kind of deconstruction, a critique and deconstruction. So the law as such can be deconstructed and has to be deconstructed (16).

In *The Cure at Troy*, the agent of this change of law is Neoptolemus. In the climactic confrontation of the play, Neoptolemus, who had shared this perspective earlier in the play: 'I'm under orders' (51), and who had lied to Philoctetes in order to obtain his bow, realizes the error of his ways and becomes a more complex character through the introduction of an ethical strand to his *persona*. In a colloquy with Odysseus, the gradual opposition between pragmatic tribal politics and a more open humanistic ethics is unveiled. In response to Neoptolemus' statement that 'I did a wrong thing and I have to right it' (52), and to his further remark that he is going to 'redress the balance' and cause the 'scales to even out' (65) by handing back the bow, Odysseus replies in clichés: 'Act your age. Be reasonable. Use your head.' The reply of Neoptolemus demonstrates the gulf that exists between the two: 'Since when did the use of reason rule out truth?' (66).

For Odysseus, 'rightness' and 'justice' are values that are immanent in the ideological perspective of the tribe or community. There is to be no critical distance between his notions of myth and history. He tells Neoptolemus that there is one last 'barrier' that will stop him handing back the bow, and that is the 'will of the Greek people,/And me here as their representative' (Heaney 1995, 66). He sees no sense of any transcendental or intersubjective form of justice in what Neoptolemus is attempting. When Neoptolemus speaks of 'doing the right thing,' he is answered by the voice of the tribe: 'What's so right about/Reneging on your Greek commission?' Their subsequent interchange deserves to be quoted in full as it is a *locus classicus* of the conflict between the force of law as a societal hegemonic tool and a broader notion of justice, dare I call it deconstructive justice: between a view of self and other as connected and mutually responsible, and that of self and other as disparate and in conflict:

> ODYSSEUS. You're under my command here. Don't you
> forget it.
> NEOPTOLEMUS. The commands that I am hearing overrule
> You and all you stand for.
> ODYSSEUS. And what about
> The Greeks? Have they no jurisdiction left?

NEOPTOLEMUS. The jurisdiction I am under here
Is justice herself. She isn't only Greek.
ODYSSEUS. You've turned yourself into a Trojan, lad (67).

In this exchange, the critical distance already spoken of is evident in the value-ethic of Neoptolemus. He has moved beyond the inter-tribal epistemology of Odysseus, where not to be Greek necessitates one's being Trojan. Such a perspective severely limits one's range of choices: one is either Greek or Trojan – a parallel with the population of Northern Ireland being divided into the adversarial binaries of Catholicism or Protestantism: nationalism or unionism: republicanism or loyalism.

In a ringing assertion earlier in the play, as he begins to have some form of sympathy with Philoctetes, Neoptolemus says 'I'm all-throughother. This isn't me. I'm sorry' (48). Here the beginnings of an ethics of identity, of a view that the self is not defined in simplistic contradistinction to the other, but rather is shot through with traces of that other, is seen as a painful and self-alienating experience. One is reminded of Levinas's statement that language is 'born in responsibility,' implying that the responsibility involved is to the other, to other traditions, other ideas, but most essentially, to other people (82). A comparison can be made between the doubt and questioning of Neoptolemus, and Odysseus's conviction that 'he's in the right' (1). For a change in the law, there must be a questioning of the existing dispensation and the symbolic language to arrive at that originary moment of change, which 'is neither legal nor illegal, just or unjust' (Derrida 234). I would argue that in his invocation of the idea of the 'allthroughother', and in his decision to invoke a different concept of justice, Neoptolemus is deconstructing the existing legal mores of his culture, and that his act of violence is one of interpretation rather than physical violence.

For Derrida, the founding moment of law, in a society or culture, is never a moment 'inscribed' in the history of that culture since it 'rips it apart with one decision', a decision which Derrida sees as a 'coup de force', a 'performative and interpretative violence' which is in itself 'neither just nor unjust' (241). As Derrida puts it 'deconstruction takes place in the interval that separates the undeconstructability of justice from the deconstructability of law', and he further asserts that justice can be seen as the possibility of deconstruction (243). The moment that a set of rules, precepts, codifications are written as text, they lose the force of authority and instead become open to the force of interpretation and hermeneutic analysis. So the original violence – the force of law that inaugurates a law – attempts to set out the conditions through which that law is to operate, or be enforced. This is what Neoptolemus does as he deconstructs the Greek-Trojan self-other binary with the force of a new law – the allthroughother. This is the interval within which a new sense of justice can be enunciated, a justice which violently overthrows the previous dispensation – it is the force of law, brought about by saying the law, and the continuous adjudication of which Heaney speaks parallels idea of the law as singular in its interpretation each and every time.

However simultaneously the interpretative force of law allows for this intention to be deconstructed in the interests of 'the possibility of justice' (249). In other words, the codification of law is not a structural machine which grinds the subject through its machinations. Instead, each individual instance requires a singular performative event, where the case is debated by lawyers, before a jury, and a judge, and where the individual circumstances of each protagonist are taken into account. In this case, there is a strong element of the undecidable to be found. Just as the law addresses itself to the polis, to the generality of the citizens of a state, so each case is about a single individual, and his or her case is interpreted on its own merits. So just as the force of law is general, the force of justice is particular: 'one must know that this justice always addresses itself to singularity, to the singularity of the other, despite, or even because, it pretends towards universality' (248). Thus Neoptolemus is acting in a single particular instance, and by so doing is changing the concept of law by an act of interpretive violence. The same is true of the central character in Heaney's other translation, *The Burial at Thebes*.

In a piece published in *The Irish Book Review*, 'Thebes via Toombridge: Retitling Antigone', Heaney sets out the connections between local and universal that motivated the title of this translation. Speaking of Francis Hughes, the dead hunger striker and neighbour of his in county Derry, Heaney stresses the body of Hughes as a site of struggle between the security forces and the nationalist crowd who came to take possession of it after he had died and his body was being brought back from prison by the security forces and handed over to his family and to Sinn Fein. Ownership of the body becomes a seminal metaphor here, as it becomes a potent signifier of the contest between the 'instinctive powers of feeling, love and kinship' and the 'daylight gods of free and self-conscious, social and political life', to quote Hegel (2005, 13). Heaney sees the motivation behind the 'surge of rage in the crowd as they faced the police' as an index of what he terms *dúchas* (13), and it is here that we come to Antigone's retitling. For her sense of propriety and integrity come from that feeling of kinship with the other as a fellow human, regardless of the political differences that separate us.

The scene is set after an invading army from Argos has been defeated by the Thebans under their new king Creon. Two of the sons of Oedipus, brothers to Antigone and Ismene, died in this battle. Eteocles perished defending Thebes but his brother, Polyneices, was part of the attacking army and hence a traitor:

> Their banners flew, the battle raged
> They fell together, their father's sons (8).

The Theban king, Creon, outraged by this treachery from one of the royal family, decrees that Polyneices shall not receive the normal purifying burial rites and places under interdict of death, anyone who will attempt to provide these rites to the corpse. He decrees that Polyneices, that 'Anti-Theban Theban', will not be accorded burial but will be left to rot in the open. The results are that 'The dogs and birds are at it day and night, spreading reek and rot'. Creon justifies this, in a manner similar to the British authorities and their treatment of the corpse of Francis Hughes:

> This is where I stand when it comes to Thebes
> Never to grant traitors and subversives
> Equal footing with loyal citizens (11).

For Antigone, the duty she has to her brother as human far surpasses her duty to the Theban notion of patriotism as laid down by Creon, and interestingly, she cites a higher law than that of Creon or Thebes itself:

> I disobeyed the law because the law was not
> The law of Zeus nor the law ordained
> By Justice. Justice dwelling deep
> Among the gods of the dead (20-1).

By positing a higher order of the treatment of the other than that of the polis, or group, Antigone is voicing the same debate between different versions of the law as was seen in the previous play.

Her stress is on the rights and duties of the individual to other individuals, or in Levenasian terms, to the face of the other. Interestingly, Creon is not depicted as some sort of political fundamentalist: he is a heroic figure in his own right who has done the state some service. He has saved Thebes from its enemies and voices a sense of patriotic philosophy which underwrites his personal ideology. His views on the polis and its need to impose order could well serve as a credo for many states in the world:

> For the patriot
> Personal loyalty always must give way
> To patriotic duty. Solidarity, friends,
> Is what we need. The whole crew must close ranks.
> The safety of our state depends upon it (10).

The stress here is on the individual as defined by his or her group. It is a sentiment similar to that of Odysseus in *The Cure at Troy,* where the choices of definition are binary: one is either Greek or Trojan. For Creon, the binary is parallel: one is either a patriot or a traitor, and this carries through in life and death:

> This is where I stand when it comes to Thebes:
> Never to grant traitors and subversives
> Equal footing with loyal citizens
> But to honour patriots in life and death (11).

The need to see these bodies as signifiers of patriotism or betrayal after death is a potent trope in nationalist rhetoric in an Irish as well as in a classical context. The images of dead martyrs or traitors are the motive forces behind so many of the commemorative parades, processions and demonstrations that have caused such tension, bloodshed and death throughout the history of Northern Ireland, as Brown and Viggiani discuss below. The honouring of one's own glorious dead and the dishonouring of those who broke the code of the tribe is a vital signifier in nationalist and unionist rhetorical structures. These bodies, like that of Francis Hughes, have lost all individual resonance: they have been transposed into ideological signifiers, and it is this process of ideological transformation that is being assayed by Creon as he refuses burial to Polyneices, that 'anti-Theban Theban' (Heaney 2004, 10). By so doing, he attempts to attenuate the humanity of Polyneices: he is to be buried without 'any ceremony whatsoever' and is adjudged to be merely a 'carcass for the dogs and birds to feed on' (Heaney 2004, 11). To treat the dead correctly and with honour, she implies, is very much an index of our own humanity. The treatment of people as less than human, as often demanded by the voice of the tribe, is the antithesis of her own actions. Hers is an evocation of a higher, intersubjective sense of ethics:

> This proclamation had your force behind it
> But it was mortal force, and I, also a mortal,
> I chose to disregard it. I abide
> By statutes utter and immutable –
> Unwritten, original, god-given laws (21).

We remember that to be just, the decision of a judge for example, must not only follow a rule of law or general law, but must also assume it, approve it, confirm its value by a reinstituting act of interpretation, as if, at the limit, the law did not exist previously – as if the judge himself invented it in each case. Each exercise of justice as law can be just only if it is a 'fresh judgment' ... This new freshness, the initiality of this inaugural judgment can very well – better yet, must very well – conform to a pre-existing law (Derrida 251). Antigone is not looking to establish a rule: what she is doing is looking for justice in this singular situation.

In death she teaches Creon that: 'until we breathe our last breath/we should keep the established law', and in this line we see the credo of both original and translation: our common humanity should transcend our differences. It is the treatment of the dead, themselves no longer part of politics as agents that is seen as wrong in the dramatic logic of the play and the translation. As Heaney calls it in his prose piece 'it is a matter of burial refused', as Polyneices is being made a 'non-person' and this is what Antigone cannot countenance, and it is this disrespect for the human in death that is the cause of the metaphorical contagion outlined by Tiresias:

> spreading reek and rot
> On every altar stone and temple step, and the gods
> Are revolted. That's why we have this plague,
> This vile pollution (44).

The result is that tapestry of the power structure that Creon is attempting to consolidate unravels in a litany of dead bodies: Antigone, Haemon, Eurydice all lie dead by the end of the play. Just as this review opened with a political contextualization of these translations, it is formally and ethically fitting that it close with a further such contextualization.

The body of Francis Hughes and the body of Polyneices are answered, in the contemporary moment, by the body of Robert McCartney, someone who was killed within his polis, but who, metaphorically, is a revenant, unable to rest. On January 30th, 2005, Robert McCartney was murdered outside Magennis' pub in the Short Strand area of Belfast. Reputedly, the murderers were members of Sinn Fein and the Provisional IRA, and in the aftermath of the murder, the pub was cleaned of fingerprints, CCTV evidence was removed and threats were issued to the witnesses of the act as to the consequences of reporting any of this to the Police Service of Northern Ireland.

The dead man's sisters – Catherine, Paula, Claire, Donna and Gemma – and his partner Bridgeen have spoken out in a campaign to see justice done, in a case that is eerily resonant of the voice of Antigone in defence of Polyneices. Their demand is for justice to be done for their brother, a demand that echoes across the centuries, and that could be spoken in the words of Antigone: 'Justice dwelling deep/Among the gods of the dead' (Heaney 2004, 20-1). It is significant that Heaney, in describing the genesis of this text, compares the treatment of the body of Polyneices with that of Francis Hughes, the hunger-striker: it is even more significant that this play deals with the voice of women, then, as now, seen as not quite part of the public sphere, women who are totally focused on obtaining justice for the dead:

> I never did a nobler thing than bury
> My brother Polyneices. And if these men
> Weren't so afraid to sound unpatriotic
> They'd say the same (23).

The partner and sisters of Robert McCartney have suffered the same fate as that of Antigone, in that they are seen as unusual voices in the public sphere. '[W]omen were never meant for this assembly' (27), says Creon, words that have a chilling echo in Martin McGuiness's warning to the sisters about being used by other political forces. Here, the ethical has engaged with the political, and the political is found wanting in the face of that imperative towards justice that has become symbolized by the name and body of Robert McCartney. In real terms this means that the force of justice is an ethical, singular and individual one, rooted in a call of an impossible future: 'justice remains *to come*, it remains *by coming*' (Derrida 256). Each individual case is an event not governed by the past applications of the rule of law but by a present and future interpretation based on singularity.

Read in the context of this event, the following lines have a double resonance, both within the text and the current political situation, as they state the role of women in the public sphere:

> Two women on our own
> Faced with a death decree –

Women, defying Creon?
It's not a woman's place.
We're weak where they are strong (5).

In a culture where women had little value, Antigone defies the law, the state and the king and ultimately triumphs by proving her point and obtaining proper burial for her brother. Again, the strength of the text is the focus on the individual. Creon is far from the two-dimensional figure of evil with whom we have become familiar over recent years as complex political issues are attenuated into a just war against 'bad guys' whose names have been almost domesticated for familiarity: Saddam, Bin Laden, Arafat. At the end of the play, as Creon ponders the wreckage of his personal and political life, he utters the poignant phrase: 'I have wived and fathered death' (54).

Hence the force of law in these two plays is a verbal one, an eruptive one, and a singular one. However, once the law has become a textual entity, it is open to the violence of interpretation, a violence that is enacted according to the call of justice, that initiates some 'irruptive violence' (Derrida 256) that deconstructs the power relationships of those structures wherein the hegemonic power resides in the shape of these politicians who make the laws. In this sense, justice relates to the law in terms of the undecidable which may deconstruct and unhinge the structural relationship between the discourses of law and power and instead operates in that temporal futurity of the perhaps – 'one must always say perhaps for justice' and perhaps no justice is possible except to the degree that 'some event is possible which, as event, exceeds calculation, rules, programmes, anticipation and so forth' (257).

Bibliography

Althusser, Louis, *Lenin and philosophy and other essays*. Second Edition (London: New Left Books, 1977).

Derrida, Jacques, 'The Force of Law: The Mystical Foundation of Authority' in *Acts of Religion*, ed. Gil Anidjar (London: Routledge, 2002): 228-298.

Fennell, Desmond, *Whatever You Say, Say Nothing* (Dublin: ELO Publications, 1991).

Freud, Sigmund, *The Standard Edition of the Complete Psychological Works of Sigmund Freud*. Volumes XII and XIII. Edited and translated by James Strachey (London: Hogarth Press, 1955).

Harris, Eoghan, 'A Nice Poet Bogged Down in the Past', Sunday Times, 8 October 1995.

Heaney, Seamus, *North* (London: Faber, 1975).

---, *Preoccupations: Selected Prose 1968-1978* (London: Faber, 1980).

---, *The Place of Writing* (Atlanta: Scholars Press, 1989).

---, *The Cure at Troy* (London: Faber, 1990).

---, *The Burial at Thebes: Sophocles' Antigone* (London: Faber, 2004).

---, 'Thebes Via Toomebridge: Retitling Antigone', in *The Irish Book Review*, Volume 1, Number 1, 2005 13-14.

Levinas, Emmanuel, *The Levinas Reader*, ed. Sean Hand (Oxford: Basil Blackwell, 1989).

Lloyd, David, ' "Pap for the Dispossessed": Seamus Heaney and the Poetics of Identity' in *Anomalous States: Irish Writing and the Postcolonial Moment* (Dublin: Lilliput, 1993) 13-40.

Morrison, Blake, *Seamus Heaney* (London: Methuen, 1982).

4 | Branding Irish Violence:
The Spectacles of Rural and Urban 'Ireland'

Kyna Hamill

The difference between the description of violence and its actualization on stage is a perpetual contention in the theatre. In the western canon, the debate began with Aristotle, who emphasized that the story should be so constructed that the events make anyone who *hears* it shudder and feel pity even without *seeing* the play (Sidnell 50-51). To Aristotle, inciting pity and fear through imitation meant to replicate an event through plot development, rather than to mimetically represent it. We generally accept this as 'keeping the violence off the stage,' where it can safely be heard and not seen. Since Aristotle asserted that we cannot undo the existence of traditional stories, we continue to listen as Medea endlessly murders her children and Oedipus repeatedly blinds himself. No matter how many times the story is told, history reminds us that humans are imperfect, and more often than not, their imperfections surface in acts of violence. The Neoclassicists also pushed violence off the stage: Giambattista Guarini, author of *Il Pastor Fido* is just one of Aristotle's neoclassic interpreters who reinforced that 'becoming accustomed to the sight of horrible things, such as blood, wounds, and deaths...does not fortify the soul, nor does it purge the fear of death' (Sidnell 155). In the theatre today, we are accustomed to the sight of horrible things, and perhaps our souls have been weakened as a result. As this paper will explore, listening is no longer enough: today, violence must be seen in order to be believed.

Thanks in part to the media, the depiction of violence has even pop culture critics contributing to the argument about how much carnage should be seen on stage. In a 2006 Slate.com review of *The*

Lieutenant of Inishmore, Zachary Pincus-Roth bemoaned the previous state of violence on stage as 'too stylized to be genuinely scary' (www.slate.com, 2006). On the kind of cinematic violence missing from the theatre which features stereotyped figures such as mobsters, bank robbers and federal agents, he continues:

> Skeptics might argue that such subjects are simply not well-suited to theater. They require too many locations. Fake fistfights are hokey. Shooting and explosions require money and the proper expertise. Battle scenes look as silly as those in Max Fischer's high-school drama club Vietnam War play in the movie *Rushmore*. Theater works better when a messenger enters and describes the horrific news. That's how the Greeks did it, and that's how it should stay. But after watching play after play in which all the fighting takes place behind closed doors, it's strangely exhilarating to see naked cruelty right before our eyes (2006).

The fascination with the 'naked cruelty' in *Inishmore* appears to have captured the critics' attention more than the message of excessive violence itself. Despite the seriousness of the topic – violence related to splinter army groups in Northern Ireland circa 1993 – critics amused themselves with witty bi-lines: 'Terrorism Meets Absurdism in a Rural Village in Ireland,' (*New York Times*): 'Gore-ious fun' (*New York Post*): and 'When Irish eyes aren't smilin'' (*USA Today*).

No one was laughing when McDonagh first proposed the play to London theatres back in 2000. His now infamous pronouncement that he would submit no new plays to the world until *Lieutenant* was produced, chided the Royal Court and the National Theatre for not being courageous enough to tackle such a sensitive subject. As Patrick Lonergan has argued, this may be part of McDonagh's skilful manipulation of the press (65-78). As early as 1997, McDonagh boasted, '*The Lieutenant of Inishmore* is ... going to get me into so much trouble. It's about the INLA and IRA ... It's the most vicious thing that has ever been written on the subject' (*Irish Tatler*, 162). It was finally the Royal Shakespeare Company that took it on in 2001, the spring and summer before September 11. At the time, all ticket holders were warned that the play was potentially disturbing, though McDonagh was lauded for bravely writing something that was 'liberal in content but conservative in politics' (*The Guardian*).

Fast forward five years, when terrorism in Ireland seems passé in the new, larger geopolitical climate. In May 2006 *Lieutenant* opened at the Atlantic Theatre and transferred to Broadway where it played for 142 performances and received a nomination for Best Play at the Tony awards. In its incarnation on Broadway, the play contained the same gun shots and the same blood bath, but ironically the same characters who seemed dangerous five years ago, appeared to be almost cartoonish in 2006. Though the play is set in Ireland, McDonagh's characters possess the charm of witty thugs seen in so much of American 1990s film. By depicting this kind of violence to a cinematically cognizant audience, the 'Ireland' depicted in the Broadway production becomes an ambiguous setting where violence overshadows the geography.

Ironically, since 2001, the consequence of violence in Northern Ireland has barely registered in world news. Taking a back seat to terrorism in the Middle East, the crisis surrounding Irish independence in the North that once captured the attention of the world, now seems eclipsed by Ireland's economic success in the European Union. Soon, plays from Ireland and Northern Ireland that incorporate violence may begin to lose their impact and identity to audiences who no longer identify the locale of 'Ireland' on stage as a dangerous place. To audiences in 1907, the violence described by Synge's Christy Mahon was taken personally – as an affront to being 'Irish' (Grene, 79). Yet, one hundred years later, the violence depicted in McDonagh's *Inishmore* has little to do with Ireland, and more in common with a Quentin Tarantino film. While audience members may have left the stalls because they felt sick, the nausea had more to do with the bloodbath on stage than the exaggerated depiction of Irish culture. Spanning one hundred years of Irish drama, representations of violence have relied upon the fact that 'Ireland' was a country of rebels, and the product of rebellion – violence – was a fact of life, one could even say tradition. As McDonagh's over-the-top bloodshed alters the way in which violence is depicted on stage, it is important to look back at the way violence on the Irish stage has not only been portrayed, but also theatrically simulated.

There was a time when the state of violence in Northern Ireland garnered both pity for the victims of violence, and fear of bombs going off anywhere at any time. Pity and fear could also be manifested for those bucolic Irish who had to sustain a meager living in a post-famine, postcolonial rural existence. We can thank the stereotypes of American film for sustaining such dialectics of Irish culture, the urban and the rural being the two most popular portrayals of 'Ireland.' The same typecasting can also be found in representations of violence in Irish drama which, for the most part, has been manifested using two contrasting representations: stylized depictions of violence pertaining to the struggle for independence, and mimetic or 'real' depictions of rough rural brawls. In the former, memory and storytelling are crucial, while in the latter, visual and visceral violence are witnessed. Examining plays which track these two representations of violence in Irish drama, I will demonstrate how 'Ireland' on stage depends very much upon violence in order to maintain a certain identity to the outside world. This tradition of violence, once a significant aspect of its cultural branding on the stage, has begun to lose its fighting reputation because Irish culture itself is so diffused throughout popular culture. J.M. Synge's *Playboy of the Western World*, Brendan Behan's *The Hostage*, John B. Keane's *The Field*, Owen McCaffrey's *Mojo Mickybo* and Martin McDonagh's *The Lieutenant of Inishmore*, each depict violence with varying levels of graphic 'imitation.' However, the more over-the-top the portrayal of violence on the stage, the less impact it appears to have in terms of a social message. When it comes to representing violence on stage, perhaps Aristotle was correct: description does make us shudder more, not because the spectacle of violence is too difficult for our souls, but because the saturation of violence has made us stop caring.

In *Stages of Terror*, Anthony Kubiak regards theatrical violence as a 'mere' representation: claiming it ceases to be transgressive because its mimetic inefficiency remains an obvious flaw (160-1). Though significant in 1991, Kubiak's work now also seems dated in our post 9/11, post-Abu Ghraib, and post-*The Passion of The Christ* civilization, where violence is objectified to gargantuan proportions with no regard for discretion. Kubiak was right that we desire violence 'more and more,' however not because we see what we most 'deeply fear,' but because fear itself is ephemeral, and does not maintain the impact it once did. In the spectacular violence of film, television, and increasingly, theatre, fear and awe may be aroused in the mimetically superb special effects that can be executed with technical superiority. It is no wonder that 'staged' violence is in direct competition with 'real' violence considering that a keyword search of 'Snuff,' 'Torture,' or 'Drunken Bum Fights' can bestow us with the demystifying images of how a violent act *can* be executed in reality.

Unfortunately for mainstream theatre, the saturation of violent images from the media has sullied our ability to listen without seeing. It is not enough to hear that Oedipus poked out his eyes. Let us have the 'black blood,' in all its gory details. We know the ill-fated story so well that we have become desensitized and incapable of fear towards the bloodshed described by the inauspicious Second Messenger. As Davey says in Martin McDonagh's bloodstained *Lieutenant of Inishmore*, 'Worse and worse and worse this story gets,' so, as the theatre becomes more blood-soaked, it is actually depicting violence not only unrealistically, but unconscionably as well. Alison Pill who played Mairead in *Inishmore* on Broadway naively sums up the phenomenon,

> We have five gallons of blood on the stage by the end of [the show] ... It's very tasty blood, though, it's made of chocolate syrup and peanut butter and Karo syrup and it's ... it's kind of like an ice-cream sundae' (www.broadway.com).

Until *Inishmore*, dramatic interpretations of violence pertaining to the IRA, Northern Ireland and the struggle for independence have, primarily, been represented stylistically. Because the violence has historically been so inconceivably horrific and unrestrained, it is actually difficult to portray on stage. Instead, storytelling, music, humour and memory have become the methods by which to communicate the details of the violence without exploiting it. Ronan McDonald acknowledges the difficulty dramatists have had in engaging with the Northern conflict on stage: 'Many of the pressures are the same as those felt by poets and novelists, the need to find an idiom or mode of expression that will address the political situation while still remaining true to artistic creation, to be a public artist without being a propagandist' (232). McDonald goes on to say that 'distancing strategies' need to be incorporated in order to avoid clichés. In the 1980s, experimental theatres such as Field Day Theatre Company and Charabanc Theatre Company became known for critically distancing the dramatization of politics on stage. In this way, unlike in film, the theatre served as a location of recollecting the hurt and harm of a given crisis without audiences having to watch it play out over and over again. The tragedy is eulogized using the memory of those who can relate to the experience first hand, and as such, approaches a clearer and more empathetic understanding of history (ibid., 235).

Earlier manifestations of critical distancing can be seen in the plays of Brendan Behan who also recognized that music and humour could be used as a way to acknowledge the issues without over-emphasizing the politics. In *The Hostage*, a musical satire situated in Dublin in 1960, Behan criticized the IRA not for its use of violence, but for being 'out of date.' Pat, the caretaker, laments the state of the IRA: 'This is nineteen-sixty, and the days of the heroes are over these forty years past. Long over, finished and done with. The IRA and the War of Independence are as dead as the Charleston' (131). The boarding house / brothel that Pat takes care of is owned by the eccentric Monsewer who thinks he is perpetually fighting in an anti-British campaign. The only truly sympathetic character is the 'boy in the Belfast Jail ... that got copped for his IRA activities' whom we never meet. In exchange for the boy's freedom, a British soldier is kidnapped and held hostage in the symbolically decaying house. It is not until the third act that the soldier actually realizes he is, in fact, a hostage. The misfits in the house keep coming to visit him and as the quasi-Brechtian songs suggest, we believe he is fated to be safe.

The English translation, originally directed by Joan Littlewood of the Theatre Workshop, was slightly different from *An Giall*, written by Behan in Irish. Though the final scene in which Leslie, the British soldier meets his death, is different in each, both versions are shocking because his safety is implied by way of the curious, though harmless, visitors as well as his relationship with the compassionate Teresa. *The Hostage* is startling when the violence finally erupts because throughout the play, we truly believe in the good-humoured atmosphere of the house. People dance, and tease each other, the IRA is mocked, and Leslie is treated by most of the group with respect. It is clear that his fate is connected to the boy in the Belfast Jail, and because we never see the boy, it is not necessary for us to believe that Leslie is in danger. In the English version, Behan tricks us with an explosion, which stirs us from our passivity. The inhabitants are not who we thought they were, and pandemonium ensues during the final climatic scene described vividly in the stage directions:

> Whistle and sirens blow, drums beat, bombs explode, bugles sound the attack, bullets ricochet and a confusion of orders are shouted all over the place. Bodies hurtle from one side of the stage to the other and, in the midst of all the chaos, the kilted figure of MONSEWER slow marches, serene and stately, playing on his bagpipes a lament for the boy in the Belfast Jail (233).

In the subsequent stand-off, Leslie makes a run for it and as he 'zig-zags across the stage...the drum echoes his runs with short rolls.

As he makes his last run there is a deafening blast of gunfire and he drops' (235). That 'he drops' is all we need to know that Leslie is dead. In the Irish version, as described by Alan Simpson, Leslie does not meet his death as listed in the stage directions, 'but in a cupboard into which he has been stuffed by Padraig, and bound and gagged to hide him from the Police. He has suffocated' (Behan 20).

Though both versions are distressing, Behan does not require a bloody depiction of the Soldier's death. In the English version, the stylized drum beat stands in for his military prowess as well as the gun that takes his life. The violence that is seen is shocking, but not bloody. Its stylized method can most likely be attributed to Joan Littlewood who, as a director, was influenced by the theatre of Bertolt Brecht. We think of Katrin in *Mother Courage* whose drum beats on the roof similarly mingle with the cannon of gun shots that kill her. In the Irish version Leslie's death is unseen by the audience, and his body is revealed afterwards. This seems more akin to torture than an execution-style killing: though concealed, his death seems more vicious because that which goes unseen arouses suspicion about his treatment towards the end, much like the fate of many victims of the crisis.

According to Kubiak, concealed violence has more impact on the audience because the nature of real violence in performance 'is not as efficient as its mimetic representation: real violence in performance, then, is not transgressive, but merely inefficient' (160). The collapse of social order through violence in *The Hostage* reflects a specific period in the history of the struggle for independence. Behan could find the humour in the situation partially because, in a rather Freudian analysis, feelings of anxiety provoke an appreciation and need for humour. In 1960, the violence depicted in *The Hostage* would have been shocking, as were the jokes about the IRA. Yet, the impact of stylized violence is no less significant, because when theatrical violence mirrors history, memory imbues that which is not seen.

A more contemporary witnessing of the conflicts, this time set in Belfast, can be seen in Owen McCafferty's *Mojo Mickybo*, commissioned by Kabosh Theatre in 1998. In it, two actors use story telling and physical action to chronicle the life of two young Belfast boys in the early 1970s, whose different religions do not seem as important as sneaking into a screening of *Butch Cassidy and the Sundance Kid*. Violence is endemic in the play, if not by bombs then by bullies, and although the boys fantasize in order to escape the violence in everyday life, their story ends, like Butch and Sundance, with death. McCafferty's drama highlights story-telling rather than spectacle. Since violence is not meant to be represented realistically, the audience is expected to recognize the accounts of terrorism through historical fact, film and even personal experience.

In this stylized approach to depicting violence, the boys' characters are played by adult men, who attempt to represent the violence as it is seen and understood by children. This reinforces the impact that violence has on gender and youth, a subject rarely encountered in Irish drama. By locating the hostility in Belfast against the backdrop of a classic American Western known for its romanticized portrayals of gun violence, we see how violence in Belfast has desensitized the boys who have grown up watching countless acts of killing. At one point they must fight the neighbourhood bullies, and the actors, portraying both the protagonists and antagonists, must physically fight each other like shadow boxers in order to play out the action. It is an inspired scene which not only highlights the talent of the actors, but also comments on the perpetuation of violence which divides both children and men. Throughout the play, we see how violence in the street has become such a fact of life that the boys need the cinema, filled with romanticized shoot-outs, in order to escape the reality of their surroundings. We finally learn of their religious differences when we discover that Mojo comes from 'up the road' while Mickybo comes from 'over the bridge.' In their imaginary world, however, they fight their battles together, like Butch and Sundance. The final imaginary shoot-out, a simulated game to the boys, becomes all too real when we learn that Mojo's dad has been coincidentally killed by a bomb in the pub. The vivid description of the aftermath is all that is needed to comprehend the impact of what will happen next. Once fantasy meets reality, the boys must grow up, part ways and remain divided by urban geography. By concealing most of the violence through story-telling and virtuoso acting, McCafferty maintains critical distance from the historical crisis in Northern Ireland. Spectacle is integrated not by simulating 'real' violence, but by having the boys physically play out 'unreal' cinematic brutality.

When it comes to rural depictions of aggression on the stage, stylized urban violence is replaced with a naturalistic representation of rowdy brutality. When the bombs and guns are removed, and only fisticuffs and shillelaghs remain, scenes of violence are vividly depicted with boisterous enthusiasm. Concealment of the violence is unnecessary because the rustic locales already appear 'invented' when compared to urban life in Dublin and Belfast. The portrayal of rural life, seen so much in a theatrical 'Ireland' incorporates elements of reverie and imagination. 'Real' violence can be articulated because it remains a necessary feature of the rural invention. Examples of these bucolic brawls can be easily located in Synge's *Playboy*, John B. Keane's *The Field* as well as any one of McDonagh's Irish plays. In each of these dramas, violence is menacingly implied and then played out with extreme consequences. The simulated violence seen in the country appears safer than the city street because potentially lethal weapons such as hand guns and bombs are removed from the scene. In the country, loys, a lighted sod, shillelaghs and pots full of oil whimsically replace the truly dangerous weapons of the city and perpetuate the folklore of the country.[1]

The rural concept of the 'Fighting Irish' is not mutually exclusive with violence, but it is one of the biggest by-products of the stereotype. Cinema has embraced this ubiquitous aspect of rural life because of the potential for spectacle. The 'Fighting Irish' has become an exaggerated emblem of how the 'Irish' behave – with feistiness and tenacity. John Wayne's portrayal of Sean Thornton in *The Quiet Man* (1952) is just such a stereotype. He returns to Ireland to find peace from his disgraced pugilistic career after killing a man, and he even attempts to stop fighting. When his masculinity is repeatedly called into question, his temper is finally provoked. Cinematic history can thank John Ford for sticking to his guns and including the over-cooked eight minute fight at the end of the film, which the producer wanted to cut.[2] The brawl, between Thornton and 'Red' Danaher, his wife's brother, sprawls all over the Irish countryside and became known as the longest fight on film in its time. It encouraged and exploited the lively Irish temper which needed a little airing out on occasion. Even John Ford capitalized on his feisty Irish heritage, and became known for his 'Fighting Irish' attitude when it came to making the kind of films he wanted to make.[3] We can also recall Tom Cruise's portrayal of the bumpkin,

---

[1] Note that tourists to Ireland can obtain a souvenir shillelagh in the airport gift store, though grenades are conspicuously missing.

[2] See Randy Roberts and James Olson, *John Wayne: American* (New York: Simon & Schuster, Inc., 1995).

[3] See Emanuel Eisenberg, 'John Ford: Fighting Irish, *New Theatre*' (April, 1936) reprinted in *John Ford Made Westerns: Filming the Legend in*

Joseph Donnelly, in the boorish film, *Far and Away* (1992). When Joseph arrives in America, he discovers that his only skill from the country that can be applied to urban life is his ability to fight. Night after night he exchanges blows in public brawls to earn money not only for the land he has always desired, but also for a collection of fashionable hats.

Fictional representations of rural communities, usually in the west, are seen as impoverished and isolated to the point that they often become grotesque locales. This grotesque representation of the rural Irish landscape and its people includes exaggerated depictions of violence which corresponds with the skewed social framework. To Synge's first audiences, *Playboy* represented Ireland as peopled by a murderous race of savages. As depictions of the rural west continue in the theatre throughout the twentieth century, however, the violence only gets worse. In J. B. Keane's *The Field*, Bull McCabe kills the Englishman without any legal consequence, and in McDonagh's Irish plays, the bored and frustrated characters carry out horrific acts which can only be rationalized by their skewed perspective on the world. The simulation of violence also becomes more graphic and bloody. Where Synge left off by satirizing heroism in murder, McDonagh pushes his characters beyond the limits of realism as we linger uncomfortably in communities filled with immodest murderers who use torturous methods in their everyday lives.

The benchmark for rural violence originated in *Playboy of the Western World*, where Synge shrewdly manipulated Aristotle's rules for spectacle. We, and the townsfolk, hear of Christy's deeds towards his father throughout the first two acts, so much so that a frustrated Pegeen exclaims 'You've told me that story six times since the dawn of day' (40). It is finally Pegeen, tired of hearing his lies and humiliated by her declaration of love who takes it upon herself to maim Christy Mahon. In defiance of Aristotle's rules, Synge now offers up 'real', performed violence after two acts of hearing about it, only to be told that no death actually occurred. Nicholas Grene has remarked that *Playboy* is a mock version of the Oedipus myth which denies Christy the successful act of parricide, noting however that this does not 'wholly disarm [the play] of its terrors' (96). Like in *Oedipus*, Christy's violence towards his father takes place offstage: however, Pegeen's torturous burning of his leg occurs in full view of

---

the Sound Era, Gaylyn Studlar and Matthew Bernstein, eds. (Bloomington: Indiana University Press, 2001).

the audience and with the complicity and encouragement of the townsfolk. While Christy's punishment for his lies may seem warranted to Pegeen, his treatment is brutal and corresponds to the viciousness Christy claims to have demonstrated towards his father.

The representation of violence in *Playboy* is often over-shadowed by the real riots which occurred during its first productions in both Ireland and America. While the word 'shift' had a great impact on the play's history, the physical struggle with Christy that occurs in Act 3 rarely receives attention, though it foreshadows gruesome acts of violence in later Irish drama (Grene 96). In fact, more attention has been paid to Christy's *claims* of violence than the actualized torture carried out on him at the end of the third act. In Synge's stage directions, Christy is 'pulled down on the floor' then 'they pull the rope tight on his arms.' It is at this point that Christy encounters the terror he inspires:

> **SHAWN.** I'm afeard of him (*To Pegeen*) Lift a lighted sod, will you and scorch his leg.
> **PEGEEN**. (*Blowing fire with the bellows*) Leave go now, young fellow, or I'll scorch your shins.
> **CHRISTY.** You're blowing for to torture me? That's your kind is it? ...
> **SHAWN**. (*In terror*) Keep a good hold, Philly. Be wary for the love of God ... Oh isn't he a Holy terror...
> **CHRISTY.** ... And won't there be crying out in Mayo the day I'm stretched upon the rope, with ladies in their silks and satins sniveling in their lacy kerchiefs, and they rhyming songs and ballads on the terror of my fate. (*He squirms round on the floor and bites Shawn's leg*).
> ...
>
> **MEN**. (*to Pegeen*) bring the sod over will you.
> **PEGEEN**. (*coming over*) God help him so. (*burns his leg*) (82-3).

The violence depicted here is articulated through simulated or 'real' pain which will emerge as a highly effective technique in naturalistic theatre. *Playboy* should even be considered a landmark play not only in Irish drama, but also in terms of its depiction of naturalistic violence. This is not the sexually charged, viscerally exaggerated violence of the Grand Guignol. The naturalistic torture carried out by Pegeen, 'that wild-looking but fine girl' from rural Ireland, is Synge's innovative way of portraying the Irish country-side with charming, and 'authentic' violence.

In Keane's depiction of rural life, the 'Fighting Irish' spirit is seen in the way many of the characters hold onto their beliefs, whether they are right or wrong. Violence is not always a by-product of this spirit, but when it does emerge in *The Field*, the episode is disturbing. The play takes place in 1965, a few years after the scene of *The Hostage*, though the community appears much more antiquated in its regard for civility and the law. In the play, the coarse Bull McCabe attempts to purchase the land he rents, which previously belonged to his ancestors. When he discovers that William, a British capitalist, plans to outbid him, Bull takes it upon himself to 'scare' the foreigner out of town by assaulting him. After confronting and beating him to death with the help of his son Tadhg, the audience observes as Bull 'whispers an act of contrition over the body.' What began as a warning becomes murder and despite Bull's on-stage prayer, neither the law nor the Church could control the outcome.

Much of the rural violence we see on stage goes unpunished. The perpetrators each carry out the acts without consideration for the jurisdiction of the law or the Church. In order to exist in this grotesque version of small town 'Ireland,' citizens take it upon themselves to use violence as a means of justice. Though the village priest is mentioned in *Playboy* he never appears on stage. In *The Field* the Church is more visible, but when the Bishop desperately appeals to the congregation to assist the police in finding the murderer, pleading, 'Among you there is a murderer! You may even know his name, you may even have seen him commit this terrible crime – through your silence, you share his guilt ... ' (Keane 149) no one comes forward. Unlike in *Playboy*, violence is not celebrated by the characters in *The Field* but rather is understood to be an inevitable outcome of the hunger for land. The scene in which Bull kills William is described explicitly with all of the technical details found in the stage directions:

> Tadhg holds William's arms and Bull hits him heavily, skillfully, three or four times. William breaks from them, weakly desperate, but Tadhg grabs him by the legs and brings him to the ground again. Bull grabs his stick and beats William across the back and head ... Tadhg pulls William up as Bull stops beating him with his stick and gives William the knee. William falls helplessly (145-6).

We begin to see in *The Field* how rural violence becomes more and more explicitly simulated on stage. We are not forewarned about the extent of the violence, though there is a sense of threat and danger that foreshadows the climactic action. Unlike in the urban centers of Ireland and the North, the execution of a fight, torture or even murder in the west is done in full view of the audience, revealing the grotesque 'reality' of rural life. This depiction of violence is the kind of cultural branding that perpetuates the idea of rural 'Ireland' as untamed and quixotic. As a result, characters who literally get away with murder only add to the charm of rural life. In the theatre, Martin McDonagh has especially capitalized on this invention more than any other playwright who uses a literary Ireland as a locale. Fighting, torture and murder are commonplace in his rural communities, and whether critics adore him or hate him for staging 'Ireland' we cannot deny his impact over the last ten years. McDonagh excels at the grotesque reality of rural 'Ireland' by treating the violence as a primary condition of life. In the plays of the *Leenane Trilogy*, as in *The Cripple of Inishmaan*, and *The Lieutenant of Inishmore*, violence is endemic and expected, not only by the staged community, but by McDonagh's own audiences. He has gone to great lengths not only to objectify violence on stage, but to draw it out with visceral simulation. As a result, thrill-seeking audience members can see horrific acts of torture, murder and dismemberment right before their eyes. Synge and Keane's depictions of violence seem like rudimentary stick figures compared to McDonagh's fully fleshed-out three-dimensional diagrams of slaughter. Though McDonagh follows a similar pattern in the invention of rural communities – isolation, poverty, and little regard for the law or the institution of the Church – I suggest that the violent spectacle envisioned by his work actually destroys the myth of the 'Fighting Irish.' In McDonagh's world, the visceral quality of violence is so closely related to American film that 'Irish' violence is actually obliterated in order to make room for something more real.

Much has been made of McDonagh's affinity for film violence, which this author need not re-visit. My interest, rather, is in the technically difficult demands that McDonagh makes in the stage directions, so sophisticated that they appear almost impossible to execute. Scenes which include blowing up a stove with a gun, pressing a hand to the stove while pouring hot oil on it and blowing up a cat do not depict 'real' violence, but exaggerated spectacle unique to the stage. His brand of stage spectacle can actually compete with violence depicted in film because of its visceral authenticity. We must not be fooled by seemingly 'real' depictions of gore, however: this is still the theatre, where illusion is crucial. Since he has been present during many of the first productions of his plays, McDonagh's theatre aesthetic has established a certain standard for simulated violence. Because his stage directions include such technically complicated details, a fight director, and often a pyrotechnics specialist are required. McDonagh's affinity for simulated violence was not always so sophisticated, however. Despite his astonishing success over the past ten years, he started out with very little experience in the theatre, and was known to overindulge in dramatizing violence. During the initial rehearsals for *The Beauty Queen of Leenane*, McDonagh wanted Marie Mullen who played Maureen to stand on Anna Manahan's (Mag) back, though she protested 'I'm sorry, Martin, but nobody is going to stand on my spine' (Marks, *New York Times*, B1). He appears to have become more discerning about staging the brutality in his plays in subsequent productions. In Fintan O'Toole's *New Yorker* profile on McDonagh in March 2006, O'Toole reveals that during the rehearsals for *Lieutenant of Inishmore*

> David Wilmot, who played Padraic, crouched over Andrew Connolly, one of his would-be assassins ... When David Brimmer, the fight director, suggested that Wilmot move the knife in such a way as to give the audience the impression that he's about to cut Connolly's ear off, McDonagh objected. 'No the ears are so "Reservoir Dogs".' 'Why don't I bite his ear off?' Wilmot asked. McDonagh shook his head. 'It's going too far. It's being too specific' (40-47).

Curiosity inspired me to interview David Brimmer to find out more about how the violence was staged. Though he was unable to reveal many of the pyrotechnical illusions, Brimmer noted that McDonagh did not want 'brutal, literal, visceral' violence. It was Wilson Milam, who also directed the original production in London, who came up with the solutions to staging the blowing up of a cat as well as the many bloody shoot-outs. Milam also had to solve the problem of the colour of the stage blood when the production moved from the Atlantic to the Lyseum Theatre. Because of the amount of blood on stage, the larger space made the red colour look fake, and a blue hue needed to be added in order to make it look real. As Brimmer has realized in his many years as a fight director, 'reality doesn't work on stage.' In *Lieutenant*, audiences experienced a comic and stylized violence which pushed the boundaries of theatrical realism. Brimmer's colleague fittingly described this experience as a 'blood pie in the face'[4]. We have seen this kind of violence throughout McDonagh's Irish plays: Mick's explosive smashing of skulls in *A Skull in Connemara*: Valene and Coleman's devastating kitchen brawl in *The Lonesome West*: and the beating of Billy in *The Cripple of Inishmaan*. Though much of this kind of violence leaves his audiences in a state of heightened anxiety, McDonagh generously proffers a helping of comic relief just when they need it the most. We may sit in his theatre stained with a bloody pie in the face, but at least we are laughing.

No play in McDonagh's repertoire has pushed the limits of violent spectacle more than *The Lieutenant of Inishmore*. Here, we have a hybrid example of the two kinds of violence seen in staged 'Ireland.' Urban violence from Belfast is relocated to the rural setting of Inishmore where guns intermingle with ignorant country philistines. As the explicit violence of the north, exaggerated through Padraic's obligation to the 'cause,' moves to the country, stylized depictions of violence mix with the 'real' to give us a hyper-real sense of authenticity. This technique is necessary in order to manifest the kind of cinematic 'reality' admired by McDonagh. By providing astonishingly real spectacle through staged illusion, McDonagh's stage becomes literally covered in blood. In McDonagh's hyper-real 'Ireland' we no longer see violence as endemic to Irish culture in its earlier stage manifestations. This is not the kind of violence that surfaces from the 'Fighting Irish,' but is rather a satirized depiction of cruelty beyond the scope of anything seen on stage in the twenty-first century. Though cases of torture and murder have been historically documented on both sides of the struggle for independence in both Ireland and Northern Ireland, staged depictions of such exploits in the 2006 production do not elicit an immediate association with the subject. The brawling 'Fighting Irish' stereotype has been replaced with sophisticated cinematic spectacle.

As violence becomes objectified, as it does in *The Lieutenant of Inishmore*, our sense of what is real is drawn not only from film, but also from the most recognizable social crisis in the collective memory. To North American audiences of the Broadway production in 2006, 'Ireland' does not necessarily register anymore. The torture in the play, for example, illicits the prisoner abuse at Abu Ghraib

---

4 Telephone interview with Mr. Brimmer on October 1, 2006.

more than the victims of the Northern Irish conflict. When the play was first produced in 2001, comparisons to 'Ireland' were remarkably different. Critical discussions focused on the sensitive issue of portraying Padraic, an Irish freedom-fighter who was too violent to be in the IRA. In 2006, however, criticism of the American production focused more on violence as entertainment than on how the play satirically depicted an actual historical crisis. Ignorance usurped the history of Northern Ireland as comparisons were made to film violence, and of course McDonagh's Academy Award for his short film dominated the publicity. Depictions of torture were not criticized, but rather applauded, because of the way 'naked cruelty' could delight a bored Broadway audience. In truth, McDonagh's commentary on terrorism seems more relevant to the crises in the Middle East than to Ireland in 2006.

By lauding the stereotype of the violent 'Irish,' in his plays, McDonagh may indeed have created a monster. The 'In-yer-face' theatrical movement of the 1990s may seem tame in comparison to what is to come. Comparisons to reality are inevitable, but just because we can put such scenes on stage does not mean that we should. Aristotle, after all, believed in torture as a means of extracting the truth from slaves, but he did not want violence on stage. We need to pay close attention to the trend of providing theatre audiences with 'real' cinematic violence on stage. 'Naked cruelty' may be enthralling, but it threatens to devour our own sense of reality.

Bibliography

Behan, Brendan, *Behan: The Complete Plays* (New York: Grove Press, 1978).

Bolger, Dermot, ed., *Druids Dudes and Beauty Queens: The Changing Face of Irish Theatre* (Dublin: New Island, 2001).

'Break a Leg! No really, break it, we need more violence onstage,' www.Slate.com, 3 May, 2006, found at: www.slate.com/toolbar.aspx?action=print&id=2140877.

Conroy, John, *Unspeakable Acts, Ordinary People: The Dynamics of Torture* (New York: Alfred A. Knopf, 2000).

'Depicting the Hurt of Love Curdling into Hate,' *New York Times*, 21 April, 1998.

Grene, Nicholas, *The Politics of Irish Drama* (Cambridge: Cambridge University Press, 1999).

Harrington, John P., and Elizabeth J. Mitchell, eds. *Politics and Performance in Contemporary Northern Ireland* (Amherst, MA: University of Massachusetts Press, 1999).

'Hybrid Handler' *Irish Tatler* (October 1997): 162.

Keane, John B., *The Field and Other Irish Plays* (Dublin: Mercier Press, 1990).

Kiberd, Declan, *Inventing Ireland* (Cambridge, MA: Harvard University Press, 1996).

---, *The Irish Writer and the World* (Cambridge: Cambridge University Press, 2005).

Kilroy, James, ed., *The Playboy Riots* (Dublin: The Doleman Press, 1971).

Kubiak, Anthony, *Stages of Terror* (Bloomington: Indiana University Press, 1991).

McCafferty, Owen, *Mojo Mickybo: Three Plays* (London: Nick Hern Books, 2003).

McDonagh, Martin, *The Lieutenant of Inishmore* (London: Methuen Publishing Ltd., 2001).

---, *A Skull in Connemara* (London: Methuen Publishing Ltd., 1997).

---, *The Lonesome West* (London: Methuen Publishing Ltd., 1997).

---, *The Cripple of Inishmaan* (London: Methuen Publishing Ltd., 1997).

---, *The Beauty Queen of Leenane* (London: Methuen Publishing Ltd., 1997).

O'Toole, Fintan, 'A Mind in Connemara: The Savage World of Martin McDonagh,' *The New Yorker*, 6 March 2006.

Roberts, Randy and James Olson, *John Wayne: American* (New York: Simon & Schuster, Inc., 1995).

'Sick-buckets in the stalls' *The Guardian*, 28 April, 2001.

Sidnell, Michael J., 'Aristotle: The Poetics.' *Sources of Dramatic Theory, 1: Plato to Congreve* (Cambridge: Cambridge University Press, 1991).

Studlar, Gaylyn and Matthew Berstein, eds., *John Ford Made Westerns: Filming the Legend in the Sound Era* (Bloomington: Indiana University Press, 2001).

Synge, J.M., *The Playboy of the Western World* (New York: W.W. Norton and Co. Inc., 1997).

5 | Fighting the Peace: Counter-Narrative, Violence, and the Work of Gary Mitchell.

Tim Miles

> 'It's this: I am free when I am free of what people want to tell me. All stories   are lies. I protest against all stories. All. I protest. A Protestant' (Welch 51).

> 'I wrote this piece in an ocean of optimism. The cease-fire was six weeks old and everybody on TV made the point of saying that the war was over and that there was peace in Northern Ireland ... It was dreadful to see world leaders shaking hands and saying that everybody was going to get on from now on' (Gibbons, REF).

> 'Why do I feel stranded? Why does everyone around me feel stranded?' (Mitchell, *Stranded*)

Gary Mitchell is a prolific playwright whose body of work includes over thirty stage plays, radio scripts and screen plays, including *In a Little World of Our Own* which won *The Irish Times* Best New Play award in 1998, and *The Force of Change*, winner of the Royal Court's Best New Play award in 2000. His plays represent the extremist Loyalist community in Northern Ireland and their response to the ceasefire. Praised in the press, his work has sold out in Ireland, England, and the United States, and was performed in the Czech Republic for the first time in 2007 as part of the British Council funded 'Diversity, Identity, Dialogue' programme of events focusing on Northern Ireland. However, despite international success, he now finds it increasingly difficult to get his work produced in the UK or Ireland. He has not had a major professional production in England since 2004, when *Loyal Women* played at the Royal Court. Many of the theatres that performed his work in the past, such as The Tricycle and Royal Court in London, the Lyric in Belfast, and the Abbey in Dublin, have turned down scripts in recent years.

This essay considers Mitchell's work as presenting a counter-narrative to the hegemonic movement towards peace and 'normalization' in Northern Ireland. In analysing Mitchell as a writer of counter-narratives, I argue that his work is best understood as a response to the marginalization of working-class Loyalists from much cultural and political discourse. This may be seen in his documentation of working-class Loyalist experience, via on-stage discussion and dramatic analyses of that community's institutions and customs. Mitchell's representation of violence is part of this documentation, in analyzing a community who may be post-war, but are not yet post-conflict. His work resists what he calls 'the peace process narrative', an ideological construct that presents peace in binary extremes of success or failure. In this way, his writing acts as a counter-narrative to recent media representations of his community.

Molly Andrews defines counter-narratives as:

> only mak[ing] sense in relation to something else, that which they are countering. The very name identifies it as a positional category. But what is dominant and what is resistant are not, of course, static questions, but rather forever shifting placements. The discussion of counter-narratives is ultimately a consideration of multiple layers of positioning (2).

> Counter-narratives, however, clearly exist beyond this definition, in a wider intellectual context. They embrace post-modernity's interest in the deconstruction of the meta-narratives of modernism, and also, implicitly, the binary oppositions that underpin much of Western thought. They connect to Barthes' idea of being 'surrounded by narratives', and link to Foucault, developing Gramsci's thinking on the problem of hegemony – that certain social groups need to be marginalized in order to maintain social order (Foucault 1965).

Peters and Lankshear suggest that:

> Counter-narratives have a strategic political function of splintering and disturbing grand stories which gain their legitimacy from foundational myths concerning the origins and

development of an unbroken history of the West based on the evolutionary idea of progress (Giroux et al 2).

The movement from war to peace, in a postcolonial context, may be seen as part of this 'evolutionary idea of progress'. Peters and Lankshear go on to refer to Lyotard and his belief that all meta-narratives mask the will-to-power, and serve to exclude the interests of others. They go on to say that 'Counter-narratives are specific and local, and offer critiques that counter the official and hegemonic narratives of everyday life, such as those legitimating stories propagated for specific political purposes to manipulate public consciousness by heralding a national set of common cultural ideals' (13). Counter narrative, they continue, are 'little stories', the stories of those individuals and groups whose knowledge and histories have been 'marginalized, excluded, subjugated or forgotten' in the telling of official narratives. So, taking these theories together, I suggest we have counter-narratives discussed in terms of positioning, as resistance to hegemonic notions of progress which are intended to 'manipulate public consciousness', serving to expose the masking of the will-to-power, and as stories of the marginalized and excluded.

At first glance, it may seem strange to regard Loyalists in Northern Ireland as marginalized and excluded. They are, after all, the majority population, in favour of maintaining the political status quo, who over centuries have gained substantially from dis-crimination against Catholics and Nationalists. Nevertheless, many commentators have written about Loyalists' marginalization. Alan Parkinson, for example, argues that from the start of the 'Troubles' the British media have misrepresented the Loyalist community which has, in turn, failed to present itself in a positive way. Parkinson cites Martin Smyth's Ulster Unionist Information Institute, the first organization specifically designed to promote an understanding of the Unionist position, which did not emerge until 1988, almost two decades after the conflict began. For a culture built on heavy industry, religious faith, and military service, he argues, such 'spin' seemed unimportant (1998, 31). Developing this point, Hutchinson argues that the peace process is problematic to many Loyalists partially because of the word 'process' itself. 'Process' as a concept is anathema to a culture that respects certainty, stead-fastness and contract, echoing the religious slogan 'today, tomorrow and forever' seen displayed outside many Protestant churches in Belfast (2006, 207).

Parkinson argues that the British media were ill-informed about Northern Ireland's history and population, so it tended to portray Loyalists as 'bigots in the bowler hats', as well as 'quizzing the government' on high profile 'miscarriages of justice', allegations of 'shoot to kill', and the abuse of Republican prisoners (78-82). As a result Loyalism looked entrenched, inflexible and irrelevant to many observers. Steve Bruce similarly claims that media commentators often failed to appreciate the strength of Loyalist identity which, in turn, led to a failure to fully understand the Troubles. He claims that during the Troubles there was a move in Loyalist self-definition from Ulster British to Ulster Protestant, and that the community's sense of isolation from the British state increased, as did its sense of perceived threat from the Irish state (vi). Indeed, there has always been a paradox at the centre of Loyalist paramilitary activity, in that it seeks to demonstrate its allegiance to the state by breaking the laws of the state. In so doing, Loyalism undermines its own loyalty, and thus increases its own marginalization. Susan MacKay, in her book *Northern Protestants: An Unsettled People*, repeatedly comments on confused identity and factionalism within the 'lost tribe' of Ulster Protestantism, showing, over many interviews, a community combining defiance with apathy, and a tendency towards negative self-definition. Its perceived exclusion from discourse, and identity discourse in particular, may perhaps be best summarized by Billy Hutchinson, former prisoner and member of the Ulster Volunteer Force (the UVF). Commenting about his teenage years he said: 'no one talked about politics ... our politicians did our thinking, our clergy did our theological thinking, and our bosses did our economic thinking. We just got on with it' (1999, British Library Sound Archive).

The lack of intellectual engagement may well have been fostered by the education system teaching the UK national curriculum. Councillor Tommy Kirkham comments in the documentary *Red, White and Blue*: 'We were taught British history in school and not Irish history. Had we been taught Irish history we might have had a better understanding of where we are today' (1998). Peter Taylor in his documentary and subsequent book, *Loyalists*, makes a similar point. Referring to Gusty Spence, the leader of the Ulster Volunteer Force (UVF) at the start of 'the Troubles', Taylor states that 'Spence knew that Loyalist prisoners had one fatal flaw. They knew about guns and bombs, but nothing about history and politics' (211). Mitchell has made a number of references to his belief that his community has no access to its own history. Speaking about his only history play, *Tearing the Loom*, set during the Protestant rebellion of 1798, he stated:

> Since I began to do all the research, it became very clear to me that, when you read Irish history, you have to be aware who is writing it, because there is no clear Protestant historian, no sense of certain times in history from a Protestant perspective. Even the iconic figures don't come through – you go from King Billy, straight into Carson and Paisley (*The Irish Times* 15/6/2000).

Returning to Andrews' point about 'layers of positioning', it is important to realize that there are a number of histories of the Protestant working-class that Mitchell ignores. He tends to position his community as excluded and as the victim of discrimination, claiming that at school he was discouraged from any ambition to be an actor or a musician, and that when he first joined an amateur dramatics group he was told that plays about working-class Ulster Protestants did not exist (*The Irish Times* 154/6/2000). Later, he claims a film producer told him that his screenplay could not be made, because Loyalists have no legitimate cause and therefore the audience would feel no empathy with the characters. He has said that the Lyric Theatre wanted his play *In a Little World of Our Own* set, not in Belfast, but in an English city like Birmingham, a position denied by the Lyric. He says he knows Protestant actors who have changed their names 'to sound more Catholic' (*The Guardian*, 5/4/2003), and in 2003 was quoted as saying that his work is 'too close for people in Northern Ireland, and too uncomfortable for British Artistic Directors' (*The Irish Post*, 7/11/2003), despite enjoying considerable success around this time. He positions himself as the outsider, seemingly attributing inabilities to get his work produced to his working-class Protestant background. Commenting on the failure of the National Theatre to produce any of his work when he was writer-in-residence there, for example, he says:

> I had to continually remind everyone that it was the national theatre of Great Britain and Northern Ireland. I was told that my plays were not Irish enough. When I explained that I was not Irish, and I wanted to do British plays, I was pretty much shown the door (interview, 2007).

Mitchell offers the following explanation for why he finds it increasingly difficult to get his plays produced:

It is in everybody's interest to keep paying me and produce nothing. I have written radio plays that cannot be made, and given my award winning status, to not even be able to get a radio play made, and yet I am still being commissioned, and I am still being paid. I am still writing them. Is this a very clever strategy to silence the voice of the people that no one wants to hear? (2007).

The BBC, he says, 'do not want to have anything to do with the Protestant community whatsoever' (2007) and he now refuses to write for them, as he refuses to allow anyone else to adapt his work for television. He finds the origins of this conspiracy in a construction of peace designed – to refer back to Peters and Lankshear – to 'manipulate public consciousness by heralding a national set of common cultural ideas', about the advent of peace.

In December 2005 Mitchell's home and car were bombed, allegedly by dissident Loyalist paramilitaries. Responding to what he considered to be limited press and public sympathy he stated:

If I was a Muslim writer whose work upset members of my community so much that some were threatening to kill me, then it would be a *cause célèbre*. There would be questions in parliament, writers would stage protests and Salman Rushdie would write letters of support. But because this is Northern Ireland what's happening to my family isn't part of the peace process narrative (McDonald, 2006).

Because his plays explore the continuing influence of Loyalist paramilitary organizations, principally the Ulster Defence Association (UDA), Mitchell claims the blame lies firmly with the highest political power:

You have a Prime Minister who is so determined that the history books will record him as the man who bought peace to Northern Ireland. Part of the process means you set up the committee and they go in to do a report on paramilitary activity. If they come back and say yes, the paramilitaries are doing everything, the peace process is failing. If they come back and say the paramilitaries are doing nothing, then the peace process is succeeding, so they're not sending in Sherlock Holmes (interview, 2007).

Although many of his allegations are difficult to assess, what is clear is that Mitchell positions himself as an outspoken maverick. He has spoken of a 'culture of victimhood' whereby, in his words, 'we can all agree to feel sorry for gays or blacks' (interview, 2007). However, he feels his community is excluded even from a public acknowledgement of its suffering and marginalization, his argument resonating with the slogans on one of the larger murals on the Shankhill Road which proclaims: 'Where are our enquiries? Where is our truth? Where is our justice?'

Mitchell argues that he is from a marginalized community, and has been discriminated against by producers and theatre companies despite considerable success. Positioning himself accordingly in the media, he argues that his treatment is the result of the construction of a hegemonic peace narrative. In interview he agrees that there is 'a lot of good work on the ground' and talks admiringly about the community work done by both the DUP and Sinn Fein, calling this a 'real' peace process. We now need to consider his assertions of a dominant 'peace process narrative', and that English people think that 'everything is fine now you have peace'. My aim here is simply to place Mitchell's counter-narratives in context.

Speaking in February 2007, Pam Brighton, Artistic Director of Dubbeljoint and producer of most of Mitchell's radio plays, claimed that 'there are only two stories the BBC wants now', these being, in her words, 'my life as a bomber', or 'Belfast is like everywhere else' (interview, 2007): that is either a sensationalization of conflict, or an acceptance of the universality, and success, of peace and normalization. Peace also requires new forms of theatre. Paula McFetridge, former artistic director of the Lyric, has spoken of the 'end of the single community drama'. Much arts funding is aimed at 'bringing people together', rendering problematic Mitchell's enclosed dramatic worlds of Protestant in-fighting.

Malachi O'Doherty has intervened into the controversial topic of arts funding, to argue that the funding bodies for the arts are involved in ideological manipulation of culture for a political purpose: 'The politician reads culture as allegiance and community as support ... To be an artist – for whom culture is a description of what we do, not a prescription of what we *ought* to do – this is repulsive' (2003, 74). He continues, claiming that: 'Political movements feel entitled to take responsibility for wider areas of our thinking and demand conformity ... There is pressure to direct arts and community funding towards those who best represent the elements of the predominant political model' (74). He goes on to suggest that 'in an effort to establish political harmony ... simplistic readings of local culture are privileged above all others' (75). These 'simplistic readings' are the representation of 'intense, monolithic and dangerous sectarianism', or its converse, peace and normality.

He concludes: 'It assumes that this society doesn't need honest reflection but can get by sufficiently on delusion' (75).

To give one example of a post-conflict Belfast drama, in March 2007 *Leaves* by Lucy Caldwell, winner of that year's George Devine award, opened at the Royal Court, having transferred from Dublin. The play is set in Belfast in the 'present day', and concerns a family's attempts to deal with the aftermath of the eldest daughter's attempted suicide. Nicholas De Jongh, reviewing the London production for the *Evening Standard*, noticed that 'any political/-religious discussion about Northern Ireland's violent history or its impact on the girl never moves beyond the minimal or anecdotal' (2007). The play represents Belfast as being much like everywhere else. Mitchell, however, is anxious to point out what he sees as the reality, positioning himself in opposition to these kinds of representations. In interview, he expresses his belief that the reality is vastly different to the popular perception:

> **MILES**. I wonder how much violence there is that is no longer reported?
> **MITCHELL**. Millions. Millions. It is exactly the opposite of what is portrayed (interview, 2007).

In a report for the Institute for Conflict Research, published in 2006 and entitled *No Longer a Problem? Sectarian Violence in Northern Ireland*, Neil Jarman states that between 1994 and 2005 there were on average five attacks per month on churches, chapels, or Orange Halls: that there were 376 riots in the interface zones of north Belfast over the same period: that the police recorded 294 sectarian incidents between April 2001 and March 2004, and these incidents were 'largely of the most serious type, while minor forms of sectarianism, such as verbal abuse, harassment, visual displays and graffiti were largely unrepresented' (2005). At least seventeen barriers (peace walls) have been built, extended or heightened in Belfast since the ceasefires of 1994. Younger people are, according to Jarman, more likely to experience sectarian harassment and violence than older age groups, and a 'very high' percentage of young people favour a segregated living, schooling and working environment. The Northern Ireland Housing Executive reported that from 1991 – 2005, an average of 1,378 people per year sought re-housing because of sectarian, racist, or paramilitary intimidation.

Peter Shirlow has published a number of studies on sectarian violence in Northern Ireland. In *'Who Fears to Speak': Fear, Mobility, and Ethno-Sectarianism in the two 'Ardoynes'* he states 'this study indicates that the implied de-territorialization needed in order to shift Northern Irish society towards more agreed and agreeable forms of political ownership and consensus-building remains distant and geographically rootless' (2006, 18). He goes on to say that:

> Despite the cessation of most paramilitary violence we are left with a situation in which the creation of territorial division and rigid ethno-sectarian communities means that fear and mistrust are still framed by a desire to create communal separation. Without doubt residential segregation still regulates ethno-sectarian animosity through complex spatial devices (84).

Similarly, John Gray states that culture exists to create 'greater mutual understanding' and to 'change ourselves and our society for the better' (2003), reflecting again this notion of the political manipulation of art. However, he too claims that arts funding has, paradoxically, increased sectarian polarization by showing equal respect for the two traditions:

> Belfast appears simultaneously to have become more Irish than anywhere else in Ireland, and more determinedly Ulster-Scots than the Scots in asserting its Scottishness. We are in danger of putting down cultural markers in a way that a newly confident Irish Republic and an emerging Scotland are moving beyond (2003, 47).

In his book *Belfast: Segregation, Violence and the City,* Shirlow reads the chilling potential of this development, arguing that 'there is Balkanization at present: in a benign way it could turn into ethnically-divided Belgium, or in a malign way, towards the former Yugoslavia' (2006, 78).

Nevertheless, the British press has voiced often unqualified statements of optimism about peace, especially in recent months. Much media coverage was given to the withdrawal of British troops in July 2007. Andrews states that 'one of the key functions of master narratives is that they offer people a way of experiencing what is assumed to be a normative experience' (1), and Mitchell has expressed his anger that 'English people think everything is fine now'. Christopher Hampton once commented that John Osborne, a playwright with whom Mitchell has much in common, wrote plays because he felt that 'the propaganda is not true' (Palmer, 2006). Mitchell claims a similar position:

MILES. How consciously are you aware when you write of countering misconceptions about Protestantism?
MITCHELL. One hundred per cent. One hundred per cent.
MILES. Are you countering different preconceptions with different audiences, or maybe they are the same?
MITCHELL. I think generally they are the same (interview, 2007).

These misconceptions are formed by a lack of reporting of violence and the continuing role of the paramilitaries in drug dealing and other forms of racketeering. But other misconceptions are evident in common cultural representations of working-class Protestants:

> The problem I had with the usual representation of Protestants would be that they were always the same, you know, the drunken, depressed man who beats up his wife, and the funny, silly UDA cowboys. All seemed to be one dimensional ... no attempt to express the very real differences within Protestantism, the fact that within one family you could have a born-again Christian and a paramilitary (Gibbons, 2000).

An example of such stereotypical characterization may be seen in the BBC television drama, *Holy Cross*. The story concerns two families caught up in the headline events of 2001 on the Ardoyne Road in Belfast where a dispute arose concerning the rights of schoolgirls from the Catholic Ardoyne area of north Belfast to walk a few hundred yards through the predominantly Protestant area of Glenbryn to the Holy Cross primary school. Local Protestants objected and the dispute escalated. *Holy Cross* won much critical praise winning three *FIPA D'Ors* at the FIPA Biarritz *Festival International de Programmes Audiovisuels*. The BBC broadcast proudly introduced the film as a 'searing indictment of sectarian hatred in Northern Ireland'. Copies are available at The Centre for Education for Racial Equality in Scotland (CERES) at the University of Edinburgh. However, the Protestant men are portrayed as vicious and amoral, even terrorizing their own children. To quote from one angered viewer whose message was posted on the BBC's website:

> I would like to comment on the portrayal of the Protestant community represented on tonight's programme, *Holy Cross*. I feel it is a disgustingly stereotypical view, one-sided and grossly inaccurate. It depicts the protesters as lolly sucking buffoons complete with combat 18 clothing. I am very disappointed at the whole program and the BBC itself (http://www.bbc.co.uk, accessed 20 Feb 2007).

Similarly, the film *Resurrection Man* which was released in 1997, and is loosely based on the lives of the 'Shankhill butchers', who tortured and murdered nineteen Catholics during the 1970s, fails to provide a social or political context. The film is slick and violent. Reviewers use such phrases as 'the Irish predisposition to violence' (Eircom, online). As Finlayson points out, 'treating people as emerging from some sort of essential nature depoliticizes the groups themselves' (73), thus linking to Foucault's belief that certain social groups need to be marginalized in order to maintain social order. Mitchell is scathing about *Resurrection Man* and others such as *The Boxer*, or *Some Mother's Son*, that include representations of Ulster Protestantism. He adopts a similar adversarial position when commenting on many plays. Marie Jones's *A Night in November*, for example, is the story of Kenneth, a Protestant civil servant. Appalled at the sectarian attitudes of his wife and father in-law, Kenneth abandons his Loyalism and adopts a new all embracing Irish identity, following his decision to support the Irish football team: 'I am free of it. I am a free man ... I am a Protestant man. I'm an Irish man' (2000, 108) he proudly declares at the end of the play. To Mitchell the play is ridiculous:

> I do not know of any Protestant who just changed over night and started supporting the Republic, unless there was money involved. I think that those kinds of plays are suggesting that corruption is a virtue. The way our community would look at that is that man is a traitor. He was born a Northern Irish Protestant! ... There are elements of our community that have moved across but they are so few and they are so dodgy. Look at the elections. David Ervine is the only ex-paramilitary ever to have been elected (interview, 2007).

However, for Mitchell's plays to work dramatically, audiences need to empathize with his hard men of Loyalist violence. In *In a Little World of Our Own*, for example, Mitchell gives us UDA member Ray, who commits a murder, and is virulently sectarian, disapproving of the 'namby pamby' ways of the new UDA leadership and their desire for peace. But Ray is also loving and protective towards his learning-disabled younger brother, Richard. Indeed, he owns up to the killing when suspicion falls on Richard, sacrificing his own life to defend his young sibling. During a post-show audience discussion with Mitchell at the Peacock in Dublin, one woman in the audience claimed that Ray could not have committed the murder because during the play she fell in love with him, and she could not fall in love with a killer. Mitchell's response was to say 'But that's the point'. He wants us to see Ray as a tragic hero, a victim of circumstances, whose flaw is one of commitment, passion and loyalty, and thus a man worthy of being loved. Mitchell has said that he believes violence to be 'a waste of time' (2007), but Ray's tragedy is inherently linked to his violence: we feel for him, in part, *because* he is compelled to be violent, to defend his community and his family. There is a line to be drawn between an attempt to understand violence, and an act of justification, and Mitchell's work can come close to that line: there is inevitably a mutual suspicion between him and anyone who sees art as an agent of social change.

Perhaps in a similar way to 1970's feminist companies who sought a female-only space to enable an internal debate, Mitchell wants to create a film and theatre company that is funded by Protestants, staffed by Protestants and presents Protestant stories, to enable debates about Protestantism while, in the words of Maguire, 'resisting pressure from outside to conform to particular perspectives on the community from within which he writes' (146). Mitchell sees his function as a playwright to create a body of work to 'challenge and ultimately replace' existing representations of Protestants during the struggle for peace (2007), to counter 'those legitimating stories propagated for specific political purposes' to again quote Lankshear and Peters. McFetridge comments about Mitchell as never having really seen him as a theatre writer, but more of a documentary maker. His work, to him, is indeed about documentation:

> **MITCHELL.** I want the history recorded. Tony Blair is writing his own history. He is so desperate to be the man who brought peace to Northern Ireland, but it is all nonsense.
> **MILES**. You're trying to be a historian?
> **MITCHELL.** Yes, I am. Yes, I am (interview, 2007).

In his plays, Mitchell's documentation of history may be said to broadly take three forms: dialogue-driven discussion about Protestant history and politics: an examination of Protestant institutions and traditions: and an analysis of the isolation and in-fighting that has come from a supposed peace. In *Remnants of Fear*, for example, the teenage Tony is impressed by the men of violence, principally his uncle Geordie who bears many similarities to Ray from *In a Little World of Our Own*. In both plays, these reactionary men of violence are given foils with whom to have discussions about a dilemma within the family. This serves as a metaphor for a problem within the wider family of the United Kingdom. Ray has his brother (a well-meaning liberal), his sister-in-law (a devout Christian) and his friend Walter (who conforms to the wishes of the UDA leadership), and they discuss what to do when Richard is suspected of murder. In *Remnants of Fear*, Geordie, argues with Charlie, Tony's father, who believes in progress and negotiation. Here is Charlie talking to Tony who has been caught in bed with his girlfriend by her father:

> You are worse than the DUP. I want you to listen very carefully without butting in. (*Pause*) I am going, as your dad, to see him, as her dad, and we are going to sit down, as adults, and sort this whole thing out. Now, he won't get exactly everything he wants from this deal and I won't get exactly everything I want from the deal but we will come to an agreement somehow, some way. And when we do, what I am telling you is that you have to stick to it this time. Can you do that? (63).

He could easily be talking about the peace process. At other times, Mitchell's documentation of history is more literal and less metaphoric. Maud is Tony's grandmother. She analyses the rift between the UDA and the DUP:

> They used to be the same but they're not any more. Too many people fell out with each other and bickering started between the two organizations. It's like the way the UDA no longer supports the DUP because it got tired of the DUP blackening their name on TV. Or the way they just don't do whatever Paisley says any more because Big Paisley also started to call them terrorists and said they were just as bad as the IRA (72).

In his radio play *Stranded* Mitchell writes a pained tone poem, documenting Protestant ignorance and isolation:

> We always believe what we are told ... why should we change? Jesus doesn't change? We are often quoted words written a long time ago, and you cannot remember when, but you know it isn't now ...when did we start saying 'Ulster says no'? 1912? 1995? If a culture refuses to change can it progress? ... Was it because someone said 'no' and we all backed them up? I can't remember. I can remember saying 'no': No United Ireland, No Pope here, No change, no, no, no ... the word Protestant implies we are against something, anything, everything. A negative word ... we know what we are not, what we are not going to do, what we are going to fight against, to break down, to destroy ... Where is our culture? Where is our identity? Where is our history? Where is our future? (2001)

These questions recur in Mitchell's work. Similarly, characters give voice to issues relating to Protestant ignorance and media misrepresentation. In *Remnants of Fear* Charlie comments on the contrasting experiences of Loyalist and Republican prisoners:

> The IRA all came out of prison with degrees and diplomas. They went on to become politicians, journalists and whatever else but what did the Prods do? Weights and drugs. That's it ... While the IRA young men were studying. They were actually bringing in lecturers from Queens. Professors. While they were doing that the UDA young men were marching in circles, playing snooker, lifting weights and doing drugs (120).

This rather overstates the case, as Billy Hutchinson's prison reading, for example, included William Wordsworth and Kier Hardy. But the perception of exclusion from learning and culture is one that recurs in these plays. The context for the above quotation is the debate between Charlie, Maud and Geordie, in which government policy and media representation is also critiqued:

> **CHARLIE.** I packed my wife in when I found out she was sleeping with someone else and I packed the UDA in when it became an illegal organization.
> **MAUD.** The government only made it illegal to suit the IRA.
> **CHARLIE.** The government had to make it illegal because it was killing innocent people and pretending they were all in the IRA. And that's only the tip of the iceberg.
> **GEORDIE.** Propaganda, propaganda, propaganda. You've been watching BBC Northern Ireland for too long (133).

Mitchell is concerned with analysing and documenting the changes happening within Unionist traditions and institutions. Many of his plays consider change and conflict within the UDA, such as *Trust* and *In a Little World of Our Own*. *The Force of Change* and the radio trilogy *Dividing Force* concern change within the traditionally Protestant dominated police services, and *Marching On* looks at the Protestant tradition of marching to celebrate victory at the battle of the Boyne. Commenting on *Marching On* Michael Billington claimed that the play: 'fulfils one of drama's most basic functions: the anthropological recording of the country's customs' (*The Guardian* 17/6/2000), and Mitchell is keen to confirm his accuracy saying 'I went to the bother of writing these plays, so I am going to be accurate. If there are words in the play it is because I have heard them. I am writing what people say' (interview, 2007).

In all of these plays power structures are collapsing, within both legal and illegal organizations. In *Marching On* there is a common Mitchell character, the police officer divided in his loyalty. Here Christopher, an RUC officer, finally breaks under the pressure, unable to combine the roles of police officer, father, brother and Protestant:

> Well, here's the thing – who's stopping them marching? – Me. And who's to bring him in? – Me. And who's to do this Scottish fucker for shagging his sister? – Me. And who's not allowed to see his own kids? Me-me-me-fucking me. Well, fuck it. Fuck it all, fuck the lot of you' (135-6).

As the Beast Sleeps is the story of Kyle, persuaded by the UDA leadership to lead a punishment squad to attack 'renegade' members of the UDA who wish to continue the war, as the leadership negotiates for peace. He is motivated, at least in part, by money, and the play asks, in the words of Stuart Graham who played Kyle both onstage and in the film version, 'what does an unemployed terrorist do?' He is also motivated by a sense of loyalty. Kyle tries to be loyal to all sides: to his wife and child, for whom he feels obliged to earn money, to his friend, Freddie, whom he is ordered to beat, and to the UDA leadership, who give this order. The play ends with Kyle alone, accused of treachery on all sides. During the war, Kyle was a thief with close friends and family, who stole for the UDA, but during the move to peace, he has become isolated and violent.

Mitchell represents violence as morally ambiguous. In so doing he offers a counter-narrative to its representation in works like *Holy Cross* and *A Night in November*, where the characters are one-dimensional heroes and villains. Ray is violent but loving: Kyle is violent but loyal and does want peace. Ray's violence is motivated, in part, by fraternal devotion, as is Kyle's by a need to provide for his family and help the UDA achieve peace. Opposing violence is, in Mitchell's plays, usually a complicated and uncertain position, involving great personal risk. The journalist in *Independent Voice*, for example, seeks to try to stand up to the local UDA and their involvement in drug dealing, but ends up being so intimidated that he agrees to their demands, and operates as little more than a mouthpiece for the paramilitaries – the UDA having realized, through the journalist's actions, the power of the press.

Mitchell represents the delivery of justice and its consequences as complicated. Caroline in *The Force of Change* attempts to purge collusion in the RUC and, in so doing, alienates a junior officer who, fearful for his future in the force, further co-operates with the men of violence. The other officers, as they become aware of this situation, use threats of violence against a prisoner to obtain the necessary information to prevent further violence. An attempt at justice, to exclude and condemn the paramilitaries, leads to corruption, which is countered with further violence, and the circle is complete. Similarly, in *Independent Voice*, the journalists' attempts to confront corruption lead to the murder of an alleged paedophile who is almost certainly innocent. Telling the truth is no easy matter.

Mitchell's plays offer a counter-narrative to the hegemonic narrative of a movement towards peace in Northern Ireland. His plays offer resistance to a construction of peace that fails to acknowledge the complexities of an Ulster that is not yet post-conflict. However, as Andrews says, writers of counter-narratives may consider their circumstances to be specific, but not unique. In his stories of conflict within families and in the work places, Mitchell offers narratives that transcend his own locality. As he says, 'I do not write about Northern Ireland, I write about people.' In so doing he counters the dominant narratives that seek a blanket condemnation of the Loyalist paramilitaries. Andrews claims that we become the stories we know, and this process produces and reproduces the master narrative. The challenge then is to avoid its internalization: 'Master narratives offer a way of identifying what is assumed to be a normative experience ... they become the blueprint for all stories. Ultimately, the power of master narratives comes from their internalization' (13). By presenting counter-narratives, Mitchell argues that the Peace Process can offer 'the very real chance to show that we are not this mass triumphalist band of bigots' (Mitchell, *The Guardian* 2006), not just to those outside Ulster Loyalism, but to themselves as well.

Primary Texts:

BBC *The Art of the Troubles*, (BBC Radio 4, 3 June, 1995).
Brozel, Mark, dir. *Holy Cross* (BBC Northern Ireland, BBC2, May 2004).
Caldwell, Lucy, *Leaves* (London: Nick Hern, 2007).
Evans, Marc, dir. *Resurrection Man* (Revolution Films, GB, 1998).
Hutchinson, Ron, *Rat in the Skull* (unpublished script).
Ibsen, Henrik, *An Enemy of the People*, adapted by Martin Lynch, dir. Roland Jaquarello, BBC Radio 3, 15 October 2006.

Jones, Marie, *A Night in November* (London: Nick Hern, 2000).

Leigh, Mike, dir., *Four Days in July* (BBC, 1985).

Lynch, Martin, *The Interrogation of Ambrose Fogarty* (Belfast: Lagan, 2003).

Lynch, Martin, and Conor Grimes, *The History of the Troubles Accordin' to my Da* (unpublished script).

McGuinness, Frank, 'Observe the Sons of Ulster Marching Towards the Somme' in *Frank McGuinness: Plays 1* (London: Faber and Faber, 1996).

Mitchell, Gary, *As the Beast Sleeps*, (London: Nick Hern, 2001).

---, *Dividing Force*, dir. Pam Brighton, BBC Radio 3, 10 – 24 May 2002.

---, *Energy* (unpublished script).

--- , *The Force of Change*, (London: Nick Hern, 2000).

---, *In a Little World of Our Own* (London: Nick Hern, 1998).

---, *Independent Voice* (unpublished script).

---, *Marching On* (unpublished 155

---, *Red, White and Blue: A Protestant Tale* (Brian Waddell Productions, BBC1, January 1998).

---, *Remnants of Fear* (unpublished script).

---, *Stranded* dir. Pam Brighton, BBC Radio 3, 4 September 2001.

---, *Tearing the Loom*, (London: Nick Hern, 1998).

Palmer, Tony, dir. *John Osborne and the Gift of Friendship* (GB: Isolde Films, 2006).

Welch, Robert, *Protestants* (Belfast: Lagan, 2006)

Secondary Texts:

Anderson, Chris, *The Billy Boy: The Life and Death of LVF Leader Billy Wright*, (Edinburgh and London: Mainstream, 2002).

Andrews, Molly, 'Counter-Narratives and the Power to Oppose' in Andrews, Molly, and Bamberg, Peter (eds.) *Considering Counter-Narratives: Narrating, Resisting, Making Sense* (John Benjamins: Amsterdam, 2004).

Bamberg, P., 'Considering Counter-Narratives' in Andrews, Molly, and Peter Bamberg, eds. *Considering Counter-Narratives: Narrating, Resisting, Making Sense* (John Benjamins: Amsterdam, 2004).

Brighton, Pam, Interview with author, 12 Feb 2007.

Bruce, Steve, *The Edge of the Union: The Ulster Loyalist Political Vision* (Oxford: Oxford, 1994).

Byrne, Ophelia, *The Stage in Ulster from the Eighteenth Century*, (Belfast: Linen Hall Library, 1997).

---, (ed.) *State of Play?* (Belfast: Linen Hall Library, 2001).

Cornell, Jennifer, 'Walking with Beasts: Gary Mitchell and the Representation of Ulster Loyalism.' *Canadian Journal of Irish Studies*, 29.2, (2003): 27-34.

Culler, Jonathon, *Barthes: A Very Short Introduction* (Oxford: Oxford University, 1993).

Carruthers, Mark, Stephen Deeds & Tim Loane, eds, *Re-Imagining Belfast: A Manifesto for the Arts* (Belfast: Cultural Resolution, 2003).

Etherton, Michael, *Contemporary Irish Dramatists* (New York: Sant Martin's, 1989).

Feldman, Allen, *Formations of Violence: The Narrative of the Body and Political Terror in Northern Ireland* (Chicago: Chicago University Press, 1991).

Finlayson, Alan, 'Discourse and Contemporary Loyalist Identity', in Shirlow, Peter and Mark McGovern, eds, *Who are 'The People'? Unionism, Protestantism, and Loyalism in Northern Ireland* (Pluto: London, 1997).

Foucault, Michael and Donald Bouchard, eds, *Language, Counter-Memory, Practice: Selected Essays and Interviews by Michel Foucault* (Ithaca: Cornell University Press, 1977).

Freeman, Mark, 'Charting the Narrative Unconscious: Cultural Memory and the Challenge of Autobiography' in Andrews, Molly, and Bamberg, Peter (eds.) *Considering Counter-Narratives: Narrating, Resisting, Making Sense* (John Benjamins: Amsterdam, 2004).

Gibbons, Fiachra, 'Truth and Nail', *The Guardian*, 10 April 2000, p.24.

Giroux, Henry A, Colin Lankshear, Peter McLaren & Michael Peters, *Counter Narratives: Cultural Studies and Critical Pedagogies in Post-Modern Spaces* (Routledge: London, 1996).

Grace, Sherrill and Jerry Wasserman, eds, *Theatre and Autobiography* (Vancouver: Talon books, 2006).

Gray, John 'Culture is for Change' in Mark Curruthers, Stephen Deeds, Tim Loane, eds., *Re-Imagining Belfast: A Manifesto for the Arts* (Belfast: Cultural Resolution, 2003).

Harrington, John P. and E. Mitchell, *Politics and Performance in Contemporary Northern Ireland* (Massachusetts: University of Massachusetts, 1999).

Holdsworth, Nadine, 'Namby Pamby Ways Don't Get Results: Cultures of Machismo and Violence in the Work of Gary Mitchell', The Twelfth Annual Central New York Conference on Language and Literature, 28 October 2002.

Hutchins, Wesley, 'Gary Mitchell's Talk Process'. *Poesie Theatre De L'Ireland Contemporanie*, 56.2 (2003): 206-218.

Hutchison, Yvette, 'Counter-Narratives: Challenging or Underpinning the Dominant', University of Winchester, Counter-Narratives: Challenging/Conflicting/Confusing Voices, April 4, 2006.

Irish Playography, http://www.irishplayography.com/, accessed 5 May 2007.

Jarman, Neil, 'No Longer a Problem? Sectarian Violence in Northern Ireland', Institute for Conflict Research, 2005 http://www.community-relations.org.uk/consultation_uploads/OFMDFM_-_Sectarian_Violence.pdf, accessed 5 May 2007.

Llewellyn-Jones, Margaret, *Contemporary Irish Drama and Cultural Identity* (Bristol: Intellect, 2002).

McDonald, Henry 'Playwright Hits Back Against Intimidation', *The Guardian*, 29 January 2006. Available at http://www.guardian.co.uk. Last accessed 15 April 2006.

McDonald, Henry, & Jim Cusack, *UDA: Inside the heart of the Loyalist Terror* (Dublin: Penguin, 2004).

McFetridge, Paula, Interview with author, 14 Feb 2004.

McKay, Susan, *Northern Protestants: An Unsettled People* (Belfast, Blackstaff, 2000).

McKenna, Bernard, *Rupture, Representation and the Refashioning of Identity in Drama from the North of Ireland, 1969-1994* (Westport, Praeger, 2003).

MacNeice, Louis, *Collected Poems* (Faber and Faber, London, 1992)

Maguire, Tom, *Making Theatre in Northern Ireland* (Exeter, Exeter University, 2006).

McDowell, Wallace, 'Traditional Routes', Irish Theatre in England, National Portrait Gallery, 17 June 2005.

Mitchell, Gary, Interview with author, 12 Feb 2007.

Morash, Christopher, *A History of Irish Theatre, 1601-2000* (Cambridge: Cambridge University, 2002).

Morrow, Duncan 'Suffering for Righteousness' Sake? Fundamentalist Protestantism and Ulster Politics' in Shirlow, Peter, & Mark McGovern eds. *Who are 'The People'? Unionism, Protestantism, and Loyalism in Northern Ireland* (Pluto: London, 1997).

Mulholland, Marc *Northern Ireland: A Very Short Introduction* (Oxford: Oxford University, 2002).

Murphy, Y., A. Leonard, G. Gillespie, and K. Brown eds, *Troubles Images: Posters and Images of the Northern Irish Conflict from the Linen Hall Library, Belfast* (Belfast: Linen Hall Library, 2001).

O'Doherty, Malachi 'A Bit of a Nuisance' in Gray, John 'Culture is for Change' in Curruthers, Mark et al (eds.), *Re-Imagining Belfast: A Manifesto for the Arts* (Belfast: Cultural Resolution, 2003).

Parkinson, Alan F., *Ulster Unionism and the British Media* (Four Courts: Dublin, 1998).

Pilkington, Lionel, 'Theatre and Cultural Politics in Northern Ireland: The Over the Bridge Controversy, 1959, *Eire-Ireland*, 30.4 (1996), 76-93.

Russell, Richard Ranking, 'Loyal to the Truth: Aesthetic Loyalism in the work of Gary Mitchell' *Modern Drama*, 48.1, (2005).

Sass, Louis A., 'The Consolations of Counter-Narrative' *Narrative Enquiry* 8.2 (1998): 429-443.

Shirlow, Peter, 'Who Fears to Speak': Fear, Mobility, and Ethno-Sectarianism in the Two 'Ardoynes' in *The Global Review of Ethnopolitics. Special Issue: Northern Ireland*, 3.1 (2003): 76-91.

Shirlow, Peter and Mark McGovern, eds, *Who are 'The People'? Unionism, Protestantism, and Loyalism in Northern Ireland* (Pluto: London, 1997).

Shirlow, Peter and Brendan Murtagh, *Belfast: Segregation, Violence and the City* (Pluto: London, 2006).

Sinnerton, Henry, *David Ervine: Uncharted Waters* (Dingle: Mount Eagle, 2002).

Tachibana, Reiko, *Narrative as Counter-Memory: A Half-Century of Post-war Writing in Germany and Japan* (Albany: State University of New York, 1998).

Taylor, Peter, *Loyalists* (Bloomsbury: London, 1999).

Whitehead, Baruch, 'Music of the Civil Rights Movement' conference paper presented at 'Counter-Narratives: Challenging/Conflicting/Confusing Voices' University of Winchester, 4 April 2006.

Wood, Ian S., *God, Guns and Ulster: A History of Loyalist Paramilitaries* (Caxton: London, 2003).

6 | Representing Acceptability: Power, Violence and Satire in Martin McDonagh's *The Lieutenant of Inishmore.*

Catherine Rees

This essay explores a variety of strategies used by playwrights and directors to represent the 'unrepresentable', focusing in particular on Martin McDonagh's *The Lieutenant of Inishmore*. It draws upon Lyotard's argument that the postmodern 'produces the feeling that there is something unrepresentable' (*The Postmodern Explained* 15), that it establishes a division between what is literally experienced and what can be imagined. Lyotard states that 'it should be made clear that it is not up to us to *provide reality*, but to invent allusions to what is conceivable but not presentable' (15). This concept of 'conceivable but not presentable' describes two separate categories of imagery and a complex relationship between them: that which is literally depicted (in this case on stage), and that which the audience can only imagine. The concept also recognizes the audience's awareness that these categories might be reconciled in an explicit representation, and their resulting fear or anticipation. In this way, the audience can be moved, terrorized, outraged or simply made uncomfortable, not necessarily by what is depicted explicitly – although this of course still plays a crucial role – but by their reactions to what they have witnessed, and their expectation of what is yet to come.

The terms this essay will use to describe these responses are 'normative representation' which refers to action or speech actually experienced in the theatre (referred to below by Wehmeyer and others as what is 'real'), and 'imaginative speculation' which describes the audience's personal and internal response to this action (referred to by Wehmeyer as 'play'). Imaginative speculation can be described in this instance as Lyotard's 'conceivable but not presentable' as it exists in the minds of the audience but not in the 'real' world of the stage action. This essay will use these terms to explore Martin McDonagh's *The Lieutenant of Inishmore* (2001) to establish a discussion of taboo theatre. This term is being used here to describe both theatre that permeates the general sphere of cultural discourse, and drama that challenges the audience in the ways described above. In many cases, the belief that a play can communicate some 'truth' or 'reality' beyond the fictional events it describes can deeply disturb the audience. This confluence of imaginative speculation and cultural resonance, beyond the text of the play, is what can make theatre controversial or notorious. This fragile balance can be further upset if the play is classified as a comedy or satire, as these genres can add to the audience's discomfort, particularly if beliefs they hold are ridiculed or mocked. This essay will discuss the use of comedy in the theatre, as well as establishing a separation between representations of comedy and satire on the stage. I will suggest that the ironic elements funda-mental to satire create different levels of audience response, as they speculate in differing ways. As Arthur Pollard puts it, the 'essence of successful satire [is] to get your victims "hopping mad" and your audience "laughing their heads off"' (12). Firstly, however, I would like to explain the terms laid out above in greater detail.

Anthony Kubiak's *Stages of Terror: Terrorism, Ideology and Coercion as Theatre History* (1991) provides a theoretical outline for the various ways in which terror operates in the theatre. Whilst his focus is clearly on modes of terrorism, his descriptions of the processes involved in creating terror and fear of violence in the audience are particularly relevant here. Kubiak's premise is that terror is an unrepresentable force and it exists only in the minds of the audience. As soon as it is realized on stage, it ceases to be terror and becomes terrorism: that is, it engages the mechanics and apparatus of the spectators' previously unrealized fears. He writes:

> [T]he terror that is the result of this terrorism – the real pain inflicted on the body – can never become a sign, can never enter a system of information and exchange. It remains unsignifiable, unrepresentable. This distinction between terror and terrorism, the difference between real pain and the techniques of its production, represents the reification and commodification of terror into terrorism (21).

This process and relationship between terror and terrorism is exemplified in theatrical representation. As Kubiak explains:

> Here we are faced with a paradox ... because in performance what cannot be articulated must be shown. And when it is shown, it ceases to be what it was. Thus when terror enters the information system of performance, it ceases, in a sense, to be terror – which is unspeakable, and unrepresentable – and becomes a mask of itself. Terror is transformed into the imaging system of terrorism (11).

Kubiak's argument that theatrical processes transform unrepresentable feelings of terror into the recognizable images of terrorism has clear implications for this analysis of McDonagh's work. If we return to Lyotard's discussion of the unrepresentable, he suggests that the postmodern should produce feelings that there is something underneath literal representation that is resistant to standard forms and modes of expression. Lyotard's later example of this in *The Differend: Phrases in Dispute* (1983) is Auschwitz, which he claims 'marks a point of absolute barbaric irrationality' (Malpas 70), and as such cannot be comprehended or discussed within the existing frames of historical discourse or empirical experience. This reminds us of Kubiak's definition of terror: that it is unrepresentable yet conceivable, but in the transformation from imagination to representation it loses its status as pure terror and becomes its dynamic application.

I intend to argue that this relationship as described by Kubiak can be applied to the above terms 'normative representation' and 'imaginative speculation'. In the transformation between the internal speculation of terror into normative representation, the unthinkable becomes depicted and converted from mere fantasy into literal action. However, theatre does not generally depict literal actions: it is instead concerned with the representation of them. Kubiak argues that theatre is involved with 'the staging of representative, mimetic *images* of life. Consequently, theatre's perverse claim to truth is that it is not 'real' but is a *true perjury* that is determined and upheld by the conventions of the stage' (28). Thus, whilst the witnessing of theatrical images creates the feeling that internal imaginings have been realized, it is important to stress that they have not been expressed in any real terms, as theatre tends to reject literal violence or terror happening in actuality. Instead, audience members are presented with fictional images which, in naturalistic theatre, are constructed to give only the impression of reality. In this way, it is the representation of actions which is powerful, as it is the means by which the audience are presented or confronted with their own expectations or assumptions.

These complex relationships constitute a paradigm attempting to explain the relationship between audience expectation and speculation on the one hand, and the world of the play in which the portrayed action might support or reject their previous assumptions about both the play and society in general. Audiences are thus involved in a symbiotic relationship between themselves and the play, as well as with cultural discourses taking place outside the theatre. Susan Bennett describes this process as consisting of two separate but related frames:

> The outer frame is concerned with theatre as a cultural construct through the idea of the theatrical event, the selection of material for production, and the audience's definitions and expectations of a performance. The inner frame contains the event itself and, in particular, the spectator's experience of the fictional stage world ... It is the intersection of these two frames which forms the spectator's cultural understanding and experience of theatre. Beyond this, the relationship between the frames is always seen as interactive. Cultural assumptions affect performances, and performances rewrite cultural assumptions (1-2).

Bennett's argument establishes a relationship between the theatrical event and the 'outer frame': the world existing beyond the theatre, which includes, I would suggest, cultural discourses surrounding the theatre from the world 'outside'. This relationship is forged through the audience's expectations and assumptions about the performance and their interaction with the theatrical event. This relationship seems to imply a powerful effect felt in the outer frame but caused by the inner — essentially a realization that theatre can affect its surroundings through the medium of its audiences. An example of this realization in operation is stage censorship, which continued in Britain until 1968.

Operating under a censorship system, plays had to obtain a licence for public performance and any offending scenes, language or subject matter could be excised by the Lord Chamberlain's office.[1] This allowed control to be exerted over what could be represented on stage, so possibly restricting the processes of imaginative

---

[1] Detailed commentaries of this process exist, for example see Findlater 1967, Johnson 1990, De Jongh 2001, Nicholson 2003 et al.

realization described above. Censorship can also affect the relationship between the outer and inner frames, since it aims to prevent stage action from influencing audience members and filtering out into the wider society. Referring to the desire to manipulate and control these relationships, Steve Nicholson writes, 'it was the actual rather than the abstract – what happened outside theatres as 'a result' of what happened inside and on stage – which was crucial to control' (6). In other words, the action within the theatre and the content of the play itself was deemed secondary to the perceived 'effect' this play could have in the 'real' world outside.

Two examples of theatrical censorship help make this point. De Jongh writes of a letter of complaint from a member of the London Morality Council in the 1920s about the portrayal of sexual activity on stage. De Jongh quotes his letter, '"I have no hesitation in stating that if these incidents were enacted in streets or parks, the participants would be promptly and rightly brought before the magisterial bench"' and remarks, 'he pretended there was no distinction between an erotic action simulated on stage and one committed in public' (73). John Johnston writes of a W. Somerset Maugham play, *Our Betters* (1917), being considered problematic for a British production by the censors 'because it made fun of Americans just when England was counting on America to enter the war' (84). Similarly, in an example of self-censorship, George Bernard Shaw deferred public production of *Heartbreak House* (1919) 'because he recognized that national morale must come first in time of war, and *Heartbreak House* might have lowered morale' (Bryden 193). Shaw writes of the connection between theatrical and world events, 'That is why I had to withhold *Heartbreak House* from the footlights during the war: for the Germans might on any night have turned the last act from the play into earnest, and even then might not have waited for their cues' ('Preface to *Heartbreak House*' 48).

However, a literal relationship between the inner and outer frame is too simplistic. Events on stage do not merely mirror those in the outside world. John Elsom writes:

> Unfortunately, if the theatre is a reflection of the times ..., it is a treacherous mirror, for where does the image we see relate to the lives we live? Have we chosen ... the correct angle of vision? If we stand in front of a mirror, we are looking at an apparently accurate picture of ourselves, but with every detail reversed (2).

Gillian Hanson makes a similar point through a discussion of censorship, 'One of the most irrational points about censorship is that it deals only with the *representation* of certain acts and not the acts themselves. Thus to show someone committing a murder (a crime) is not a crime, but to show someone making love to his wife (not a crime) is one' (30). This has resonances with the infamous case brought against Michael Bogdanov, the director of Howard Brenton's *The Romans in Britain* (1980), for 'procuring acts of gross indecency' (de Jongh 132) as the play contains a simulation of male rape. The case did not go to trial, but, in theory at least, the Sexual Offences Act of 1956 could have been brought against the production (de Jongh 246). This 'refus[al] to distinguish between the simulated and the actual ... implied that ... an aspect of the offence might lie in the spectacle of the offence' (de Jongh 246). In other words, there was a false conflation between the representation of an act and the act itself, and there was the suggestion that the depiction of it was as troubling and offensive as witnessing the thing itself.

In the (arguably mistaken) belief or conviction that theatrical images are actual, plays are often at the centre of controversy or protest. Indeed, when members of the public react violently towards a play it is a potent example of the inner frame creating tangible effects in the outer. Some of the most famous theatrical examples of this involve early twentieth century Irish theatre. The first production of J. M. Synge's *The Playboy of the Western World* at the Abbey Theatre in 1907 caused such offence that 'by the third night fifty policemen were insufficient to quell the disturbance. Several members of the audience were arrested and subsequently fined. The controversy filled the news columns of Irish and British newspapers for several weeks' (Fitz-Simon 30). This riot was echoed in 1926 when Sean O'Casey's *The Plough and the Stars* caused similar problems, again at the Abbey. The audience 'booed and catcalled' (Welch 96) during the play and at one stage 'a dozen or so women got up on stage, and were followed by young men. A fight broke out amongst the players and the demonstrators' (Welch 96). The causes of these riots are well documented: the Synge play was controversial because of its strong language and suggestion of the sexual licentiousness of Irish girls and *The Plough and the Stars* caused great offence due to its unfavourable representation of the 1916 Easter Rising volunteers. In both cases, it was the question of national representation which caused riots in the auditorium, as the audience objected to the way in which the playwrights chose to portray the national character. As we have seen, representation is critical, as, although it has the suggestion of objective fact, it is in fact an aesthetic choice made by the playwright and, as such, can cause great offence amongst the audience who take it to be meaningful beyond the world of the play and into their own personal worlds. It is an example of the moment in which fragile boundaries are transgressed and the theatrical representation is understood as a comment upon the actual world.

McDonagh's plays are often deemed controversial. Subject matter such as death in *A Skull in Connemara*, the use of violence in *The Beauty Queen of Leenane*, *The Cripple of Inishmaan*, and *The Pillowman*, and the discussion of the Catholic Church and the representation of religion in *The Lonesome West* are all potentially challenging areas for theatrical representation. If audiences interpret certain elements of a play as literal truth rather than artistic creation, controversy is often the result. For example, Luckhurst's criticism of the terrorists and the Inishmore locals in *The Lieutenant of Inishmore* as 'psychopathic morons' and 'hopelessly dumb' (Luckhurst 36) suggests that they are not portrayed 'realistically', but rather they are exaggerated creations, transcending the boundaries of naturalistic behaviour. In this regard, audience expectation can play a considerable part in the reception of a play, as Bennett has described above. In a model describing the series of relationships between stage and audience, Bennett refers to the 'horizon of expectations' in the audience interacting with the 'internal horizon of expectations (*mise en scène*)' of the 'fictional stage world' (210). These terms refer to the exchange of meanings and signs from the staging of the play and the reactions in the audience. These boundaries can be upheld and the audience remains essentially passive, or they can be transgressed in the ways described above, and the audience can protest or react against a performance, breaking the conventional separation between them and the stage-world.

McDonagh's plays have yet to create protest but one reviewer provides an example of the way in which these boundaries can be exposed. Reviewing *A Skull in Connemara*, Ben Brantley asks, 'is that a piece of tibia that's just landed in my lap?' (407) and remarks that 'it's only natural that some of those soiled white fragments [the human remains exhumed by the principal characters] would fly past the proscenium arch' (408). The grisly image of human bones flying

from the stage into the auditorium provides a salient reminder of
the complex relationship between the stage and the audience, and
the breaking of these traditional and conventional physical
boundaries. Kubiak's descriptions of terror and its transformation
into terrorism remain pertinent here. The audience's interaction
with the play, and the occasional transgression of their usual
boundaries, describe a dynamic relationship with theatre, the
audience responding actively to the work. This could include
enjoyment and laughter as well as terror and fear. Crucially, the
spectators own imaginations remain central as they are concerned
with Lyotard's 'conceivable but not presentable', and their imaginative speculation interacts with the normative representation to
cement their personal responses to the play.

The dismemberment of five terrorists at the end of *The
Lieutenant of Inishmore* is the most discussed aspect of the extreme

Kubiak argues that on-stage violence is a significant aspect in
provoking audience response, writing: 'When terror and pain
assume signification, they assume meaning: when they cease to be
meaningless, they are no longer terror and pain. When terror moves
into signifying systems it is consequently transformed into terrorism' (38). We have already explored his separation between terror
and terrorism, and the imaginative elements of terror over the literal
depiction of terrorism, and here it can be applied more directly to
McDonagh's plays. In *The Lieutenant of Inishmore* violence is both
signified and suggested, allowing for this complex relationship to
flourish. A close reading of two key passages in the text will
elucidate further.

The dismemberment of five terrorists at the end of *The
Lieutenant of Inishmore* is the most discussed aspect of the extreme
violence in the play. Wehmeyer described it as 'the bloodiest [act]
ever staged since Shakespeare let Titus loose on Rome' (92).
However, whilst the ending is often the most memorable violent
aspect to this play, there are numerous other scenes which are
similarly explicit. The scene in which Padraic tortures James is self-
consciously reminiscent of Tarantino films, with the stage directions
communicating violent menace instantly:

> *James, a bare-chested, bloody and bruised man, hangs upside
> down from the ceiling, his feet bare and bloody. Padraic idles
> near him, wielding a cut-throat razor, his hands bloody.
> Around Padraic's chest are strapped two empty holsters and
> there are two handguns on the table stage left. James is
> crying.*

However, despite this opening, and the fact that there has been injury inflicted on James before the scene begins, the audience witness no more physical violence, apart from Padraic shooting his own mobile phone. In fact, the scene consists of a discussion between the two men, comically undermined by Padraic's despair when he learns his cat is ill. Furthermore, a bizarre convention of politeness is adhered to when Padraic explains to James who is on the phone and even apologizes for keeping him waiting and for the delay in their interaction. The communication between the two men is frequently interrupted by comic exchanges and finally Padraic lets James go with some change to get to the hospital to have his injuries taken care of.

In this case, the construction of the scene indicated to the audience at the beginning that it would be horrifically violent, but the reality undermined the expectation. Here, the expectation of an explicit representation of violence unsettles the audience, yet nothing particularly unpleasant is portrayed on stage. The play uses the *mise-en-scène* of violence to agitate the audience into believing they will be perturbed by what they will see, but comically undercuts that with the almost friendly banter between the torturer and his victim. The play's power to direct the audience's imaginative speculation arouses their expectations without having to stage violence which might be difficult to watch by simply suggesting it might happen, causing disquiet without having to show anything. The audience's imaginative engagement with what has happened before the scene opened, and with what has the potential to happen whilst they are watching, is enough to create unease: the scene activates the audiences' expectations without ever meeting them.

However, the final scene works in an opposing way as the violence is graphically represented. Although some violence is committed off-stage, such as the blinding of the terrorists and torture of Christy, the most discussed violence in *The Lieutenant of Inishmore* is the '*blood-soaked living room strewn with body parts*' and the dismemberment of the terrorists by the surviving characters. Again, the scene is comedic, challenging its audiences' ability and desire to laugh at the grotesque and revolting absurdity of two Inishmore locals hacking to pieces the visiting terrorists. One of the play's most quoted lines, delivered when Padraic is about to murder his father for the death of his cat, 'Come on in ahead of yourselves. I'm just in the middle of shooting me dad' (45) and 'I was all set to blow his [Davey's] head off now ... but seeing as he's family I won't. I'll have some respect. I'll kill me dad on his own' (53) are funny lines structured to create laughter in the auditorium, and yet they refer directly to patricide, a subject not usually considered humorous[2].

Whilst the setting of the earlier torture scene indicated violence but delivered very little, the opposite is true of this scene. The setting of Donny's house is deliberately idealistic, to subvert both the myths of rural Irish perfection and to disrupt audience expectation. We may expect to see violence in 'A desolate Northern Irish warehouse', but the connotations of 'A cottage on Inishmore … A clock somewhere on the back wall along with some framed embroidery reading 'Home Sweet Home'' does not suggest murder and dismemberment. As we have seen, in McDonagh's plays the inverse is often the case and expectations are subverted in the staging of these two scenes. The graphic violence of this final scene certainly pushes the boundaries of what might be shown on stage, and the dodging of audience preconception further intensifies the horror when it finally arrives. These two scenes, although different in style, both exploit and manipulate audience expectation by requiring them to make imaginative leaps, while McDonagh controls their reactions by intensifying their imaginative speculation in the first scene and deferring any normative representation, whilst signifying their horror in the final scene, and exemplifying Kubiak's transformation between the imaginative elements of terror and the depiction of terrorism, in the case of this play, literally so.

The violence in McDonagh's plays has attracted a great deal of critical attention. However, equally important are his simultaneous use of comedy and the effect of the two blended together as we have seen in the above two extracts. This leads us onto a brief examination of comedy and of its sub-genre satire, as both play significant roles in McDonagh's work. I would like to suggest that satire operates within the difference between how things are and how they may appear. The difference established here between appearance and reality allows for a more direct relationship with the audience who should understand that what they are witnessing is not literal (normative representation) but an artistic response to attitudes or belief (imaginative speculation). In this way, audiences must 'jump

---

[2] This is also the case in The Beauty Queen of Leenane, in which Maureen tortures and finally murders her mother, but although this play is ostensibly comedic too, these particular scenes are far more melodramatic and serious, thus creating more conventional shock in the audience.

the gap' between the more literal presentations given to them by comedy and the ironic, once-removed humour of satire.

Audiences are thus crucial in giving satire its meaning, for example Swift's *A Modest Proposal* which requires the audience to understand the nature of Swift's satire to appreciate his form of attack. Unless the reader is aware of the direction of Swift's criticism of attitudes towards Ireland, they would no doubt be appalled by his notions. However, once the audience understands the irony, they give Swift's work its full meaning. In this way, satire makes more use of speculative imagination than straightforward comedy, because it relies upon what is *not* said and expects the audience to draw their own conclusions – this is what gives satire its distinctive savagery. Thus satire has more in common with the forms of theatre outlined above: it involves the audience enjoying what is not explicitly de-monstrated, but instead taking meaning from their own imaginative responses to it.

McDonagh's work has been commonly associated with what we might term 'comic unsuitability' – a use of comedy which seems designed to make the audience feel uncomfortable or uneasy. Rebecca Wilson provides a useful description:

> McDonagh has intermeshed: a double-edged, interlocking re-invention and inversion of much ideology, iconography and topography of 'classic melodrama': thematics of Gothic melodrama flavoured with elements of Grand Guignol: *a macabre 'gallows humour'* and streaks of lasciviousness recalling those lode veins of the Irish comic tradition (131 italics mine).

The aspect of 'gallows humour' is perhaps the most relevant to discuss here, as it encapsulates the complex independency between comedy and 'unacceptability'. The interrelation of these two factors creates the challenge for the audience, as they are traditionally and conventionally kept separate, yet combined in these plays. It is this combination that makes McDonagh's plays testing for audiences and critics, and pushes the boundaries of their speculative imagination as they are forced to conceive of humour where there may logically be none.

The Power of Laughter: Comedy and Contemporary Irish Theatre (2004) edited by Eric Weitz provides some useful discussion surrounding these questions. In the introduction, Weitz asks 'the morally valid question, "What are we laughing at and what purpose does it serve?"' (5). Other contributors attempt to answer this question, suggesting, 'The fact that laughter has a function in relieving stress might lead us to speculate whether the point of comedy, of humour, is to create tiny moments of artificial stress that can be instantly relieved. The relief, here, is essential' (Johnston 176). This argument suggests that moments of laughter are ends within themselves, created for the purpose of relieving stressful situations experienced through the play. However, whilst this may be true for certain plays, it does little to explain or account for McDonagh's comedy, in which the humour itself is the moment of stress and laughter does nothing to relieve it. In fact, the laughter amplifies the audience's unease, creating a position of 'moral anxiety', as Howard Barker argues in *Theatre of Catastrophe*. He explains that audiences at his work experience anxiety that 'comes from what's said and what's done, because [the plays] are profoundly resistant to conventional morality' (33). In this way, the audience discovers a gap between what they witness, and their normative expectations brought with them from the 'outside world'. This gap constitutes their imaginative speculation, as they have to take personal responsibility for their imaginative responses to the play. To take an example from McDonagh's work, the joke about patricide in *Lieutenant*, discussed above, does not relieve stress. In finding the joke funny, the audience experiences the horror of the relationship between acceptability and unacceptability, their own imaginations and what they are witnessing on stage, and laughing at something which is usually deemed particularly serious. The comedy merely reinforces the anxiety of thinking about patricide in a humorous way.

Wehmeyer argues that comedy is the only way to address certain sensitive subjects: that in certain situations rationality breaks down and 'Laughter is the only release mechanism' (90). Wehmeyer's use of the term 'release mechanism', however, again implies the audience experience relief in laughter. Although this is certainly valid, it cannot be argued that laughter about patricide can in any way relieve stress: surely it must complicate and confront the audience's moral boundaries and shock them into behaving in ways in the theatre that they would reject in other social spheres. I would answer Weitz's question by suggesting that the function of comedic representations of painful or taboo subject matter is to confuse the audience's normative and conventional ethical standards by provoking laughter at subjects they would not normally consider comic or within the realms of comic acceptability. At all times, the presence of the audience is essential in the consideration of comedy, to measure the parameters for a discussion of acceptability. Bernadette Sweeney states that

> The comic 'value' of dramatic material can be measured most clearly in performance, and can lend an audience an element of complicity, a permission to play, which has, on occasion, pushed the boundaries of theatrical form in Irish theatre' (8).

She goes on, '[laughter] makes real the presence of the audience, and marks key moments of response' (9).

This implies a collective response on the part of the audience, however, as well as the use of dramaturgical strategies by the playwright to elicit that response. Such objectives are strenuously denied by Howard Barker, who says he finds, 'one of the most depressing sounds in the theatre is that of the audience in the unified pursuit of a single goal – the laugh, for example – which is so easily achieved' (81). However, he agrees that laughter can be 'more complex and creative' (81) if 'the laugh, when it occurs, is accompanied by a sense of the faux pas, or where it comes from the unbidden, from an amazement that comedy exists at all' (82).

This seems to explain or describe much of the comedy of *The Lieutenant of Inishmore*. The use of faux pas or amazement that comedy could be found in certain situations, seems to provide a useful description of the conflicting responses audiences experience when witnessing the 'unacceptable comedy' on stage: the desire to laugh and also the horror that they can find humour in the situation being described. This is again usefully explained by the gap between the audience's imaginative speculation and what is actually witnessed on stage. Potentially troubling images of human misery and pain are framed and represented in such a way that they provoke laughter. The audience must somehow jump an imaginative gap in order to laugh, but the theatre can be seen to provide a security in this process. While no-one (we would assume) would laugh at the dismemberment of humans in the 'real' world, the theatrical space provides a safe environment to participate in the comedic representation of dismemberment without having to assume any responsibility.

Wehmeyer discusses McDonagh's blending of violence and comedy with reference to Mikhail Bakhtin's *Rabelais and His World* (1984). He uses Bakhtin's notion of 'play' to explain the chaotic and anarchic elements of carnivalesque crisis with the plays, the moments of the unreal which refer to the 'breaking point of the cycle' (Wehmeyer 93) and the new possibilities and renewal which follow this. Crucial for Wehmeyer though, is 'the possibility of distinguishing between these two worlds' (93) and allowing the theatrical audience to make critical judgments. He argues that the violence of McDonagh's plays is so extreme that violence becomes the norm rather than the exception. As Wehmeyer puts it, 'The excess of violence and pain as a normal state loses its transformative power, becomes aesthetic and sensational and is as such gratuitous' (92). He continues:

> A distinction between the real and play is no longer clearly visible [in McDonagh's plays]. Play, with all its attributes of excess and liberating mimicry is not distinctly framed within a tangible reality to which an audience can relate. In a sense, carnival characterized in McDonagh by parody and excessive spectacle becomes a permanent condition. The excess becomes the norm. Only by accepting the presented characters as different from ourselves, as inferior, as our Other are we able to laugh at their hideousness (93).

Wehmeyer argues that the violence is too extreme to be considered 'realistic' and thus cannot be understood by the audience as the 'play' rather than the norm. In McDonagh's work the violence is too all-encompassing and therefore the audience is lost as to how to react to it, as it defines Bakhtin's categories of carnival rather than reality. For Wehmeyer, in McDonagh's dramatic worlds the carnival, not reality, is the consistent element.

However, as I have argued above, violence in McDonagh's plays is not as pervasive as we might expect from a review of the critical response. The scene between James and Padraic explained earlier, for example, could easily be a horrific gangster-style bloodbath. Similarly, the torture of Mag by Maureen in *The Beauty Queen of Leenane* described by Rebecca Wilson as 'a harrowing scene steeped in the horror of Grand Guignol' (139) is, although a shocking moment, not strictly representative of the play as a whole, as violence is not used or referred to often in the rest of the play. The same is true of *A Skull in Connemara*, and *The Lonesome West*, in which violent acts tend to be discussed rather than portrayed on stage. The point here is obviously not to argue that violence is not significant in McDonagh's plays, as clearly it is a key feature, but rather to suggest that the effect of witnessing the violence for the audience is still intense as it is delayed throughout the action of the play, and kept as a moment of terror and alarm. For example, the '*pained screams*' (67) from Billy in *The Cripple of Inishmaan* when he is beaten by Bobby with a lead pipe are all the more shocking – and not at all humorous – because the rest of the violence is slapstick, involving the breaking of eggs and Chinese burns. It would therefore not be accurate to argue that the representation of violence in McDonagh's work never registers with the audience.

Wehmeyer's essay on McDonagh does indicate some interesting interactions between representation and the audience, however, as he clearly demonstrates the distinction between 'the real and play' (93). To suggest that any element of a play is 'real' is somewhat problematic, but it is more straightforward to argue, as I have, that the 'real' indicates normative representation and that 'play' refers to acts of audience imaginative speculation. The potential gap between these two can cause, in the case of the examples considered in this chapter, offence, anger, or upset. Simple description does not always have this effect: rather, artistic representation seems to heighten the audience's responses. Thus the discussion and narration of violent events, and verbal or physically expressive threats, are effective in confronting the audience with the limits of their desire to witness violence on stage. As discussed above, however, shocking theatre challenges levels of acceptability by crossing over from the world of fictional depiction into the speculative imagination of the audience, problematizing the conventional boundaries which traditionally accept these two phenomena to be one and the same. The imagination of the audience can bring greater horror to a dramatic situation: for example, *The Pillowman* coincidentally premiered during the trial of a Soham school caretaker who had sexually assaulted and murdered two young girls in the summer of 2002[3]. The line, 'Are you saying I shouldn't write stories with child-killings in because in the real world there are child-killings?' (26), was met with a sharp intake of breath at the two performances I watched, providing grisly proof of the problematic boundaries between artistic representation and contemporary events.

It has been argued by some theatre critics that the creation of violence on stage creates a safe space for the audience in which to be shocked and horrified without experiencing the terror in an external

---

[3] The trial of Ian Huntley for the murder of Holly Wells and Jessica Chapman began on 3rd November 2003 at the Old Bailey in London. *The Pillowman* opened ten days later, on 13th November 2003 at the National Theatre in London, linking the events both temporally and spatially.

reality themselves. Frequently the example relied upon is that of the Grand Guignol, a sensationally graphic form of theatre originating in Paris in 1897 and coming to London in the next century. James M. Callahan writes of the Grand Guignol audiences:

> the Grand-Guignol offered a chance to be scared in complete safety ... Most people are vicarious lovers of violence and danger and the majority of people find the theatrical depiction of violence to be cathartic. People went to the Grand Guignol to be scared ... People have enjoyed, and always will enjoy, being stimulated and scared (166-167).

However, other critics disagree as to the extent of this simplistic division between art and life, and its reception by the audience. Grand Guignol was so powerfully violent that it infamously had a profound effect on those who saw it. Richard J. Hand and Michael Wilson claim that 'the horror was so intense that audiences would flee the auditorium or lose consciousness' (12). They go on to provide a fascinating example of the power of horrific theatre to upset audiences in very real ways. The producers at the Grand Guignol played with the audience by creating the role of a house doctor to attend to the audience members who found the plays too horrific to cope with and required real medical assistance. As Hand and Wilson explain:

> While masquerading as a comfort, the result of such measures was probably entirely disconcerting. The significance of such stunts is that they break down the border between art and life ... By employing a doctor, Maurey [the theatre's publicist] told the Grand-Guignol audience that there was the potential of *real* danger. The implied danger would manifest itself in spectators being 'overcome' by what they will witness. This functions as an ingenious strategy in the suspension of disbelief as it strives to prove that, although the theatrical spectacle may only be art, even art can seriously damage your health (72).

Just the suggestion that the theatre might create physical discomfort might be enough to provoke it. The presence of a real doctor is not even necessarily required: modern revivals of the Grand Guignol have subjected audiences to 'a "medical examination" by two actors playing the roles of doctor and nurse, before being admitted to the theatre' (Hand and Wilson, 72), suggesting that the audience experience of the suggestion that they might be in danger, even though no real doctor is there to attend to them, is an element of their participation in the theatrical event. The existence of the actors performing roles outside the auditorium (which the audience could conceivably take to be a real medical check) further elaborates the complex relationship between the normative theatrical representation and the importance of the audience's imagination. Here the creation of horror in the minds of the audience is achieved directly by the suggestion that they will find something shocking – they jump the imaginative gap themselves, and create feelings of anxiety long before anything is literally demonstrated on stage.

McDonagh's representation of theatrical violence complicates his use of comedy considerably. His juxtaposition of violence and comedy often challenges what can be considered 'acceptable', as it causes offence or crosses the line of 'good taste', thus confronting the audience with their own preconception of comic acceptability and, again, asking them to engage with their own expectations and interaction with the play. McDonagh demonstrates the potency in challenging drama to bridge a gap between normative representation and imaginative speculation, making controversial aspects within his work stretch the traditional boundaries established between literal depiction and audience expectation, confronting them with images which may undermine or defy their notions of acceptability. By transcending these preconceptions, he can suggest alternative narratives and go beyond the world of the play, compelling the audience to engage with the drama and take it out of the realm of literal representation and into their own personal imaginations. Controversial theatre communicates to the audience by creating a powerful narrative capable of resembling reality but crucially separate from it, to challenge the audience to explore the conflicting narratives presented to them. This can be difficult to watch and cause great discomfort in the auditorium, as violent and unpleasant acts are created in front of the audience. It may offer a catharsis, in allowing the spectator to interact with extreme behaviour, action and emotion. It will, however, always be a conflicting experience, in which equal forces compel the audience to look away yet also to enjoy the horrors presented to them. In acknowledging these competing desires, the spectators are allowing themselves to experience contradictory representations, which might challenge their own desires to be shocked and appalled as well as to enjoy and be entertained. As such, controversial drama will always be difficult to watch. Brantley's review of *A Skull in Connemara* continues to express these contrasting impulses,

'Audience members should be prepared to duck. On the other hand, who could possibly take his eyes off such a morbid and oddly ecstatic spectacle?' (408).

Bibliography

Barker, Howard, *Arguments for a Theatre* (Manchester: Manchester University Press, 1997) (Third edition).

Barker, Howard, 'Howard Barker in Conversation'. *Theatre of Catastrophe*. Ed. Karoline Gritzner and David Ian Rabey (London: Oberon, 2006).

Bennett, Susan, *Theatre Audiences: A Theory of Production and Reception* (London and New York: Routledge, 1997. Second edition)

Brantley, Ben, '*A Skull in Connemara*: Leenane III, Bones Flying'. *Martin McDonagh: A World of Savage Stories*, eds Lilian Chambers and Eamonn Jordan (Dublin: Carysfort Press, 2006).

Bryden, Ronald. 'The roads to *Heartbreak House'* in *The Cambridge Companion to George Bernard Shaw*, ed. Christopher Innes (Cambridge: Cambridge University Press, 1998).

Callahan, John M., 'The Ultimate in Theatre Violence'. *Violence in Drama*, ed. James Redmond (Cambridge: Cambridge University Press, 1991).

De Jongh, Nicholas, *Politics, Prudery and Perversions: The Censoring of the English Stage 1901-1968* (London: Methuen, 2001).

Elsom, John, *Erotic Theatre* (London: Secker and Warburg, 1973).

Fitz-Simon, Christopher, *The Abbey Theatre: Ireland's National Theatre the First 100 Years* (London: Thames and Hudson, 2003).

Hand, Richard J. and Michael Wilson, *Grand Guignol: The French Theatre of Horror* (Exeter: University of Exeter Press, 2002).

Hanson, Gillian, *Original Sin: Nudity and Sex in Cinema and Theatre* (London: Tom Stacey, 1970).

Johnston, John, *The Lord Chamberlain's Blue Pencil* (London et al: Hodder and Stoughton, 1990).

Kubiak, Anthony, *Stages of Terror: Terrorism, Ideology and Coercion as Theatre History* (Bloomington and Indianapolis: Indiana University Press, 1991).

Luckhurst, Mary, 'Martin McDonagh's *Lieutenant of Inishmore*: Selling(-Out) to the English'. *New Theatre Quarterly*. Vol. 14 (4), 2004, 34-41.

Lyotard, Jean-François, *The Postmodern Explained: Correspondence 1982-1985* (Minneapolis and London: University of Minnesota Press, 1992).

Malpas, Simon. *Jean-François Lyotard* (London and New York: Routledge, 2003).

McDonagh, Martin. *The Cripple of Inishmaan* (London: Methuen, 1997).

---, *The Lieutenant of Inishmore* (London: Methuen, 2001).

---, *The Pillowman* (London: Faber and Faber, 2003).

Nicholson, Steve, *The Censorship of British Drama 1900-1968*, Volume One 1900-1932 (Exeter: University of Exeter Press 2003).

Pollard, Arthur, *Satire* (London and New York: Methuen, 1970).

Shaw, George Bernard, 'Heartbreak House and Horseback Hall'. *Heartbreak House* (Middlesex et al: Penguin, 1977).

Sierz, Aleks, 'Believe it or not. Dispatches: Holy Offensive'. http://www.channel4.com/culture. Accessed: 11th November 2005.

Sweeney, Bernadette, 'Form and Comedy in Contemporary Irish Theatre' in *The Power of Laughter: Comedy and Contemporary Irish Theatre*. Ed. Eric Weitz (Dublin: Carysfort Press, 2004).

Wehmeyer, Jan-Hendrik, '"Good luck to ya": Fast-food comedy at McDonagh's' in *The Power of Laughter: Comedy and Contemporary Irish Theatre*. Ed. Eric Weitz (Dublin: Carysfort Press, 2004).

Weitz, Eric. 'Introduction'. *The Power of Laughter: Comedy and Contemporary Irish Theatre*, ed. Eric Weitz (Dublin: Carysfort Press, 2004).

Welch, Robert, *The Abbey Theatre 1899-1999: Form and Pressure* (Oxford: Oxford University Press, 1999).

Wilson, Rebecca, 'Macabre Merriment in McDonagh's Melodrama, *The Beauty Queen of Leenane* in *The Power of Laughter: Comedy and Contemporary Irish Theatre*, ed. Eric Weitz (Dublin: Carysfort Press, 2004).

7 | Speaking Violence in Conor McPherson's *Rum and Vodka* and *The Good Thief*

Tom Maguire

Introduction

In Conor McPherson's two plays for a solo performer, *Rum and Vodka* (1994) and *The Good Thief* (first staged as *The Light of Jesus*, 1994), we hear from two male narrators who recount sprees of violence that match much of the excesses of the British In-Yer-Face theatre (Sierz) and the extremes of McPherson's contemporary Martin McDonagh. Yet performances of these plays rarely re-enact the events they describe: they are primarily diegetic rather than mimetic experiences.[1] Lyn Gardner's review of a double bill production of McPherson's plays at London's Soho Theatre in 2001 noted: 'But even when performed as well as they are here, the question hovers – as it does over much of McPherson's work – whether these stories might be read as well off the stage' (558). This is echoed in a number of reviews of the same production: 'Bar a few moments of expressive acting, the result could have been delivered on a page – if not an audio book' (Espiner 559): 'both pieces ... have a certain awkwardness on stage [...such] voice plays come to the stage when they would have been better served on the radio' (Brown 559). Ian Johns began his review for *The Times* with the question, 'is an actor talking without interruption any more than a spoken short story?' (559). So what I want to explore here, is the speaking of

---

[1] Of course, talking about violence has a long history in Irish theatre, most notably in the play which I think serves as the prototype for much of the subsequent stage representations of violence, Synge's *The Playboy of the Western World*.

violence in these plays, and the ethical dimensions these embodied performances bring to the spectator's experience of the violence they speak.

Acts of Violence

In *Rum and Vodka*, we follow three days in the life of a twenty-four year-old Dublin male, from the moment when he throws his computer terminal out the window of the Dublin corporation department where he works, through the course of a massive drinking binge, to his eventual return to his wife and two young daughters back home in Raheny. As well as downing copious amounts of drink, he rapes his sleeping wife, pukes repeatedly, has casual sex with Myfanwy, a younger woman from Clontarf, spends the night with her and goes to a party at the house of one of her friends. His story is littered with acts of violence. For example, when he tells his wife that he has lost his job in the middle of the supermarket, he recounts that:

> She hit me across the eye with a can of tuna.
> I think I blacked out.
> I tumbled backwards into a freezer with Bird's Eye fishfingers and pizzas and shit.
> I could hear Maria screaming and she was thumping my legs and stomach.
> People were watching.
> The kids started crying.
> I managed to crawl out the far side and stepped into someone's trolley.
> They had left a child in the seat part and I toppled it over.
> The child skidded across the floor and banged its head on a low shelf with raisins.
> And I ran (21-2).

Brutal and messy though this incident is, it pales by comparison with the events in The *Good Thief*. Here the narrator is a low level thug sent to threaten a local businessman, Mitchell. However, when he arrives at Mitchell's house, armed with a sawn-off shotgun and a revolver, to find two other hoods already there, the violence begins and it spirals quickly out of control. By the time he leaves, taking Mitchell's wife and her daughter west, four men have been killed. This is only the start of the body count.

Swearing as Verbal Violence

One of the characteristics of each piece is the use of colloquial working-class language, itself replete with swear words. *Rum and Vodka* opens with the line, 'I think my overall fucked-upness is my impatience' (9). The narrator describes his state of marital bliss: 'If I wanted to I could drink 'til three in the morning, watch videos 'til dawn, fuck my missus' (12). On taking Myfanwy away from her friends at a concert, he asks, 'Couldn't they see there was a silent bond, a communication beyond words going on here? Cunts' (30). *The Good Thief* contains just as much swearing. Fixated with the promiscuity of his ex-girlfriend, he decides 'Fuck them' (50). Considering that she might be having anal sex with his employer, he muses, 'I thought about Joe Murray putting it up her arse./ I called her a fucking bitch and apologised to Mrs Mitchell' (61). When he attacks a councillor who is extorting money from his friend Jeff, he remembers, 'I wanted to fuck him up generally so that he'd be too scared to do anything to anybody' (65).

Aleks Sierz argues that swearing is itself an act of violence since the use of sexual swear-words contravenes general cultural taboos:

> Because they refer to sex, but are violent in intent, those words pack a double punch. Unlike euphemism, which is a way of defusing difficult subjects, of circling around a meaning, the swearword aims to compact more than one hatred, becoming a verbal act of aggression, a slap in the mouth. In the theatre, 'bad language' seems even stronger because it is used openly. (8)

However, this account overlooks the extent to which swear words within specific speech forms and contexts become detached from their sexual referents, and serve as empty signifiers which can be imbued with meaning by their use rather than by reference to the initial act they referred to. Even where they retain their original referent, their capacity to shock will be determined as much by the linguistic competences of the audience as by any innate reference. For example, within British culture a survey into swearing in the media noted that, 'a concern was expressed that the high level of swearing and offensive language all around them had produced a deadening effect. Many participants suggested that such language now offended them less than in the past' (Millwood Hargrave online). Indeed, a number of the respondents noted that swearing was to be regarded as 'common', an indication of their recognition of it as a marker of class. Within Ireland swearing is so common-place

that a recruitment web-site providing advice for people wishing to
work in Ireland cautions:

> Swear words tend to have a different (and often less strong)
> meaning in Ireland, so you can't even be sure you have
> understood what you have heard. Also, swearing is not
> considered offensive by everyone, although it is fair to say that
> not everyone approves of it. The best advice is to be aware that
> unexpected people may swear: try not to be offended, find out
> from someone you trust what it means and avoid falling into
> the same habit (Houston 2002: online).

So for Irish audiences watching these plays, or for audiences
elsewhere watching them as 'Irish plays', the sense in which swearing might be regarded as violent needs to be treated cautiously. It is
perhaps more accurate to regard it as less a cause of offence than as
a marker of a specifically and authentically Irish working-class mode
of speaking.

Textual Narrative and the Limits of Ethics

In each of these respects, the description of violent incidents and the
use of swearing, the narrative is available directly through the
written text. This is particularly problematic in an ethical sense.
Here, I draw on Labov's classic analysis of the structure of narrative
which identifies six common elements:

> An abstract (summary of the substance of the narrative),
> orientation (time, place, situation, participants), complicating
> action (sequence of events), evaluation (significance and
> meaning of the action, attitude of the narrator), resolution
> (what finally happened), and coda (returns the perspective to
> the present). With these structures, a teller constructs a story
> from a primary experience and interprets the significance of
> events in clauses and embedded evaluation (Riessman 18).

I want to focus specifically here on the function of evaluation.
'Narrators say in evaluation clauses (the soul of the narrative) how
they want to be understood and what the point is' (ibid: 20).
Evaluation is the process by which the narrator assigns values and
meaning and directs the audience to how the events described
should be interpreted (Cortazzi 46). The distinction here is not to
suggest that the enactment of violence is in its own right more
ethical than its rendition in words. In slapstick, for example, it is the
refusal to play out the consequence of violent actions that provides

the distance between the spectator and the characters, and that allows for laughter. This suggests that irrespective of whether the violence is enacted or spoken, it is in the evaluation of it within the performance that the spectator is interpellated ethically. So, how are the acts of violence in these narratives evaluated? In *Rum and Vodka*, the narrator discovers at a party that someone has taken the bottle of vodka which he had earlier stolen from Myfanwy's brother's house:

> I went over to the couch.
> The muckers looked at me.
> One of them had the bottle between his legs, trying to hide it.
> I grabbed it away from him and swung it at his face.
> The bottom of it hit his nose right on the bridge.
> That really fucked up his face.
> The bottle hadn't smashed so I heaved it against the side of another bloke's head.
> It broke with a pop and glass went everywhere.
> Someone screamed.
> I went to find Myfanwy (43).

In *The Good Thief*, the narrator is tortured by his ex-employer's henchmen:

> Vinnie Rourke grabbed my bollocks and gave them a good wrench.
> It was agony, but it was sort of funny.
> I asked him if he was enjoying himself.
> He got a bit annoyed.
> I said I never knew he was a poof.
> That did the job. He let go and told me he'd show me who was a poof.
> He kicked my legs so hard I was leaping in Seamus Parker's arms.
> Then I was on the floor (74).

In each instance, there is some element of external evaluation. In the first, it is in the narrating of an evaluative action, where what is described is 'what the character did rather than what they said' (Cortazzi 48): someone screaming and then the narrator leaving. In the second, it is an example of an interpretive remark made by both the narrator – 'it was sort of funny' – and another character at the time – 'He let go and told me he'd show me who was a poof'. Yet such evaluation does not give any ethical judgement on the act of violence either at the point at which it happened or retold in retrospect. The narrative moves away from these moments immediately, without dwelling on them or making sense of them. They just happen, and the narration moves on. Thus the consequences of the acts, for either the perpetrators or the victims, even with the passing of time, are left unexplored in the language of the telling. The violence is treated textually, therefore, as of no more significance than the downing of beer, stealing a car or buying a take away. It is just another piece in the mosaic of experiences that make up these stories.

Performed Narrative and Ethics

However, I want to suggest that it is in performance that an ethical perspective might be added. Firstly, I want to examine the performative dimensions that speaking a narrative in person has. Goffman suggests that:

> Everyone knows that when individuals in the presence of others respond to events, their glances, looks and postural shifts carry all kinds of implication and meaning. When in these settings words are spoken, then tone of voice, manner of uptake, restarts and the variously positioned pauses similarly qualify. As does manner of listening. Every adult is wonderfully accomplished in producing all of these effects, and wonderfully perceptive in catching their significance when performed by accessible others (2).

He argues elsewhere that the 'animator of a narrative effectively gives a "performance", a notion emphasizing the on-the-spot attempt to influence the audience through impression management' (qtd Cortazzi 38). Narration is, above all else, a performance of self. Similarly, Sample argues that:

> The body, then, through kinesis, vocalization, and facial expression, presents physiognomic aspects the perception of which, however subconscious, helps constitute the felt context of a communicative situation. It is by existing in such a felt context that words come to life in a particular situation, so that we understand how propositional contents fit into the situation at hand (119).

Performance of these narratives, then, constitutes 'corporeal encounters' (Cubilié 76) between bodies which are in communicative interaction with each other, not just words spoken and heard neutrally. Thus McPherson, in his author's note to the plays, can state:

The first problem for the actor performing these pieces is probably 'Where am I?' Where is the play set? I've made up my mind about this. These plays are set 'in a theatre'. Why mess about? The character is on stage, perfectly aware he is talking to a group of people.

I've always tried to reflect that simplicity in productions. And what I have found is that they work best when kept conversational, understated. That's what makes them believable. The temptation may be to launch into a one man 'performance', to 'act things out'. But such a performance will never be as interesting as one where the actor trusts the story to do the work.

McPherson is confident that the skilful conversationalist can deploy the capacities of everyday conversation to imbue the performance with its vitality and that this can be recognized by the attentive spectator. McPherson of course directed the first production of each play, and so managed its transition from script to stage. Certainly, the ability of the narrators to manage the experience of the audience in the 2001 production was recognized in reviews. *The Scotsman* reviewer called the performances 'Sophisticatedly colloquial, often profound and finely acted' (Brown 559). Sierz's *Tribune* review comments that:

There will always be people who say that a monologue isn't real theatre. Yet, as you watch actors Alan Mooney and Brendan Fleming gradually win over the audience, using non-verbal devices as well as words, you realize that the emotional charge coming from the stage couldn't possibly work on radio, nor would it spring from the page (559).

Thus, in the deployment of the repertoire of non-verbal gestures, as well as in the specific dimensions of live speech (pitch, tone, pause, elongated vowels, repetition) the opportunity opens up for forms of commentary on what is said that fulfil the functions of evaluation without being articulated in words.[2] It is precisely this dimension that the performative provides.

I want to look specifically now at the use of pauses within performance, pauses which are not marked at all in the play text. The typology of the text breaks the narration into stanzas which seem to correlate with units of thought or experience but there is nothing indicated to suggest how these might be connected or

---

[2] Labov terms these forms of internal evaluation as intensifiers (Cortazzi 1993: 48).

disrupted in the playing. Goffman's comments in relation to lectures are pertinent here: 'Print conventions for laying out a text provide for coherence in ways unavailable to oral delivery. Talk has no obvious paragraph markers or section headings' (190). Worthen discusses the process of reading play texts 'spatially, to account for the rhetoric of typographic space' (218) in an attempt to work out what and how a written text instructs the actor to *do*. He discusses in particular Pinter's use of the *pause* to argue for the status of the written text in defining 'the limits of Authority as they are understood by readers, actors, directors, for instance' (226). The limits of his argument regarding the importance of the text, however, are emphasized by Virginia Woolf's discussion of the relationship between the experience of reading the text and attending a performance of *Twelfth Night*:

> as the actors pause, or topple over a barrel, or stretch their hands out, the flatness of the print is broken up as by crevasses or precipices: all the proportions are changed. Perhaps the most impressive effect is achieved by the long pause which Sebastian and Viola make as they stand looking at each other in a silent ecstasy of recognition. The reader's eye may have slipped over that moment entirely. Here we are made to pause and think about it. Shakespeare wrote for the body and the mind simultaneously (323).

As Woolf demonstrates, this is not an abstract issue. Director and actor have to make pragmatic decisions here as to how the narration will be broken up in performance, irrespective of the typological conventions of the written text. Fiona Shaw in commenting on her role within *Happy Days*, for example, noted that irrespective of Beckett's very precise written text:

> The problem with all stage directions is that they appear to solve the play ... There are two problems: one is that times change. And the other is that you can have the illusion that if you follow exactly what is written the play will respond. It won't necessarily, because pauses are pauses. They have to be filled with life, or thought or imagination (*Start the Week*, BBC Radio, 22 January 2006).

These pragmatic decisions manage the audience's impression not just of the events described – what he did in the past – but also the narrator's telling now – how he views them today. Consequently, they are crucial in determining the relationships between narrator and narration: between the narrated events and the spectator: and between narrator and spectator. There is something different then, in the first example above, if the performing narrator pauses between the screaming and the decision to go find Myfanwy:

> The bottle hadn't smashed so I heaved it against the side of another bloke's head.
> It broke with a pop and glass went everywhere.
> Someone screamed. [PAUSE]
> I went to find Myfanwy. (43)[3]

or places it before the screaming:

> The bottle hadn't smashed so I heaved it against the side of another bloke's head.
> It broke with a pop and glass went everywhere. [PAUSE]
> Someone screamed.
> I went to find Myfanwy. (43)

Such a pause creates a moment of silence in performance which has ethical implications. Silence is conventionally used within dramatic performance as a means of signalling the formulation of thought within the character's mind, an encounter with the difficulty of contemplating or conceptualizing an experience, or a response to it immediately. Thus, as each character recalls the events which he has instigated, or in which he played a part, the use of pauses to signal areas which are difficult for the character to formulate in words or contemplate convey a sense of ethical recognition. According to Ian Johns's London review:

> It's a credit to much of McPherson's writing and the performances ... that a tension builds in both pieces. Not in the stories, which are too predictable, but in the audience as our feelings for McPherson's anti-heroes are constantly challenged: they are selfish creeps who are barely aware of the damage they are causing, yet they can be honest, vulnerable and sympathetic. (2001: 559)

It is precisely through the placing of the silences and pauses of performance as expressions of the difficulties faced by the character in recalling and recounting his story that such vulnerability is demonstrated and sympathy won.

---

[3] The typology here is meant to be taken as indicative of the distinctions to which I am drawing attention rather than engaging directly and specifically with the complexity explored by Worthen.

Silence and Witness

There is a further aspect to this. In work on trauma narratives, attention is drawn to the importance of silence within the testimonies of survivors.[4] Such moments of silence are regarded as 'sites of witnessing which are bounded by but not articulated within language' (Cubilié 10). They open up unfilled gaps or lacunae within the story, marking the impossibility of telling the untellable. These fictional accounts take the form of personal testimonials, albeit to largely or entirely self-inflicted trails of destruction. The violence which each narrator experiences and/or inflicts has disrupted their sense of self, destroyed their identity: the character narrating is only tangentially the same character with whom the story begins. It is an attempt to reconstitute a disintegrated self. Each is a surviving witness to events which he can contemplate only in part in a form of testimony in 'language which no longer signifies' (Cubilié 3). His remembering is an attempt to reconstitute an identity through the formation of some kind of authentic account of what they have gone through while still failing to find ways to express that which has hitherto been inexpressible.

Thus, just as the direct audience address of narration places the spectator in a direct relationship with the narrator, pauses and silence provide aporia which disrupt that relationship, requiring the spectator to see beyond the words of the telling to the areas which the narrator cannot find the words to talk about. One of the most chilling moments in the two plays occurs in *The Good Thief*. The narrator has escaped to a hideout in Leitrim with Mrs Mitchell and her daughter. After an idyllic day in which they have had a picnic by the river, he is captured by his former boss's men and tortured:

> And I suppose you want to know about flat chest Mitchell and
> the sprog,' said Murray and the way he said it told me
> everything.
> When I was out cold, they'd had a party. (75)

There are two dimensions to this: one concerning the spectatorial relationship to absences within the narrative: the other to do with the narrator's relationship to such gaps. Firstly then, the lack of information invites the spectator to consider just what had happened. This invitation provokes the possibility of a literally unspeakable

---

[4] Clearly, I am in no way drawing comparison between the fictional events here and testimonials of survivors of historical events with which much of the literature in the area engages.

but nonetheless imaginable horror for the spectator. This will be highly personalized, each spectator generating a particular vision. That vision in turn situates the spectator as a witness to an event at which they have never been present. Pausing is crucial here. It allows time and mental space for the imagination of the spectator to work. Moreover, in returning the spectatorial gaze, the actor/character's silence implicates the audience in the moment. Peggy Phelan notes that 'To solicit an ethical witness in a theatre event requires one to trust that the border of the performance exceeds its spatial and temporal boundaries' (13). Tim Etchells suggests that 'To witness an event is to be present at it in some fundamentally ethical way, to feel the weight of things and one's own place in them, even if that place is simply, for the moment, as an onlooker ... The art-work that turns us into witness leaves us, above all, unable to stop thinking, talking, reporting what we've seen' (17-18). Here then, the spectator feels the weight of what they have seen precisely because they have generated the vision.

Goulish elaborates on this sense of witness:

> we may consider the Etchells' event ethical exactly because of its initial ethics-defying nature, forcing the Witness, at a loss for an immediate 'correct' response, into a position of choice, either dismissal of the event, or an unsought worldview adjustment. This adjustment may at first appear aesthetic ... but with the passing of time, it inevitably becomes ethical (147-8).

Yet in this recounting of events to which the audience has no empirical access, the spectator is being invited also to *bear witness* to the act of narration, to the difficulty in recalling these experiences, to the effect of these experiences on the narrator and from these the extent of the violence which is left unspoken. In bearing witness, the spectator confirms and legitimates the very identity of the narrator which is jeopardized by the events which they are trying to speak about. This is a fundamentally ethical position, recognizing as human the Other, even where, as in this case, that Other is culpable of the most terrible acts of violence. These are not monsters, just men. Patrick Marmion's review for *The Evening Standard* captures this: 'it is a tribute to McPherson's writing and the fluent performances in Justin Young's production that however ugly the characters become, their unselfconscious pathos keeps them sympathetic' (558). If we reserve our empathy for and bear witness only to the deserving victims, then we are in danger too of reserving rights only for the deserving not for all.[5]

Conclusion

It is difficult in an era of theatre as spectacle where the enactment of violence on the stage is ever more prevalent in its gory detail, to give due attention to the ways in which narrated violence, that most ancient convention, may itself have a fundamental function in situating the spectator ethically. What I hope to have begun to show is that in the direct engagement of the spectator through the performed word and the performed silence, the spoken and the unspoken, the present and the absent, that the representation of violence in narration nonetheless makes fundamental demands on the spectator which have implications for the world beyond the auditorium doors.

Bibliography

Brown, Mark, Review of 'Rum & Vodka and The Good Thief', *Scotsman* 10 March 2001, in *Theatre Record* 23 April – 6 May 2001.

Cortazzi, Martin, *Narrative Analysis* (London, Washington D.C.: The Falmer Press, 1993).

Cubilié, Anne, *Women Witnessing Terror: Testimony and The Cultural Politics of Human Rights* (New York, NY: Fordham University Press, 2005).

Espiner, Mark, Review of 'Rum & Vodka' and 'The Good Thief', *Time Out* 7 May 2001, in *Theatre Record* 23 April – 6 May 2001.

Gardner, Lyn, Review of 'Rum & Vodka and 'The Good Thief', *The Guardian* 3 May 2001, in *Theatre Record* 23 April – 6 May.

Goffman, Erving, *Forms of Talk* (Philadelphia, PA: University of Pennsylvania Press, 1983).

Gould, Thomas, 'The Uses of Violence in Drama', in *Themes in Drama 13: Violence in Drama*, ed. James Redmond (Cambridge: CUP, 1991): 1-14.

Goulish, M., 'Compendium: a Forced Entertainment Glossary' in *Performance Research* 5 (3), 2000: 140-48.

Houston, Eugenie, A Taste of Irish culture [online]. <http://working.monster.ie/articles/relocating_living/-adjust_culture/culture/2/>. Last accessed 13 March 2007.

---

[5] A feature of policy initiatives by western governments in the so-called 'war on terror' has been the declaration of states of exception which allow practices such as extraordinary rendition which stand outside agreed international legal frameworks.

Johns, Ian, Review of 'Rum & Vodka' and 'The Good Thief', *The Times* 7 May 2001, in *Theatre Record* 23 April-6 May 2001.

Marmion, Patrick, Review of 'Rum & Vodka' and 'The Good Thief', *Evening Standard* 2 May 2001, in *Theatre Record* 23 April-6 May 2001.

McPherson, Conor, *This Lime Tree Bower, Rum and Vodka and The Good Thief* (London: Nick Hern Books: Dublin New Island Books, 1996).

Millwood Hargrave, Andrea, *Delete Expletives?* (London: Advertising Standards Authority, 2000).

Phelan, Peggy, 'Performing Questions, Producing Witnesses', in *Certain Fragments: Contemporary Performance and Forced Entertainment*, Tim Etchells (London: Routledge, 1999): 9-14.

Riessman, Catherine Kohler, *Narrative Analysis* (London: Sage, 1993).

Sample, Colin, 'Living Words: Physiognomy and Aesthetic Language', in *The Incorporated Self: Interdisciplinary Perspectives on Embodiment*, ed. Michael O'Donovan-Anderson (Lanham, MD: Rowan and Littlefield, 1996): 119-26.

Sierz, Aleks, *In-Yer-Face Theatre: British Drama Today* (London: Faber and Faber, 2001).

---, Review of 'Rum & Vodka' and 'The Good Thief', in *Theatre Record* 23 April – 6 May 2001.

Woolf, Virginia, 'Twelfth Night at the Old Vic', in *Specimens of English Dramatic Criticism, XVII – XX Centuries*, ed. A.C. Ward (London: Oxford University Press, 1945): 321-325.

Worthen, William B. 'The Imprint of Performance', in *Theorizing Practice: Redefining Theatre History*, eds. William B. Worthen and Peter Holland (London: Palgrave Macmillan, 2003): 213-34.

8 | 'Stap Fightin'': Accents of Violence in the Work of James Young

Paul Moore

> In the hierarchy of the senses, the epistemological status of hearing has come a poor second to that of vision. (2003, 1)

This comment by Michael Bull and Les Back in the introduction to their edited volume *The Auditory Culture Reader* captures perfectly the attitude of much of the academy to sound and the sonic environment. Other than in the fields of sound as music or radio there has been a marked indifference to the role that sound plays in developing and cementing both our identity and our relationship to a particular geographical place. Bull and Back go on to quote Joachim-Ernst Berendt from his book *The Third Ear* where the author claims that this primacy of the visual limits the imagination and argues for what he terms 'a democracy of the senses' (Berendt, 1998; qtd. 2003, 2).

The focus of this essay is a comedian who lived and worked in Northern Ireland and who, through his use of character and performance, articulated the sonic ecology of the country in which he worked. Like Bull and Back, and Berendt, this article calls not just for a move to a democracy of the senses but to a point where the reader can think with the ears.

The point of listening for this 'ear thinking' is James Young, a comedian who is held in deep affection by those who grew up in post-war Northern Ireland. This affection stems from his ability to highlight social difference and everyday politics in a way which appeared to locate him in a ground removed from the sectarian matrix that dominates this place. He himself was born in Ballymoney in 1918 and, despite a few 'influentially important' forays into rep in England and the obligatory tours of Canada and America, spent all his working life performing live and on radio and television in Northern Ireland. Through to his death in 1974 he continued to represent elements of the area's life, constantly appealing to his audiences to 'stap fightin''.

Yet James Young was very much a product of his comedic age. Young's career straddles the fifties' comic tradition with its general avoidance of any critique of working-class life and its affection for the dysfunctional loner who was somehow 'of the people', and the sixties where the working classes and their habitats became the base for comedic situations. A marked attempt to analyze and represent the interior life of the different social classes emerged in the 1960s, a shift that had much to do with the rise of the post-war working-class academic, and which was informed by, and celebrated in, Richard Hoggart's crucially important *Uses of Literacy*.

Unfortunately, however, James Young never grasped the complex and contradictory politics of working-class life in the way that Johnny Speight did in the character of Alf Garnett:

> Speight worked through a complex and contradictory politics, wishing partly to celebrate working-class life and partly to ridicule the reactionary elements within it (Wagg 10).

Young never undertook this kind of 'working through'. This was partly due to his expressed belief that entertainment was the antidote to sectarian politics in Northern Ireland but it is also due in no small part to his inability to break out of his unionist background and ideologies. It is no coincidence that Young was supported and lauded by a series of Unionist Prime Ministers, particularly Lord Brookeborough. Young's humour was quintessentially Ulster in the unionist sense – articulating a form of working-class life that did belong to only 'one side of the house' and representing the 'other' only as a foil for the class he knew and understood best. Hence his best known monologue – *I Loved a Papist* – is about the ability of an Orangeman to be tolerant of his love's religion while holding on to his known birthright.

John Hill has shown in his study of the singer and actor Richard Hayward that this use of public entertainers by unionist politicians, usually through the offices of The Ulster Tourist Development Association (UDTA) to promote a particular view of Northern Ireland, is not new. On the one hand, while Northern Ireland continued to be part of the United Kingdom, the Unionist regime was continually beset by the indifference of the British public and politicians towards it and the problem that this created in being accepted as legitimately 'British'. As a result, the regime was continually concerned to establish its 'British' credentials and emphasize, as Craigavon himself put it, that they were not a 'separate people' but 'full-born fellow-citizens of the United Kingdom and immensely proud of it.' At the same time (and interlinked with this desire for 'Britishness'), the regime was also at pains to disavow its Irishness and assert its cultural distinctiveness from the rest of Ireland. This in turn encouraged an emphasis upon the peculiar cultural character of Ulster (Hill 12-13).

In the case of Hayward the impact of this patronage, both at home and internationally, was more complex and ambivalent but for James Young his work was invariably 'Ulster' in tone and context. It always cemented the view that life in Northern Ireland is about what loyalists think of nationalists and how nationalists can be made to accept their place in the social order.

This 'cementing' was done not in any conscious way but through Young's ability to represent the sound of an Ulster that had come to be associated with a particular political regime and social order. Forrester in his seminal article on 'Auditory Perception and Sound as Event' explains that this is not surprising since we 'don't hear acoustic signals or sound waves, we hear events: the sounds of people and things moving, changing, beginning and ending, forever interdependent with the dynamics of the present moment' (1.2, online). More importantly, however, we do not hear those sounds as 'pure' sonic inputs since 'our knowledge of such sounds has come from the cultural repertoire of all those available imaginable sounds' (1.4, online). These sounds become part of our cultural memory and suggest not specific occasions or venues but a constructed sonic space which is the repository for a range of other cultural memories, ideologies and beliefs. As Ong points out: the visual world is an object world – the sonic world is an event world (Ong 1971; cited Forrester, online).

This constructed sonic repertoire is very much part of the Northern Irish public imagination. Indeed it could be argued that the sonic landscape of Northern Ireland has been imagined in such a way as to reflect and reinforce ingrained sectarian notions and divisions:

> The Historical representations of the loyalist and nationalist communities resonate with opposing sounds and sound patterns. The Protestant community has always been associated with industrialisation and Protestant communities in Antrim, Down and parts of Derry are represented as being immersed in the harsh sounds of engineering works, industrial machinery, regulated rhythms and urban volume ... Nationalist Ireland, on the other hand, is represented as being awash with pastoral sounds: the animals in the field, the soft 'shuck' of farm machinery immortalised by Seamus Heaney, the natural rhythms of the seasonal weather and, at the far reaches of the island, the relaxing coming and going of the tides (Moore 268-269)

Young's ability to re-present aspects of this sound world was established in his childhood and his mother remembered with embarrassment his mimicking of visitors to the family home in Ballymoney. The platform on which he would ultimately play out this sonic skill was, unsurprisingly, Belfast. This was not merely because Belfast was the capital city and home to the arts and media in the region, but, more importantly, because it was a microcosm for life in Northern Ireland, a gathering point for all the accents, sounds, idioms and slang that were a crucial aspect of identity in this place. This sonic ecology has come to be known, principally through the work of Murray Schafer, as the soundscape. Each geographical area has a unique soundscape inhabited by a range of particular sounds which both denote place and connote identity.

Murray Schafer calls these sounds 'soundmarks'. He defines this concept as 'a community sound which is unique or possesses qualities which make it specially regarded or noticed by the people in that community' (1994: 10) and he argues that 'whatever we may think of such soundmarks, they reflect a community character. Every community will have its own sound arguments about soundmarks, even though they may not always be beautiful' (239). Young's genius was in identifying and re-presenting through comedic performance the oral soundmarks that were peculiar to Belfast. The foundations for the characters who would explore these soundmarks were no doubt laid during the period when the youthful James Young travelled around the terraced streets of Belfast collecting rent for the estate agency where he gained his first employment. It was in this atmosphere that he would hear the voice of Belfast and Northern Ireland and come to understand that this is a region that creates its meanings through sound in a way that many other regions may not. The primacy of radio as the medium of choice in the area, the preservation of the oral tradition, and the degree of telephone use in comparison to e-mail for the area (see Richards et al, 2006) all suggest a region that is immersed in the oral. There may, nevertheless, be an interesting class dimension here because Young does share this ability with a number of working-class English comedians. The most notable of these is a man who Young actually worked with during one of his short stays in England. Frank Randle from Manchester had been illustrating for years the importance of the regional comedian who acted as a safety valve for 'ordinary decent people' and their 'unsophisticated' ways, but he was only one of a number of working-class regional comedians who by dint of their voices were intrinsically part of the community they lampooned: men like Harry Lauder, Arthur Lucan (aka Old Mother Riley), Tommy Trinder and, of course, Max Miller.

It is also worth remarking that during the 1950s and 1960s there was a marked absence of female comedians. This may be because, as many studies of comedy have indicated, female stereotypes (the paradigm being the mother-in-law) have served as the basic in-gredient of male humour or it could be that, as Laraine Porter argues, there 'are currently huge gaps in documentation, historical accounting and records of early women comic performers' (67). In the case of James Young the representation of female characters is particularly problematic give the unspoken (but widely recognized) speculation about his sexuality. Young's female characters moved beyond what Porter calls the 'exaggerated dumb blondes and squeaky bimbos on the one hand or moaning harridans and ugly hags on the other' that have been the mainstay of British comedy or 'the male cross-dressers or drag artistes [acting as] female surrogates' (65). Young does this by combining a knowledge of working-class urban life with an understanding of the sonic nuances of his geography.

Hence Young understands intrinsically the role of the city itself as an intense social, economic and architectural hub for the more general sonic environment. This environment has been examined by Emily Thompson in *The Soundscape of Modernity* (2002). Thompson argues that a soundscape 'like a landscape, ultimately has more to do with civilization than with nature' (2) and she charts the ways in which the soundscape of America was transformed by technological, architectural and particularly acoustic developments during the twentieth century. Hence she suggests that 'a soundscape's cultural aspects incorporate scientific and aesthetic ways of listening, a listener's relationship to their environment, and the social circumstances that dictate who gets to hear what' (1). Crucially the sounds that remain constant, if at times literally drowned out, are the organic sounds of the human voice.

What Young did was to take these organic sounds and use them as a geographic mapping of Belfast, creating characters that used tones and accents which positioned them in a particular area of Belfast and a particular social class and, at times, religion. To link in some simplistic way, then, Young's sexuality with his creation of female characters is a misrepresentation which fails to recognize the complexity of the creative act in which Young is engaging. Young's female characters cannot be judged in the context of contemporary drag performance sensibilities. He used female characters because they were crucial to the sonic landscape of Belfast (or Derry or Portadown, or Ballymena), the women who had to make everyday life work, often in the harshest of circumstances. Hence it was that when Young finally moved to television his work was never fully successful. Some have blamed the quality of the writing but I would argue that, ironically, the introduction of the visual element undermined the key oral aspect of Young's work turning him into just another drag artist who, like Dick Emery or Les Dawson created laughs by parodying rather than representing his alter egos. It is worth remembering that the records of James Young sold more than any other Northern Irish recording artist and in many households this is the form in which he is remembered.

This sonic geography of Belfast and Northern Ireland was encapsulated then in the differing sounds the characters made. The people who populated Young's Belfast became the personification of Roland Barthes' 'corporality of speech, the voice ... located at the articulation of body and discourse', the voice that 'permits those who know how to listen to it to hear what we can call the grain ... that materiality of the body emerging from the throat, a site where the phonic metal hardens and takes shape' (1984, 255).

The voice, in relation to silence, is like writing on blank paper. Listening to the voice inaugurates the relation to the other: the voice by which we recognize others indicates to us their way of being, their joy or their pain, their condition: it bears an image of their body and, beyond, a whole psychology. Sometimes an interlocutor's voice strikes us more than the content of his discourse, and we catch ourselves listening to the modulations and harmonics of that voice without hearing what it is saying to us.

Often then it is the modulations and harmonics of Young's characters we hear and listen to rather than the content. This is the reason why, I would suggest, his presence in the ground-breaking BBC Northern Ireland radio series *The McCooeys* was so short-lived. His reign as Derek the window cleaner (a perfect piece of casting since the window cleaner is never a part of the society – he merely critiques it from the outside) lasted only five weeks because the writers maintained they did not know what to give him to do. In fact Young <u>did</u> nothing – it was not what he said, but how he said it.

Young was aware that the structure and cadence of a sentence often tells us more about meaning than the semantics. This theme is explored by Mladen Dolar in an article entitled 'Six Lessons on Voice and Meaning' (2006). The article examines the work of Roman Jakobson, in particular the lecture that is seen as 'one of the mythical birthplaces of structuralism' (28), '*Six leçons sur le sons et le sens*'. Dolar argues that this lecture illustrates how the 'voice is something that points towards meaning' (29) but that at the very moment of seeking meaning 'there is an antinomy between the signifier and the voice: the signifier is that part of the voice which participates in making sense, while the voice is precisely that which 'doesn't make sense'. Dolar goes on to argue that the aspects that do not contribute directly to meaning – rhythms, rhymes, sound echoes, metric patterns – all contribute meaning through poetics.

> The voice is the source of an aesthetic effect which stands quite apart from the referential or informational function of language ... yet there is a second level where the sounds start to make sense themselves, another kind of sense than words achieve, an additional sense, a surplus sense, and this is the bonus of good poetry – as if first the sound echoes were the bonus of 'taking care of the sense,' and then another meaning emerges as the bonus of 'taking care of the sounds (33).

It is no coincidence that Dolar should cite as the prime example of this effect Lewis Carroll's *Jabberwocky* proving as he says 'that it's not the absence of sense that is the problem, but rather that there is too much of it' (33).

Similarly the work of the theatre director and performer Robert Wilson illustrates this notion of nonsense having too much sense. Performing the work of Christopher Knowles for a commissioned volume called *Other Rooms, Other Voices* (Kurjakovic and Lohse

1999) Wilson utilizes Knowles's 'quasi-mathematical logic in dealing with language' (19) to generate a form of meaning unconnected to the onomatopoeic poems he is reading.

However, Wilson is less interested in an instrumental understanding of language. In his performance-like reading, Wilson differentiates various forms of significance within Knowles' texts through the modulation of his voice, differing rhythms and other means (1999: 19). This then was the type of meaning that Young was manifesting in his comedy, a meaning which had as much to do with signification through modulation as it had to do with sense or meaning. In the following passage, I make reference to specific tracks by James Young which illustrate the points under discussion. I suggest that the reader listen to the track in each case, before reading on; if the reader does not have access to these specific tracks, however, other online material will give a flavour of Young's comedy.

The sound is important because it was in the micro-geography of Belfast that Young found his most memorable sonic characters. Characters like Mrs O'Condriac, less than patiently waiting her turn in any doctor's surgery in the east or west sectors of the city (Young And Foolish, 1966: Track 2), while at the same moment the Belfast working Man – a corporation man – was carefully making his way up the Antrim Road (Live In Canada, 1971: Track 7). And in some school in the middle class outskirts of Belfast, a place where, as Young says, 'they have no rates, only the occasional mouse', a grammar school educated man who had 'done well for himself' was giving a history lesson (The Young Ulsterman, 1973: Track 6). None of this, however, was of interest to Orange Lily who, to the music hall tune of 'Daisy, Daisy' was bemoaning her lack of willpower for her new diet regime (Behind the Barricades, 1970: Track 12).

This small excursion around Belfast and surrounding district gives only a flavour of the depth of sonic understanding James Young had. Those who do not understand the context or the accent can take heart from the fact that, ultimately, the content does not matter: the key to understanding Young is an understanding of how the sounds of the city map class, culture, religion and national identity.

Urban geographer Paul Rodaway in a wonderfully evocative phrase calls this mapping 'sensuous geographies' and points out that 'not only is auditory information acquired about a world, an environment of sounding things and organisms in interrelationship, but also things and people emit sounds, or have a voice, which projects them into that world. Expressed alternatively, we not only perceive of a world, but have a presence in it'. He goes on to argue that we attach a complexity of meanings to the sounds we hear that are not merely related to listening or hearing in a specific signified sense but which 'we participate in [through] a geography of the living world, an auditory world, and so distinguish places and identity relationships across space' (1994).

And yet while James Young literally articulated this sense of meaning through sound – what scientists refer to as the *proprioceptive* function of listening – the man was himself a contradiction. Part of the unionist hegemonic tradition that ensured the presence of leading political figures such as Lord Brookborough at important performances and opening nights, he was nevertheless set apart because of his unspoken sexuality and his understanding that audiences were voices rather than religious groupings. Despite his living in a rigidly patriarchal society his strongest and most memorable characters were all female. And try as he might he could never escape the very thing he invoked his audiences to turn from – an ingrained sense of tribalism. His most famous monologues, especially 'I Loved a Papist', are invariably about what Protestants feel about Catholics in a process that serves to not only 'other' the nationalist community but illustrates that James Young had virtually no understanding of what Ernie the Shipyard worker would have called 'the other side'.

It is no surprise, either, that, as mentioned earlier, the records of James Young (check your attic, every home had some) sold over a quarter of a million copies. His comedy was about the spoken word, about sound, about how we heard each other. The characters were merely vehicles through which the sound of Northern Ireland was proclaimed and it was a form of communication that could not survive the collapse of the theatrical music hall tradition or the advent of television, despite the superb situation writing of people like Sam Cree. James Young didn't need situations: he needed characters and more importantly characters that spoke directly to a like-minded audience.

Ultimately James Young's characters were part of an on-going process of definition. By drawing attention to the peculiarities of the region he was helping to define that which made Northern Ireland different, that which set it apart from the rest of the United Kingdom and more importantly, from the Republic. For his part

James Young may have believed the romantic notion that people could solve their differences without reference to social, cultural or economic circumstances if they would simply resolve to 'stap fightin'. By the time of his death in 1974 James Young would have heard enough to know that, like Johnny Speight's great creation Alf Garnett, most people in Northern Ireland not only laughed at his characters, but also had come to believe that they were also telling the truth. Ironically then, the speaker that James Young held up to Northern Ireland echoed a truth that turned out to be far from universal. But he may have had the last laugh since, as Murray Schafer pointed out, in a phrase the sentimentality of which Young would have enjoyed:

> No one can hear everything – unless God can. Beyond what fascinates your ear today is something else, incessantly and obdurately present, although you cannot or do not hear it yet – but whoever hears it first has a good chance of inheriting the future.

Bibliography

Barthes, R., *The Responsibility of Forms: Critical Essays on Music, Art and Representation*. Trans. Richard Howard (New York: Hill and Wang, 1984).

Berendt, J-E *The Third Ear: on listening to the world*. Trans. Tim Nevill (Shaftesbury: Element, 1988).

Bull, M. & L. Back, eds, *The Auditory Culture Reader* (Oxford: Berg Publishers, 2003)

Dolar, M., 'Six Lessons on Voice and Meaning' in *A Voice and Nothing More* (Cambridge, Mass: Massachusetts Institute of Technology Press, 2006).

Forrester, Michael A., 'Auditory Perception and Sound as Event' in *Sound Journal* April 2005. Available online at http://www.kent.ac.uk/sdfva/sound-journal/forrester001.html. Last accessed 1/7/2009.

Hill, J., *Cinema and Northern Ireland: Film, culture and politics* (London: BFi Publishing, 2006).

Hoggart, R.,*Uses of Literacy* (Harmondsworth: Penguin, 1958).

Kurjakovic, D. & S. Lohse, eds, *Other Rooms, Other Voices* (Zurich: Memory/Cage, 1999)

Porter, L., 'Tarts, Tampons and Tyrants' in S. Wagg ed. *Because I Tell A Joke Or Two: comedy, politics and social difference* (London & New York: Routledge, 1998).

Richards, E., R. Foster & T. Kiedrowski, eds, *Communications: The next decade* (UK Office of Communications (OFCOM), 2006).

Rodaway, P., *Sensuous Geographies: body, sense and place* (London & New York: Routledge 1994).

Schafer, M., *The Soundscape: Our Sonic Environment and the Tuning of the World* (Rochester, Vermont: Destiny Books, 1994).

---, 'Open Ears', *Canadian Association for Sound Ecology.* Available online http.//ecousticecology.ca/. Last accessed 28/11/2009.

Thompson, E., *The Soundscape of Modernity* (Cambridge, MA: MIT Press, 2002).

Young, James, *James Young 25th Commemorative Edition* Vol 1, (ERTVCD 025, 1994).

---, *James Young 25th Commemorative Edition* Vol 2, (ERTVCD 026, 1999).

---, *The Very Best of James Young*, (EMBCD 501, 2002).

Wagg, S., ed., *Because I Tell A Joke Or Two: comedy, politics and social difference* (London & New York: Routledge, 1998).

9 | The representation of violence in Irish opera: Ian Wilson's *Hamelin*

Cormac Newark

> [L]o, as they reached the mountain's side,
> A wondrous portal opened wide,
> As if a cavern was suddenly hollowed:
> And the Piper advanced and the children followed,
> And when all were in to the very last,
> The door in the mountain side shut fast.
> Did I say, all? No! One was lame,
> And could not dance the whole of the way:
> And in after years, if you would blame
> His sadness, he was used to say, –
> 'It's dull in our town since my playmates left!
> 'I can't forget that I'm bereft
> 'Of all the pleasant sights they see,
> 'Which the Piper also promised me.' (Browning, ll. 226-239)

In Robert Browning's poem *The Pied Piper of Hamelin*, perhaps the most famous retelling of the myth, we hear of a city ravaged by vermin, an angry populace and a powerless municipality – powerless, that is, until the arrival of the eponymous musician, who strikes a bargain with the desperate councillors to rid Hamelin of its rats for the trifling sum of a thousand guilders. The sad story of the Mayor's retraction (in the end he offers just fifty guilders) and the Piper's revenge is framed by Browning as a simple cautionary tale appropriate for its young dedicatee, 'W. M. the younger'.[1] The straightforward moral – that one should always keep one's promises – is expressed in the inspired rhyme of the penultimate couplet: 'So,

---

[1] W[illiam] M[acready] the younger was the son of Browning's friend, actor William Macready.

Willy, let you and me be wipers/Of scores out with all men –
especially pipers'.

Ian Wilson's chamber opera, *Hamelin* (first performed by the
Schleswig-Holsteinisches Landestheater and by Opera Theatre
Company of Dublin in 2003),[2] relates a much darker history, one set
against a vague but threatening background of war and disease. The
Piper has apparently been and gone: we are faced with a lame child,
left behind, alone, outside the town, lamenting her fate: 'O Piper',
she sings, 'pray look back at this poor maid' (Act 1, scene 1, bb. 47-
56). She is joined by two men, the Mayor and a Doctor, whose very
first remarks hint menacingly at a much more violent tale than the
one we know from Browning: 'She can't go far ... she won't escape ...
she's simple and naïve ... who knows what nonsense that young fool
believes!' (Act 1, scene 1, bb. 206-21). As in Browning, the other
children are definitely gone, done away with by some mysterious
power, which explains the men's uncomfortably predatory interest
in the Girl – or, rather, in her future importance for the community:
both refer again and again to her vital role in re-establishing the
population after its tragic losses. What does seem progressively less
clear in the first scenes of the opera is exactly who (or what) is to
blame for those losses: while the Girl sings of nothing but the Piper
and his captivating music, the men mention food shortages, a
conflict that has lasted decades, plague-ridden vermin overrunning
the city and stores of grain that have gone bad, infected with fungus.

For the characters, the main motivation is thus explanation: what
exactly, among Hamelin's many recent misfortunes, has resulted in
the disappearance of the children and the present appalling trauma?
The rationalizations offered by the two men represent the violence
done to Hamelin in a plausible, prosaic way: the Girl's lament hints
at a more mysterious crime, a kind of rape – in which music itself
may somehow have been complicit. For the composer, indeed,
exposing this crime is a meta-compositional project, requiring a
musical language capable of speaking about – testifying against –
another, quite different, music. And not just any music: one
powerful enough to have wreaked legendary devastation upon
Hamelin and its inhabitants. As the work unfolds, the sound of the
pipe remains tantalizingly distant, but music's power is nonetheless

[2] The productions were directed by Christian Marten-Molnár (Flensburg,
Schleswig, Rendsburg) and Gavin Quinn (Sligo, Dublin, Belfast)
respectively.

manifestly at work, moving seductively back and forth between narrative object, descriptive agent and poetic trope.

Music about music

Historically opera has relished opportunities for reflexivity, especially in the form of stage-songs: Cherubino's 'Voi che sapete' in *Le nozze di Figaro* and the Duke's 'La donna è mobile' in *Rigoletto* are only a couple of the most famous examples of what was a common feature of eighteenth- and nineteenth-century works.[3] There are also a number of canonic operatic scenes involving diegetic instrumental music – including that played on pipes: the shepherd's tune that Tristan sings about so movingly as he lies wounded is perhaps the best-known instance.[4] The first ever surviving work in the genre, indeed, Monteverdi's *L'Orfeo*, shows the eponymous mythical musician very much in action in his professional capacity, using his virtuoso playing of the lyre to lull Charon to sleep and thus gain access to Hades and his beloved Eurydice[5].

The compositional challenge of a music so mesmerizing that it is capable of controlling the actions of a whole population of children, however, is something else again, and it comes as no surprise that Ian Wilson chose to represent this magic melody at one remove. We experience the music initially only through the Girl's desire to find it in other plausible sounds: Example 1 is from the beginning of Act 1, scene 2.

As the opera goes on, though the parts of the score intended to evoke the Piper's playing are obvious enough, always cued by references in the text and always involving the flute, it becomes just as obvious that they are to be understood as somehow emanating from the lame Girl herself rather than directly from the mythical pipe: they stand not for the music but for her desperate – and unsuccessful – attempts to recall it.

Meanwhile, the lame Girl has refused the entreaties of the two men, who want her to come back to the city with them: they decide that a night in the open will soon bring her to her senses. Act 1, scene 2 is split between her obsessive apostrophizing of the Piper,

---

[3] Wolfgang Amadeus Mozart, *Le nozze di Figaro* (1786), Act 2: Giuseppe Verdi, *Rigoletto* (1851), Act 3.

[4] Richard Wagner, *Tristan und Isolde* (1865), Act 3.

[5] Claudio Monteverdi, 'Possente spirto' in Act 3 of *L'Orfeo* (1607).

Example 1 Copyright 2002 by Universal Edition (London) Ltd., London. Reproduced by permission. All rights reserved.

which little by little resolves itself into a kind of erotic fixation, and the conversation of the Mayor and the Doctor, notionally set in the latter's library, from which we begin to learn more of the terrible goings-on in Hamelin. The music is similarly split into two distinct vocal languages. In contrast to the free chromaticism of the Girl's line, each of the men has a deliberately circumscribed range of expression: the tenor playing the role of the Mayor sings substantially within octatonic scales, and the part of the bass playing the Doctor is largely whole-tone[1].

Example 2: octatonic and whole-tone scales in the versions used in Example 3 below.

Mayor: e, f#, g, a, a# (or b♭), c, c# (or d♭), d# (or e♭)
Doctor: a, b, c# (or d♭), d# (or e♭), f, g.

This musical characterization emerges as an expressive metaphor as we gather that the men see their position as carrying with it the responsibility to hold everything together: they need clear structures in order to function properly. As they put it later in the scene, their duty is to 'steer things through. / The town would fall apart without us two' (Act 1, scene 2, bb. 671-5). A further expression of this conviction is that they frequently sing together in rhythmic unison. The ostensible need for this united front is hinted at in the following catalogue of Hamelin's woes, beginning 'The war has ravaged us for thirty years.

---

[1] The octatonic scale, a regular alternation of tones and semitones, was exploited by some nineteenth-century composers, notably Liszt, but is most often discussed in relation to the music of Messiaen, Bartók and (especially) Stravinsky: the whole-tone scale is found in a great deal of late-nineteenth- and twentieth-century Russian and French music, particularly that of Debussy.

Example 3: *Hamelin,* Act 1, scene 2, bb. 498-527. ©
Copyright 2002 by Universal Edition (London) Ltd., London.
Reproduced by permission. All rights reserved.

But there is also a musical clue to the repressed violence of Hamelin's recent history: the flute/clarinet sonority and characteristic rising semiquaver flourishes heard at the beginning of Example 1 and the end of Example 3 (also just before Example 3: see Act 1, scene 2, bb. 490-92). This passage functions as a kind of leitmotif: it is heard at moments almost throughout the length of the opera, always apparently eliciting a response from the characters on stage. If in Example 1 it could conceivably be construed as 'real' sound – the Girl hears something, listens, doesn't hear it again but *does* hear an owl, realistically quoted by flutter-tongued flute, and concludes she must have been mistaken – a little later in the scene (Example 3) it seems to function more abstractly, as a metaphor for the men's anxiety, forcing them to justify themselves. Its representative status is therefore ambiguous: given that it is apparently in some sense 'audible' in the operatic world of the work (and given its suggestive woodwind scoring) it would appear to stand for some kind of echo, real or remembered, of the famous pipe: its insistent repetition subsequently points rather to a more complicated significance. While the Girl, who passionately wants to experience the ecstasy of the Piper's music again, cannot recall it, the men cannot avoid it. For them it obviously means something very different.

Sure enough, later in the scene the Doctor gives a lengthy explanation of one particular misfortune suffered by the town: ergotism, a condition brought on by eating bread made from grain infected with the fungus ergot (Act 1, scene 2, bb. 602-52). Although, as he explains, citing various early scientific authorities, the fungus does have medicinal uses, for example to treat haemorrhaging in childbirth, it is very dangerous. In fact ergot is the naturally-occurring source of lysergic acid: as the Mayor puts it, interrupting his companion, 'The rye will send you mad' (Act 1, scene 2, bb. 656-7). The Doctor and the Mayor congratulate themselves on the soundness of their own food supplies – they 'remain in health' – but the precise result of this outbreak of madness remains suspiciously unidentified, not least because the Doctor says, in reply to the Mayor, 'Indeed, my friend, it's a convincing line' (Act 1, scene 2, bb. 659-60). Towards the end of Act 1 this ambiguity is further stressed by the Doctor's trying to drown out the (by this stage increasingly frequent and insistent) 'pipe' motif (Example 4).

Example 4: *Hamelin*, Act 1, scene 2, bb. 703-9. © Copyright 2002 by Universal Edition (London) Ltd. London. Reproduced by permission. All rights reserved.

Music about myth (and myths about music)

The librettist of the opera, Lavinia Greenlaw, has written that *Hamelin* is an exploration of how myths are made, and certainly the text skillfully keeps elements of more-or-less plausible explanations of the trauma in question circling anxiously about until almost the very last moment. Its dark, violent centre, hinted at a number of times but never made explicit, is contained within the ominous line 'And in a bowl of stew, a tiny hand that could have been...' (Act 1, scene 2, bb. 518-23 and 714-9). Not surprisingly, the authority figures in the drama constantly turn away from this terrible explanation of what happened to their children, by emphasizing that *their* food supplies were untainted – that they themselves were not victims of any temporary madness – and by evasively breaking into what becomes a familiar chorus of head-shaking and excuses: 'I've/We've seen such sights, such suffering, such crimes' (Act 1, scene 2, bb. 496-8 and 661-3: Act 2, scene 1, bb. 141-3, 258-60, etc). Their aim, which becomes increasingly definite following their first encounter with the Girl, is to get their story straight – without initially seeming to be able either to confront what really happened or understand quite how any of the less damning alternative narratives might be made to seem coherent. Their one certainty, given the appalling secrets they share, is that they must stick together – sing from the same hymn-sheet, as it were.

Thus the opera, just like the real-life aftermath of major acts of violence, becomes a collection of competing narratives, with the men trying to find the least incriminating. The Girl, whose grief-stricken wailing about the Piper is that of the distressed survivor, quite naturally engages with the tragedy in a much less structured, not to say hysterical, way. But over the course of the central part of the opera, a process of ordering is nonetheless at work as she develops her imagined love affair with, and rejection by, the Piper into a story of self-determination. She spends Act 1, scene 2 and Act 2, scene 1 gradually getting over her sense of loss, so successfully as to arrive eventually at a point where she is able to take possession of the story: 'the clue to freedom is not him but me', she concludes in the final scene (Act 2, scene 2, bb. 726-30). The position of the one who has lived to tell the tale is, as she now realizes, an empowered one.

The director of the Opera Theatre Company production of *Hamelin*, Gavin Quinn, placed strong emphasis on this aspect of the work as a story in the process of construction. The performers are portrayed as if in a workshop situation (complete with fag-breaks and tidying up after scenes), engaged in the process of devising the work we are watching. On stage, the conductor and the instrumental ensemble are clearly visible, representing in physical space that this is a story built around music – or rather a certain poetic idea of music, one eminently suited to the making of legend.

And, finally, it is the music that effects the eventual establishment of a common version of events. The men begin to see how the Girl's fantastic Pied Piper story could represent the solution to their problem, and accordingly they gradually assimilate it. The rigid rhythmic ensemble of the Mayor and the Doctor wins the day, though, and by the final scene of the opera the Girl has been drawn into the mantra and is singing along with them. Not only does she sing the same words, in fact, there are even passages in *melodic*

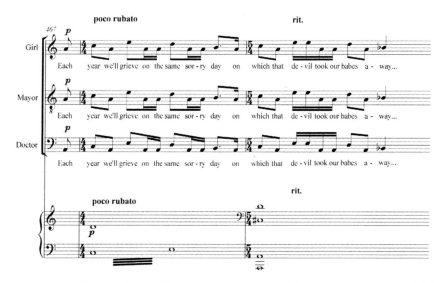

Example 5: *Hamelin*, Act 2, scene 2, bb. 465-7, repeated bb. 745-7. © Copyright 2002 by Universal Edition (London) Ltd. London. Reproduced by permission. All rights reserved.

unison (unexpected, given the independence of line usual in contemporary opera), so nearly have the narratives converged.

Similarly, the disorientating chromaticism of the opening scenes of the work has disappeared, to be replaced by a much more stable harmonic language. After some disturbing revelations and some uncomfortable music to match, it would seem that the opera has, after all, rejoined the more straightforward (and much less disconcerting) version of the tale favoured by Browning. Even if its more troubling aspects remain unresolved, each of the characters in the opera seems to find solace in a common survivor narrative which, if not necessarily the whole truth, is no less tragic. For Browning too, this straightforwardness is both the key to and, crucially, the *result of* being in a position to pass the story on:

> [O]pposite the place of the cavern
> They wrote the story on a column,
> And on the Great Church Window painted
> The same, to make the world acquainted
> How their children were stolen away:
> And there it stands to this very day (ll. 283-8).

For the nineteenth-century poet, untroubled by the obligation to represent the sound of the pipe except via the lame child's vision of the 'pleasant sights' it conjured up, music could remain in its habitual position: mysterious and unknowable, but magically vital – an appealing metaphor for poetry itself, in fact[1]. For the twenty-first-century composer, however, music's complicity in the tragedy is an issue that cannot be ducked. In the end Wilson expresses it not so much by gestures towards the unrepresentable music of the Piper (though some of those gestures *are* to be heard in the course of the opera), but, far more insidiously, by the legitimacy lent to his legend, when it is at last in a version that everyone can agree on, by an inexorable and entirely musical progression towards stability and resolution. It is in this way – rather than through any self-consciously 'enchanting' tune to represent the Piper's seductive appeal – that Wilson renders the coercion, the act of musical violence, lying at the heart of the story.

Wilson's *Hamelin* is an opera about the representation of violence, yet no violence is staged. More importantly, it is also an opera about the representation of music, in which the expressive ambiguity of leitmotivic procedure is fully exploited: the flute and clarinet passages heard at key moments in the score are *about* the Piper's music rather than actually *being* that music. This is all the more appropriate because, as becomes more and more clear as the opera goes on, the Piper's Pipe may not have ever really existed.

Bibliography

Browning, Robert,'The Pied Piper of Hamelin', *Bells and Pomegranates* vol. 3 (1842).

Monteverdi, Claudio, *L'Orfeo*. Ed. Denis Stevens (London: Novello, 1968).

Mozart, Wolfgang Amadeus, *Le nozze di Figaro*, ed. Ludwig Finscher. *Wolfgang Amadeus Mozart: Neue Ausgabe sämtlicher Werke* II:5/xvi (Kassel: Internationale Stiftung Mozarteum Salzburg, 1955-91).

Verdi, Giuseppe, *Rigoletto*, ed. Martin Chusid. *The Works of Giuseppe Verdi* I:17 (Chicago: University of Chicago Press/Milan: Ricordi, 1983).

Wagner, Richard, *Tristan und Isolde*. Ed. Isolde Vetter. *Sämtliche Werke* 8 (Mainz: B. Schott's Söhne, 1990-93).

Wilson, Ian, *Hamelin* (London: Universal Edition, 2002).

---

[1] In this context it seems worth noting that this nineteenth-century music-poetry identification was nowhere more cultivated than in Ireland: see Harry White, *Music and the Irish Literary Imagination* (New York: Oxford University Press, 2009).

10 | Framing Reality: A Case Study in Prison Theatre in Northern Ireland

David Grant

Introduction

In June 2006, Frank McGuinness's powerful evocation of the experience of Protestant soldiers from Northern Ireland during the First World War, *Observe the Sons of Ulster Marching Towards the Somme*, was performed by prisoners in Hydebank Young Offenders Centre in Belfast. Beyond the frames of the world of the play and the production was the dominant frame of the prison itself. Based on interviews with key participants and the experience of working with the cast in the six months after the production, this article considers the impact and legacy of the project. *Observe the Sons of Ulster Marching Towards the Somme* deals with one of the defining episodes in Northern Ireland Protestant culture. As such, it might have seemed too aligned to one side of the community to have enjoyed full support among a group of prisoners from both sides of the region's cultural divide. Moreover, those familiar with the play, could not fail to be aware of the potential sensitivity within a prison of its homoerotic dimension. Experience was to show, however, that these anxieties were themselves functions of 'the view'. This article recounts the use of a version of Boal's *Rainbow of Desire* technique to explore the expanding perspective of the prisoner-participants and examines the experience of both them and the artistic team to suggest that the theatrical value system that both groups came to share, allowed the project to avoid the pitfall of becoming a public performance of punishment.

The Project

In June 2006, eight prisoners in Hydebank Young Offenders Centre in Belfast performed Frank McGuinness's iconic account of Protestantism in the north of Ireland, *Observe the Sons of Ulster Marching Towards the Somme*. In addition to the conventional concentric theatrical frames of the world of the play, the production and the venue, the visiting audience were also palpably aware of the additional framing provided by the prison itself.[1] They experienced this in material form as they negotiated the security procedures before taking their seats and also in the presence with them in the performance space of prison inmates and staff. In addition to these multiple layers of reality, yet another frame was evidenced by the presence of television cameras, before, during and after the play. For me as a member of the audience, however, such was the conviction of the actors (a conscious but I hope forgivable pun) that all but the frame of the play were sublimated in the moment of performance. Reflecting on the experience afterwards, I found myself making connections between the world of the young volunteers in the trenches and that of their present-day peers on the stage, but as the action unfolded I was only intermittently aware of the production context. Based on interviews with key protagonists Mike Moloney, Dan Gordon, and Brendan Byrne, and the experience of six months spent working with the cast after the event, this article will consider the impact and legacy of the overall project (of which the production and eventually a BBC documentary are only the more visible parts) in relation to James Thompson's idea of 'the view': that 'we need over time to learn to look, not to be told what to look at' and that 'reflection needs a set of experiences against which judgment can be made' (2003: 71-3).

The idea for the production came from Brendan Byrne of Hotshot Films, an independent production company based in Belfast. His initial interest was in a documentary about a rehearsal process and the idea for this to be of a production of the McGuinness play performed by young prisoners came later: but by his own account, once *Observe the Sons* became the basis of the project the idea sold itself. The BBC responded fairly readily to the proposal for four short films documenting the process. The prison authorities were also enthusiastic. They regularly receive requests

---

[1] See John O'Toole, *The Process of Drama*, (London: Routledge, 1992): 51-53 for an excellent analysis of contextual frames.

from broadcasters to film in the prison and rarely agree, but they could see the inherent attraction of so challenging a project. Indeed, it was arguably this sense of challenge that made the proposal so attractive.

Observe the Sons of Ulster Marching Towards the Somme deals with one of the defining episodes in Northern Ireland Protestant culture. As such, it might have seemed too aligned to one side of the community to have enjoyed full support among a group of prisoners drawn from both sides of the region's cultural divide. Moreover, those familiar with the play, could not fail to be aware of the potential sensitivity within a prison of its homoerotic dimension. Experience was to show, however, that these anxieties were themselves functions of 'the view'.

In *Applied Theatre: Bewilderment and Beyond*, Thompson articulates this concept through a series of anecdotes. He recalls a visit to the Grand Canyon and how, while he and his wife marvelled at the uniquely breathtaking vista, his infant children played in the sand by the road, unmoved by the epic spectacle before them. He relates this to his own indifference, when a teenager, to the remarkable topography of Edinburgh – a city that now enthralls him – and argues that we learn through a lifetime of experience to contextualize what we see. He concludes that the range of perspective of the young is generally more limited than that of older observers. I would add cultural experience and education as other factors that define the extent and nature of an individual's view.

To apply this in my own case, although I had directed a play in Maghabery Prison in 1993, I had no direct experience of Hydebank Young Offenders Centre. I had developed a strong respect for the prisoners I had worked with in Maghabery, but in those pre-Ceasefire days it was easy to romanticize the entire prison population as politically driven. I made a point of not knowing what offences the prisoners I was working with had been convicted of, but imagined them all as having paramilitary pasts. I vividly recall my first meeting with them. I stood alone at one end of the large education room: they stood at the other end, clumped together, a phalanx of tattooed forearms. Suddenly one of them inched forward. 'Mr Grant, we've just got one question for you. (*Pause*) You're not going to shout at us, are you?' They were clearly much more apprehensive than I was. Dan Gordon, who directed *Observe the Sons*, recounted a similar sense of ambiguity about his first exposure to the prison environment in an article for the Northern Ireland

Association for the Care and Resettlement of Offenders (NIACRO) newsletter:

> What also bothers me is I've liked the people I've met so far. I don't know who they are or what they've done and really I don't want to. And I'm certainly not a victim so I don't feel I have any right to judge – but when I meet them and talk to them I've liked them ... all of them. It's very confusing – they don't have horns or tails or try to steal my watch, they just want to break the routine for a few minutes with talk ... But when we talk – when the masks come off – I'm shocked by my ignorance and their ordinariness. Every day we interact on a human level – I know nothing other than what they tell me about how they feel about themselves and the worlds they know ... I'm learning every day that people and life are a lot more complicated than I thought (16).

My own expectations of the Hydebank prisoners were, I realize now, just as contradictory. On one hand, I imagined that they would be mainly 'hoods' (young anti-social hooligans with a propensity for joyriding). On the other hand, I assumed that they would be strongly sectarian with paramilitary connections. Having worked in the centre on and off for six months, my view has broadened. The range of offences is much wider than I had imagined and levels of sectarianism are remarkably low – not least, I now understand, because many of the inmates are the principal targets of paramilitary punishment regimes. Nevertheless, *Observe the Sons* presented obvious difficulties. As Margaret Llewellyn-Jones has observed, for instance, 'the iconographic significance of the donning of an Orange sash ... will evoke different and potentially challenging responses' depending on the context of the production (10). At the start of each performance of *Observe the Sons,* Dan Gordon addressed the audience explaining that the play contained 'emblems' and 'language', but with hindsight, I think this was more for the benefit of the guests than the prisoners. Apart from one quite performative episode during the rehearsal period, when a Catholic member of the cast refused to wear an Orange sash until he had permission from his mother, there was little evidence of sectarianism among the mixed cast. Dan and Mike Moloney (the coordinator of the project and Director of the Prison Arts Foundation) are both adamant that this was 'never about the sash' but part of an elaborate games-manship that characterized much of the rehearsal process. As his peers caustically commented, the prisoner concerned hadn't asked his mother's permission for his armed robbery! Similarly, the play's treatment of sexuality was acknowledged in the rehearsal room but not fetishized. Although the cast, as the only openly homosexual member of the cast put it to me, 'were not keen on the gay stuff', the subject was far from taboo and a powerful tenderness was evident on stage.

What I imagined to be major obstacles, then, the production took in its stride. Far more significant was the institutional environment. Dan Gordon has attributed the success of the whole project to 'a series of happy accidents'. Firstly, the Chief Security Officer at Hydebank turned out to be a 'Somme fanatic'. He agreed to give a talk to the cast in the first week of rehearsals and they later noted – from the rushes of the Hotshot Films documentary for the BBC – how visibly moved he was by what he told them. Secondly, it proved possible to transform the somewhat sterile environment of the prison chapel where they rehearsed by use of camouflage netting which could be stowed in a duvet cover between sessions. A Brechtian half-curtain was also used to disguise offices at one end of the room.

The third fortuitous element was the casting process. More than a hundred and fifty prisoners saw a promotional DVD of Dan at the commemorative Somme Centre in which he appeared both as himself and as Red Hand Luke, a satirical loyalist character he plays on the popular BBC Northern Ireland comedy series, *Give My Head Peace*. Dan had been ambivalent about using this television persona, but the rushes of the documentary show that this provided an immediate point of contact for the prisoners who saw it. One hundred and twenty expressed initial interest as a result: fifty turned up to the prison gym for a briefing session. Of these, not all were eligible to participate for legal reasons: for example, because they were on remand and a television appearance might unfairly influence a future trial. In the end, however, twenty-five signed up for audition and eighteen actually came forward. In the audition process, the artistic team consistently referred to popular television parallels, coming up with the idea of *Prison Idol*. With various changes throughout the early weeks of the process, this eighteen became the core of the final company.

Dan's fourth happy circumstance was the play itself, which required all the actors to be on stage throughout the performance. This allowed him to insist that they all listen in rehearsal all the time. The fact that the characters formed four distinct pairings also proved useful and the process became driven by competition between pairs. The analogy of prison cellmates was noted by one participant – when you're locked up in a small room with someone, you have to get on. In retrospect, Dan 'felt a great sense of disappointment' that they never became one team. But the pairings produced some superb moments like one exultant 'high fives' at the end of a successful run of a scene.

Dan's final explanation for the success of the production lay in his own background as a P.E. teacher. This enabled him to join in the rigorous military style physical preparation that began the process and to engage with the P.E. teachers on the prison staff. He understood the culture of the gym and respected it. In response to the question, '[h]ow do the practices of drama and theatre best engage with the systems of formalized power to create a space of radical freedom[?]' (Kershaw, 36), Baz Kershaw has concluded that they have a greater chance of doing so when they 'fully and directly engage with the discourses of power in their particular settings' (49). It seems clear from the above account, that the success of *Observe the Sons* derived not least from the way in which the idea of the play made an impact on the prison authorities, most obviously in the person of the Chief Security Officer and in which the production style connected with the centre's prevailing gymnasium culture.

Perhaps the greatest challenge in creating theatre inside a prison is the capacity of the institution to deaden the imagination. If the Benthamite ideal of a jail is the all-seeing panopticon, the vision thus provided is entirely literal, with little scope for metaphor or analogy. Mike Moloney recalled a moment when he was showing the mother and grandmother of one of the cast their son/grandson's picture in First World War uniform, on display in the performance space after the show. They had clearly been moved by the play and were proud of their offspring, so Mike tried to engage them in an imaginative journey. 'Do you see that soldier?' he asked, and they played along. And then he asked if they saw their own boy. They shook their heads in sad denial. The idea of re-imagining him as other than a criminal was too great a leap for them to take.

James Thompson's idea of 'the view' is helpful in understanding this situation. In the case of the mother and grandmother described above, they lacked a relevant 'set of experiences' to allow them to look with a significative eye. They needed the opportunity 'to learn to look, not to be told what to look at'. Those of us whose daily lives are preoccupied with theatre often underestimate the extent to which we are required to frame and process a theatrical event, both as spectators and practitioners. Bert States's pithy comparison of phenomenological and semiotic modes of understanding is instructive here:

> If we think of semiotics and phenomenology as modes of seeing, we might say that they constitute a kind of binocular vision: one eye enables us to see the world phenomenally: the other eye enables us to see significatively ... Lose the sight of your phenomenal eye and you become a Don Quixote (everything is something else). Lose the sight of your significative eye and you become Sartre's Roquentin (everything is nothing but itself) (8).

Most mainstream theatre assumes its audience to have some sort of theatrical education, without much thought to how these theatrical sign systems are created, propagated and managed. One way of illustrating this, by analogy, is to look at the experience of a newcomer to the prison system. The prison enjoys its own rich semiotic system. The clothes that prisoners wear carry a wide extended meaning. Prisoners wearing polo-shirts and jeans are in standard prison issue. Those in sportswear are wearing their own clothes. But as was explained to me by Mike Moloney, the prison issue has the additional significance that these prisoners have probably little support or contact with the outside world. So, in a drama workshop I held in the prison shortly after the end of the production of *Observe the Sons*, when one of the participants drew attention to the new t-shirt being worn by another member of the group, this carried the additional meaning that that prisoner had had a recent visit. In fact, the t-shirt had been provided by one of the play's professional production team, who had come to understand the psychological importance of prisoners being able to wear their own clothes.

Another powerful example of this prison semiosis occurred late in the rehearsal process. Unusually for non-prison staff, Mike and Dan were given permission to walk prisoners around the grounds without escort. In the final run-up to the production, Dan realized that one of the stage crew would be more valuable in the theatre than in the rehearsal room. He asked the prison officer on duty if he could walk the prisoner concerned across to the other building without waiting for another officer to be summoned. This was agreed to, provided that Dan took the prisoner's identifying 'T-Card' with him. These cards are held by an officer in respect of any prisoner for whom he has responsibility at any given time. On Dan's return, a member of the cast grew angry, castigating Dan for having become a 'screw'. In that prisoner's eyes, the powerful symbolism of the T-Card (what for Dan had seemed at most an administrative irrelevance), had transformed him from benign outsider to an integral part of the prison system.

If the view of artists working in the prison was altered through the process of working on the production, that of the prisoners also underwent change. By Dan's account, the rehearsal process depended heavily on him demonstrating approaches to the performance, sometimes line by line. The prisoners lacked the experience and the terminological shorthand to translate the written text into performance without this kind of painstaking mediation. But they were extremely adept at negotiating the social context of the production. In particular, the presence of the documentary cameras created an unusual rehearsal dynamic. Part of the drama training process involved rigorous quasi-military physical workouts and Dan and Mike both commented on the total dedication that followed from the prisoners' awareness that they were being filmed.

One episode illustrated the sophisticated understanding of the filming process that at least one prisoner developed. This cast member (the one whose mother and grandmother had been looking at his picture and who had temporarily refused to wear the sash) had been consistently the most difficult in rehearsal, regularly bridling against the discipline required by the process and eventually refusing to come down for rehearsal at all. Mike went to reason with him accompanied by the camera, but to begin with, the cameraman held back, recording sound only while Mike talked to the prisoner in his cell. Eventually, as negotiations reached an advanced stage, the camera tentatively invaded the prisoner's private space. Clearly aware of the camera, but without directly acknowledging it, the prisoner reiterated the main points of his argument which we had already heard off-camera, demonstrating a subtle understanding of the editing process.

The combination of engaging in a drama-based process while simultaneously being filmed shattered the monocular perspective that constrains most prisoners. Instead of a tunnel-visioned preoccupation with their release date, the play offered its participants a temporary imaginative respite, while the camera created an extended digital view – a sense of virtual perspective. One powerful example of this came early in the rehearsal process when some of the cast made a pop video. This proved crucial in building their confidence in the whole production process. As Dan and Mike put it, once they saw the finished product they knew that they could be made to look good.

Caoimhe McAvinchey has noted a similar phenomenon while working with women prisoners in England and Brazil as part of 'Staging Human Rights' (221-225). Her original role was to document a broadly-based creative project and her intention was to make herself as unobtrusive as possible. But her digital camera and laptop computer soon generated more interest among the prisoners than the substantive activities themselves. In fact, the prisoners' evident interest in their own images became the catalyst for a collaboration with Jan Platun and Rachel Hale (a photographer and visual artist), 'Handheld 3', a project in the women's wing of Hydebank in November 2006. In prison, one's sense of oneself is necessarily circumscribed and the women prisoners in Belfast demonstrated a clear appreciation of the opportunity to create symbolic images of themselves using Polaroid photographs when I was among the guests invited in to see their work.

Observe the Sons of Ulster created similar opportunities for the participants to stretch their imaginations. I recall, as a member of the audience, the heightened symbolism of an early exchange between Craig and Pyper:

PYPER.	Have you ever looked at an apple?
CRAIG.	Yes.
PYPER.	What did you see?
CRAIG.	An apple.
PYPER.	I don't. I see through it.
CRAIG.	The skin, you mean?
PYPER.	The flesh, the flesh, the flesh.
CRAIG.	What about it?
PYPER.	Beautiful. Hard. White (104-105).

What struck me was not so much the homoerotic subtext, as the simple power of imagery – the possibility of the apple being something other than it was. For a few months, these prisoners, through the medium of the production, were allowed to discover a renewed sense of themselves – to look with a semiotic as well as a phenomenological eye.

In a workshop with most of the cast and crew, a few weeks after the final performance, I sought to explore this idea of extended perspective using a variant of Boal's 'Rainbow of Desire' technique

(Boal, 150-6). Boal developed this technique to 'examine individual, internalized oppressions' (Jackson in Boal, xviii) as distinct from the more public oppressions associated with his earlier development of Forum Theatre, but I have found it a useful rehearsal technique when applied to fictional situations. By engaging the group in an interactive process, I hoped I could avoid any resistance to more conventional discussion within a group that for the most part had had a bad experience of formal education.

We restaged a moment towards the end of the play, just before the soldiers go 'over the top' to almost certain death, when the hard-line Orangeman, Anderson, hands Pyper, the play's narrator, an orange sash. I asked the group to suggest different things that Pyper might want in that moment (his 'desires', however strong or weak these might be). At first, the actor playing Pyper was resistant to the notion that his character could be anything other than fully committed to his comrades – a fixity natural in someone who had evoked the moment before a series of audiences. But eventually the following additional 'desires' were teased out: Pyper's desire to be his own man (I), his desire to conform to Orangism (O), his commitment to Craig (C), his commitment to his family (F) and his reluctance to be drawn into 'Carson's Dance' (McGuinness, 163) (R). A striking feature of the discussion was the way in which many of the group quoted fluently and freely from the text, having clearly fully internalized it. In accordance with Boal's methodology, all of these 'desires' were then represented by different members of the group and the actor playing Pyper engaged in an improvised dialogue with each, before arranging them in the performance space according to how he perceived their importance for his character. The improvisations revealed a strong sense of collective responsibility, which seemed to apply as much to the group of prisoners themselves as to the characters they were portraying.

Once the 'Rainbow Image' was created, many of the group were quick to comment on it. One prisoner noted that all the 'Desires' were pointing towards Pyper: another that he had placed the 'family' image very far away. I then noted that the Craig image, although at a distance was in Pyper's eyeline and also the nearest element to the figure representing Pyper's family: that Anderson stood with the sash between Pyper and his family, perhaps suggesting Pyper's new sense of allegiance: that the figure representing Pyper's reluctance to get drawn in was nearest the audience, echoing his character's attitude in the play's prologue: and that the figure representing his

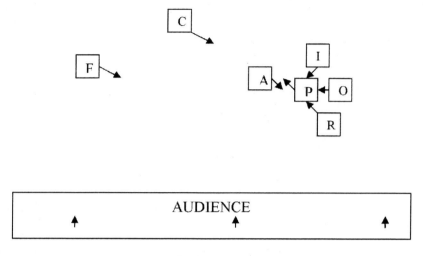

Key: P = Pyper: I = Desire to be his own man: O = desire to conform to Orangism: C = commitment to Craig: A = Anderson giving him the Sash: R = reluctance to get drawn in Carson's Dance: F = Commitment to Family

sense of independence was positioned nearest the figure representing his commitment to Craig.The group seemed fairly ready to accept these readings.

In preparation for the image theatre of the 'Rainbow of Desire', I took the group through a series of image-based exercises, including the 'Image of the Hour' (Boal, 112-3). This entails each participant enacting a simple mime, indicating what they would be doing at each hour of a typical day. Knowing more now about the system of 'compacts' that rewards prisoners for good behaviour with increasing levels of privileges, I would be able to understand more fully than I did then the significance of certain prisoners showing themselves playing video games, but I still think I rightly interpreted the high incidence of masturbatory images in the 'wee small hours', as a genuine part of the exercise rather than a commentary on the workshop itself. The fact was that these young men had become remarkably comfortable with drama-based modes of expression.

When I followed this exercise up by asking them to represent an image, hour-by-hour, of the best day they could remember, the results were predictably hedonistic, with the memorable exception of one young man who spent the entire exercise nursing a small child in his arms. I subsequently discovered that, like a remarkably high proportion of the 18-23 year olds in Hydebank, he was a father and that he had seen his daughter the previous week for the first time in several years. In subsequent meetings with him, it became clear that this was not something that he discussed with his peers. I found it all the more remarkable, therefore, that the drama exercise had created a safe enough space for him to demonstrate these feelings imagistically.

My intention had been that this workshop would be the start of a follow-up project with the *Observe the Sons* cast and crew, aimed at building on the extraordinary achievement of the production. But within weeks, in response to an escape attempt, the prison authorities vividly displayed their own point of view by transferring half of the cast to other prisons. I have no evidence that cast members were deliberately targeted and it is clear from talking to prison officials at various levels of authority that there was an exceptional sense of collective pride in the production. But that an emergency movement of 10% of the prison population included 50% of the cast of the play seems statistically remarkable. On one level, this simply reflects the over-riding importance of security within the prison system. The transferred prisoners also included two about to sit exams, but educational considerations carry little weight when security issues are invoked. But Mike Moloney has suggested to me that there is also an extent to which the prison system reacts, almost intuitively, against anything that encourages prisoners to feel part of a group. Isolation is an important instrument of control. As Baz Kershaw has observed in relation to his own work in prisons, 'creative work... is customarily an unwelcome challenge to authority, an unpredictable disruption of norms' (35).

There have been many important positive legacies of the production, however. For the duration of the production, all participants achieved 'Enhanced Status', giving them access to the maximum level of privileges. But since the production, each prisoner's story has been different. Of the four cast members who remained in Hydebank, three withdrew from further drama activities, but one of these has been motivated by the production to pursue vocational training as a P.E. instructor. In a recent court appearance, one of the stage crew attracted a much lighter sentence than expected – a decision influenced, I understand, by a character witness from the production team. Another prisoner is now released and keen to seek further training opportunities in theatre. Of the prisoners transferred from Hydebank, one feels a strong sense of betrayal at his treatment by a prison service he believed he has served well through the production and this has undone much of the benefit of it to him. But another is actively applying to drama schools. Here is an extract from a personal statement he has written for one of his application forms:

> I've found from doing the play that to look believable you just have to let yourself go and lose yourself in the performance, which at first, was very challenging. Doing the play has taught me a greater confidence in myself and also that I enjoy rising to the challenge. If I'm accepted into Drama School I hope to develop new techniques and evolve as an actor and a person. I believe in life you learn more about your character by challenging yourself and no doubt Drama School would do just that. I hope to learn how to drop the self-protecting barriers I have created for myself from having hard life experiences and to learn the ability to let go of my inhibitions and become a professional actor. I want to be a successful actor because I love the buzz you get when you see the anticipation on the faces of the audience and you can see them hanging on every word you say and making them feel just what your character is feeling. Then when you receive that standing ovation it is like no other feeling in the world. You feel so much satisfaction from knowing that the audience has enjoyed something you've put so much hard work into.

I find this statement very moving. It testifies to the life-enhancing impact of the production. And it also illustrates this prisoner's extended 'view' of himself.

There are many 'views' addressed in this article. The 'view' of the prisoners who participated in the production can be seen to have changed, both through the experience of the event itself and the digital extension of that process in the presence of the documentary camera. The 'view' of the prisoners who did not perform, but who saw the play also changed in the respect that many showed for the performers. One actor acquired the nickname 'Shakespeare' on his prison landing, but the tone of delivery changed from sarcasm to appreciation once his fellow prisoners had seen the play. The view of the prison authorities also changed, best evidenced by the decision to allow the use of real bayonets on stage, but the widening of vision was short-lived and the longer-term value of the production was not realized.

The final point of view I want to consider is that of the wider public, in a number of its forms. James Thompson has suggested that 'the popularity of certain forms of prison theatre could be understood as a response to the invisibility of the body of the prisoner in contemporary performances of punishment' (61). He is concerned that however well intentioned, prison plays may serve as a contemporary 'performance of punishment', in the tradition of public hangings and the stocks and he questions the value system governing such events. For the audiences that attended performances of *Observe the Sons* in Hydebank, the quality of the work prevented this becoming an issue. That is, the event was subject to a theatrical value system, which made the prison context largely incidental. I believe that this is a particular feature of prison arts in Northern Ireland, where there is seamless connection with the mainstream theatre, exemplified by the involvement of an artist like Dan Gordon, who is at the pinnacle of the local professional arts establishment. The following comment by one drama student who participated in a workshop at Hydebank reinforces the importance of the immediate human connection that is possible within a live event:

> I found it very surprising that such a friendly group of interesting and charismatic men could be in this institution. The workshop broke down my social stereotypes of young offenders' institutions and has made me really interested in doing more projects like this.

What may prove more problematic is the reception of the BBC documentary being made about the production process. While the presence of the camera provided the prisoners an extended 'virtual view' by allowing them to imagine themselves being seen by unknown others, the actual transmission of these images will lack the human immediacy of the live theatre event. In part to prepare the cast for the experience of seeing the documentaries, a special screening of an edited version of the recorded performances of *Observe the Sons of Ulster* was held in the chapel of Hydebank Young Offenders Centre in March 2007, a full year after the rehearsal process began.

Conclusion

It is hoped by Mike Moloney that this experience of seeing themselves look good on screen will equip the participants to negotiate the aftermath of the broadcast of the documentaries themselves. Watching the performance again, this time having got to know some of the young men involved (that is, with my own 'view' broadened) I was struck by the fact that the authority figures mimicked by the characters in the play – the army officer and the preacher – are both shown shouting, while the words of the imagined Orange speaker at 'the Field' (the traditional destination of Belfast's 12th July march) are delivered with equal virulence. I was reminded of a comment by one of my former students who spent some time working with two of the cast after they had been transferred to Magilligan Prison near Derry. He was struck by the prisoners' evident need simply to talk to him. 'No-one', he concluded, 'has ever listened to these guys, ever!' His comment brings to mind the definition of oppression quoted by the founder of Playback Theatre, Jonathan Fox – that being oppressed is having nowhere to tell your story (Fox, 6).

Be that as it may, the means by which the story is told is also crucial. It seemed to me, both watching the production and observing the participants at various times thereafter, that the indirect telling of that story through McGuinness's play had a profound impact on all those involved, usually for the good. The more direct retelling of their story through four thirty-minute documentaries is a different matter entirely. It will inevitably objectify the participants and runs the risk of distancing the television viewers from the humanity they and those in prison share. On the other hand, if the documentary can capture not just the prestige and excitement of the production itself, but also the problematic diversity of its legacy and aftermath, then I think the full story of *Observe the Sons of Ulster* at Hydebank may still be served.

Bibliography

Bentham, Jeremy, *Panopticon (Preface)*. In Miran Bozovic (ed.), *The Panopticon Writings* (London: Verso, 1995).

Boal, Augusto, *The Rainbow of Desire*. Translated & Introduced by Adrian Jackson (London: Routledge, 1993).

Fox, Jonathan, *Acts of Service: spontaneity, commitment, tradition in the nonscripted theatre* (New Paltz, NY : Tusitala Pub, 1994).

Gordon, Dan, 'Thinking about Prison' *NIACRO News* 14 (Spring 2006).

Grant, David Unpublished Interview with Dan Gordon and Mike Moloney. Belfast, 22 June 2006.

---, Unpublished interview with Brendan Byrne. Belfast, 28 June 2006.

Kershaw, Baz, 'Pathologies of Hope in Drama and Theatre' in Michael Balfour, ed., *Theatre in Prison: Theory and Practice* (Bristol: Intellect Books, 2004).

Llewellyn-Jones, Margaret, *Contemporary Irish Drama and Cultural Identity* (Bristol: Intellect, 2002).

McAvinchey, Caoimhe, 'Unexpected Acts: Women, prison and performance' in Michael Balfour and John Somers, eds, *Drama As Social Intervention* (Concord, ON: Captus Press Inc., 2006).

McGuinness, Frank, 'Observe the Sons of Ulster Marching towards the Somme' in *Frank McGuinness: Plays 1* (London: Faber, 1996).

O'Toole, John, *The Process of Drama*, (London: Routledge, 1992).

States, Bert O., *Great Reckonings in Little Rooms*, (University of California Press, 1985).

Thompson, James, *Applied Theatre* (Bern: Peter Lang LG, 2003).

---, 'From the Stocks to the Stage: Prison Theatre and the Theatre of Prison' in Michael Balfour, ed., *Theatre in Prison: Theory and Practice* (Bristol: Intellect Books, 2004).

Part II: Site, Social Space, and Place

11 | Restaging Violence: H-Block as Abu Ghraib, Castlereagh as Camp X-Ray

Paul Devlin

[Panopticon:] A perimeter building in the form of ring. At the centre of this a tower, pierced by large windows opening onto the inner face of the ring. The outer building is divided into cells each of which traverses the whole thickness of the building. These cells have two windows, one opening onto the inside, facing the windows of the central tower, the other, outer one allowing daylight to pass through the whole cell. All that is then needed is to put an overseer in the tower and place in each of the cells a lunatic, a patient, a convict, a worker, or a schoolboy. The back lighting enables one to pick out from the central tower the little captive silhouettes in the ring of cells. In short the principle of the dungeon is reversed: daylight and the overseer's gaze captures the inmate more effectively than darkness, which afforded after all a sort of protection (Michel Foucault qtd. Mills 45).

The time for a revival of Martin Lynch's cantankerous classic 'Troubles Play' may now be ripe. First staged at the Lyric Theatre in Belfast in 1982, *The Interrogation of Ambrose Fogarty's* dramatization of provocative images of police brutality and institutional malpractice, depicting the use and abuse of Emergency Powers legislation in Northern Ireland in the aftermath of the Hunger Strikes, attempted to force its audiences into an ethical (re)alignment in opposition to, or against, the acts of violence the play made them witness. In a period when anti-torture guidelines provided for in the Geneva Conventions are becoming increasingly aspirational and ideal rather than obligatory and standard, where the dilution of once seemingly inalienable human rights is justified as necessary in a post 9/11 world,[1] and where the existence of extraordinary rendition flights implicates us all in human rights abuses,[2] this essay explores three hypothetical theatrical strategies for reviving/revising *Fogarty*, ultimately suggesting an approach designed to resonate with current global ethico-political urgencies. The ideas under discussion here, it is acknowledged from the beginning, are discursive and, in particular, temporally sensitive explorations of some of the many and demanding issues inherent in the dramaturgy of revival.[3]

Dislocating the performance of a play from the specific time-space and socio-political contexts of its original and defining production has pronounced implications for any potential drama-turgical strategies pursued in restaging that work as a new theatrical event. Foucault's conception of heterotopic spaces will form the basis of a theoretical way here to think through the issues and tensions generated by such processes:

> The heterotopia is capable of juxtaposing in a single real place several spaces, several sites that are in themselves incom-patible. Thus it is that the theatre brings onto the rectangle of the stage, one after the other, a whole series of places that are foreign to one another . . . ('Of Other Spaces' n.p.)

Heterotopia is a usefully unstable concept. In applying it, Foucault moves away from spatial discourse which treats the analysis of space as something, he says, that is seen as 'the dead, the undialectical, the immobile' (70). Heterotopic spaces are conceived of as fluid, changeable, and dynamic points of multiplicity:

> The present epoch will perhaps be above all the epoch of space. We are in the epoch of simultaneity: we are in the epoch of juxtaposition, the epoch of the near and the far, of the side-by-

---

[1] Eyal Press notes: 'Recent revelations in the media suggest that torture is becoming acceptable in some quarters of the U.S. government, with terrorism replacing communism as the official rationale. And as during the cold war when U.S. trainers taught torture techniques, Washington's tolerance of such practices could have a ripple effect around the world.' (n.p.).

[2] For a brief account of the pertinent issues surrounding the transport of suspected terrorist detainees to U.S. managed detention centres in Poland, Afghanistan, Syria, Egypt, and Romania, see: http://www.channel4.com/news/special-reports/rendition.html

[3] The wisdom of a temporally sensitive theoretical model here, I hope, will become increasingly apparent as this essay proceeds.

side, of the dispersed. We are at a moment, I believe, when our experience of the world is less that of a long life developing through time than that of a network that connects points and intersects with its own skein. ('Of Other Spaces' n.p.)

Foucault, then, may provide a theoretical bridge between original and revived theatrical productions. Moreover, Edward Soja's appropriation and refurbishment of the concept of heterotopia, reimagined by Soja as 'Thirdspace', is a particularly insightful means of thinking about spatial dynamics in relation to theatrical revivals: because of the ways in which it allows spatiality to be conceived of, in Soja's terms, trialectically – that is, in terms that foreground the interrelationships between the spatial-historical and social (or, in more strictly Foucauldian terms: space, knowledge, and power). 'Thirdspace is a purposefully tentative and flexible term that attempts to capture what is actually a constantly shifting and changing milieu of ideas, events, appearances, and meanings' (2). Soja's theory, too, though not explicitly cited, nonetheless inflects much of the reasoning in what follows, especially in considerations of what effect a restaging of this seminal work might have on Northern Irish audiences after twenty five years of additional history since the play's original and defining production.

Staged amid the socio-political fallout following the Hunger Strikes in the early 1980s, when ten IRA prisoners starved to death in the H-Block,[4] *Fogarty* is the first play by a Northern Irish playwright to directly challenge an institution of the Northern Irish state, in this case the Royal Ulster Constabulary (RUC).[5] It was produced after a decade of 'extraordinary' and 'emergency' internal security measures had been employed in the day to day policing of the state.[6] The Northern Irish administration, based at Stormont, had previously made use of extensive Special Powers legislation on several other notable occasions: at the point of partition,[7] when

[4] For a detailed chronology of the major events of the Hunger Strikes see: http://cain.ulst.ac.uk/events/hstrike/chronology.htm

[5] The RUC was established as Northern Ireland's police force in 1922 and remained so until November 2000, at which point, in part in line with the recommendations of the Patten Report, it was integrated into the newly formed Police Service of Northern Ireland (PSNI).

[6] Internment without trial was introduced in Northern Ireland on 9 August 1971.

[7] Following the Government of Ireland Act (1920) the thirty two counties of Ireland were divided into the Northern Irish State and the Republic of Ireland. The Republic of Ireland consisted of twenty-six counties, while

extensive and sustained intercommunal discord threatened to undermine the infant state, in the early 1930s after a period of prolonged and widespread unemployment, economic depression, and subsequent rioting in Belfast, and in the 1950s during the IRA's border campaign. The latest use of Emergency Powers legislation, however, in some ways contradicted unfolding changes to British policy in relation to the province during the mid-1970s, which aimed to move away from Willie Whitelaw's Special Category Status for internees and political prisoners,[8] toward a policy of dealing with IRA and Loyalist prisoners as 'ordinary criminals'. The intention of this was, in part, to attempt to politically and socially conceptualize Northern Ireland as an ordinary bourgeois state. However, despite the intention of creating a veneer of 'normality', emergency security measures were renewed throughout the 1970s: most notably when the Emergency Provisions Act (1973) and later the Prevention of Terrorism Act (1976) were enacted.

Lynch's play, then, was premiered not only in a climate of heightened sectarian and state hostilities, exacerbated by the impact of the Hunger Strikes, but also following a decade of a series of (by then) institutionalized 'Emergency' provisions that had been designed as short-term, interim solutions, not a sustainable long-term Policing system. Reports of the RUC's frequent abuse of those powers had also deeply alienated a substantial portion of the Catholic/nationalist and republican population of Northern Ireland. It had also left the RUC institutionally hampered and struggling to function under the weight of accusations of malpractice and human rights abuses. The state, however, fiercely defended the RUC's position. Just three years before *Fogarty* was staged, for example, the Report of the Committee of Inquiry into Police Interrogation Procedures in Northern Ireland, despite countless allegations of police brutality and misuse of Emergency Powers, exonerated the RUC of all allegations and concluded that there was in fact a systematic campaign to discredit the police as an institution in Northern Ireland. They also suggested that 'No other police force in

---

Northern Ireland was made up of six counties. These political divisions were further ratified and consolidated by the outcomes of the Boundary Commission in 1925 and remain in place to the present day.

8 Willie Whitelaw, Northern Ireland's first Secretary of State, was appointed to office by Edward Heath following the imposition of Direct Rule in Northern Ireland in March 1972. He remained in office until November 1973.

the United Kingdom is called on to deal with so much violent crime in such unpromising circumstances ... the normal methods of detection of crime are hampered by special difficulties'.[9]

In a cultural climate not yet malleable or open to debate on the issue of policing in the north, *Fogarty* was to be a contentious theatrical proposition from the outset. Others had addressed the north's socio-political problems dramatically before, however Lynch's work had a theatrical bluntness previously unused. Writing from a position keenly aware of contemporaneous conflicts and tensions, the palpably flesh and blood characters he creates and the heightened sense of realism of his *mise-en-scène* gave *Fogarty* a charge of present tense and dramatic immediacy. Its dramatization of Willy Lagan and Ambrose Fogarty's interrogation in a west Belfast police station, and the subsequent images of brutality and systematic human rights abuses that follow, had a socio-political currency across the city. However, the production was also far from a theatrical exercise in anti-RUC propaganda. As a piece of theatre it is a deliberately ambiguous and provocatively even-handed work. As one reviewer noted:

> blunt, brutal and very thought provoking ... most certainly not an anti-police or pro-terrorist play ... Those who believe that anyone who is taken in for questioning deserves whatever is coming to him will have second thoughts ... So will those who think that the RUC are not flesh and blood (Review, qtd. Byrne 63).

However, it is perhaps equally fair to note that although *Fogarty* demonstrates a willingness in Lynch to use his creative processes to travel someway out of his own republican comfort zone and to engage empathetically with those he believed were guilty of human rights abuses, at its core this play concurs with and supports the placing of a ring fence around such debates. An ethical line in the sand perhaps comparable to Dr Clare Palley's statement, an independent expert nominated to speak to the United Nation's Sub-

---

[9] The findings of the report are particularly questionable in light of the series of recent and damning reports issued by the Office of the Police Ombudsman in Northern Ireland. For example, see the Ombudsman's findings on the much-publicized 'Operation Ballast' available for download at: http://www.policeombudsman.org/-Publication.cfm?CatID=10&action=list . A full copy of the Report of the Committee of Inquiry into the Police Interrogation Procedures in Northern Ireland is available at: http://cain.ulst.ac.uk/hmso/bennett.htm

Committee of the Prevention of Discrimination and Protection of
Minorities, made in August 1993:

> [It is] hypocritical conduct, justifying lower human rights
> standards by reason of the situation of terrorism, while at the
> same time declining internationally to admit that there is such
> a breakdown of order as to require a full derogation [from the
> European Convention] and that a state of emergency exists
> (qtd. McVeigh 12).

While Lynch's play clearly had a strong sense of its own
contemporaneous theatrical efficacy, what might a revival of a
twenty-five year old play achieve in today's climate of seemingly
ever-closer political accommodations? After all, don't the issues
Fogarty trades in belong to Northern Ireland's atavistic past? There
may still be a few political thorns to pull out since the Patten Report
was almost implemented – plastic bullets, collusion, thirty million
pound bank robberies, and 'the disappeared', to name a few – but
generally speaking everyday life in the province, with political
negotiations now close behind, have entered a discernibly post-
conflict phase. Sinn Fein, historically, has voted to support policing
in Northern Ireland for the first time in the party's history. Ian
Paisley and Martin McGuiness moved into the offices of Castle
Buildings as First Minister and Deputy First Minister of Northern
Ireland respectively: and with the retirement of Paisley and the
election of Peter Robinson as First Minister, the concept of power-
sharing and cooperation is becoming an unremarkable part of the
political landscape. The final pieces of the Peace Process jigsaw
seem to be falling into place. So why stage *Fogarty* at all? Let us
answer this cautiously at first.

In a straightforward revival of *Fogarty* planned for production in
late spring as part of, for example, Belfast's Lyric Theatre programme, staged in a manner plainly aping the original production,
Lynch's classic could arguably fulfil a valuable social function. At a
local level it might work as a theatrical yardstick to gauge how far
our relative communities have come since the heady days of no-
warning bombs and the endemic collusion of the 1980s: a theatrical
pause and 'look at us then' moment for reflection. Detached from
the daily grind of emergency provisions we could wonder how it was
all ever allowed to get so far out of hand. From the comfort of the
Police Ombudsman's office, amongst other places, we can feel
secure in what have been genuinely revolutionary changes in
Northern Irish society. Yet in terms of an actual performance of

Fogarty this all seems a bit anodyne. One of the most interesting things Lynch himself said of his play was that 'every night there is tension in the audience. There are people who identify strongly with the prisoner. Others draw back ... People have to make a choice going out the door' (qtd. Byrne 62).

The essentially historical revival proposed here seems stripped of the urgency of the original theatrical event. Partly this seems to occur as a natural result of the passage of time. But the implication of this is that political theatre is somehow inherently unrevivable. However, if our intention aims to retain the essence and verve that defined the original production, then our dramaturgy may need to alter accordingly.

What happens if we put Willy Lagan and Ambrose Fogarty in orange jump suits? What happens if, instead of presenting the key image of the original production where we see Ambrose lying on the floor of the interrogation room with his trousers around his ankles, we put Willy and Ambrose into stress positions? What if we stand them on barrels and throw black hoods over their heads? With this, then, the character of our dramaturgy is clearly changing and evolving into a second performance strategy. Contemporary re-sonances become pronounced. The question of the effectiveness of this theatrical simultaneity, however, remains open to debate. Can a west Belfast police station be a detention centre in Santiago, Robben Island, or, in this second proposed revival, Camp X-Ray or Abu Ghraib? Moreover, will Northern Irish audiences look from the local imperatives suggested by staging Lynch's play outward to more internationally aligned debates? How post-conflict, if at all, has our gaze become? Have contemporary northern iconographies shifted emphasis, for example, to the extent that the image of Hunger Strikers 'on the blanket' during the dirty protest might now, in performance, give way to that of Abu Ghraib's 'Shitboy'?[10]

The logical extreme of this position is perhaps the suggestion that local political imperatives are becoming obsolete in light of pressing international dimensions and that, by extension, political theatre must focus its energies on the bigger picture. However, as Tom Burvill suggests, it may in fact be at the intersections of the local and the global that contemporary political theatre will find its most powerful expression:

---

[10] A detainee of Abu Ghraib given this 'nickname' because he habitually covered himself with his own faeces.

[A] ... powerful vector ... can develop through electronic media between a particular local event and an international regional issue along sensitive ideological fault lines – an important aspect of postmodern global-local relationships. One role for political theatre is to work these fault lines, these contradictions (242).

Foucault's heterotopic spaces may offer us a theoretical way to work 'the fault lines' between regional and international politics and in doing so, in the staging of political theatre, a means to expose apparent contradictions through performance. By cautiously thinking of heterotopias not as sites of postmodern limitlessness, but in terms of temporally dependent (and therefore nonetheless permanently fluid) hierarchical structures, we open the door to the possibility of performances more keenly attuned to the historicity, the political, the socio-cultural and the spatial dimensions of any given moment of theatre production. This can never be exact, of course. But this does not seem a compelling enough reason to dismiss the idea completely out of hand. Foucault asks us to:

Think of a ship ... it is a floating part of space, a placeless place ... The ship is the heterotopia par excellence. In civilizations where it is lacking, dreams dry up, adventure is replaced by espionage, and privateers by the police ('Of Other Spaces', n.p.).

Extending this metaphor, we might think of the structures as the sea on which the ship is sailing. While we cannot control that sea, we can feel its eddies, gauge its moods, and even harness its currents. Can these structures then be worked to engage spectatorship? This is not to deny the spectator's individual agency, or an attempt to make any erroneous claims of homogenized responses. But rather this is an exercise in thinking out loud about the ways in which the polysemic possibilities of the theatrical space might be put into a hierarchy in a manner allowing the gaze of the spectator to be channelled in certain temporally dependent directions.

Janelle Reinelt speculates on the complicated action and operations of political theatre in liberal democracies:

I begin with the assumption that the optimal relationship between theatre and society is one in which theatre, as a cultural practice, has an active role to play in the discovery, construction, maintenance, and critique of forms of sociality appropriate to that society. When the goal is radical democracy, this involves intervening in the imaginative life of that society by producing mediations on its current balance of that equality

with liberty, staging contradictions between democratic principles and the material conditions they purport to describe, or
creating images of possible alternative configurations, other
worlds. Radical democratic theory poses questions about the
nature of membership in the political community – what does
such citizenship mean and what does it entail? (283)

Reinelt's assessment clearly harmonizes with Lynch's remarks
with regard to his intention of engendering an ethico-political
response in his spectatorship. From this point, then, the second
proposal for reviving *Fogarty* begins to look increasingly pedestrian.
If, as Reinelt seems to imply, the purpose of contemporary political
theatre practice is in part to bring liberal democracies to heel, to ask
them to give account, then this second dramaturgical strategy
clearly fails. If the essence of democratic hegemony is the principal
of consent, the disruption of this consent in contemporary political
theatre practice is crucial. This second revival strategy is unlikely to
create a suitable crisis of consent. It is simply not vital enough.

A third dramaturgical strategy, then, necessarily begins to assert
itself. There remains another fault line that might be productively
worked. The demolition of the Maze Prison[11] began in October 2006.
In a year from that time H-Block, as it has come to be known during
'the Troubles', will no longer exist. Spatially speaking, Long Kesh
has much to recommend it. Not just because it is three hundred and
sixty acres of prime development opportunity, but also because it is
a site of considerable heterotopic import. A one time Royal Air Force
base, the prison has been variously reimagined as an impoverished
detention centre,[12] at one time lauded as a model of a modern
European prison, and by its prison population known as a university
of terror, the Maze is set to be razed to the ground only to be rebuilt
in a similarly heterotopic – if refocused – vision of modernity. The
site, under the design of the company responsible for London's
successful bid for the 2012 Olympics, will now become many places
for many people. Amongst other things the prison and its surrounding site are to become: a forty-four thousand seater multi-
purpose sports stadium (housing rugby, football, and Gaelic football
games), a five thousand seater indoor arena, an equestrian centre, a
hotel, a restaurant, public housing, cafés, shops, multi-screen

---

[11] AKA H-Block and Long Kesh.
[12] Used as a site to house internees from the early 1970s, the prison's H-
    Block wing was in fact constructed as a permanent replacement to the
    Nissan huts previously used to hold detainees.

cinemas, offices, an industrial park, recreational parklands, a conflict resolution centre, and, most controversially of all, a museum depicting the role of the prison during 'the Troubles'[13].

There may, however, be one more purpose to which this prized site might be put: as the location for a possible third staging of *Fogarty*. Perhaps, though, this may also mark the point where our revival becomes less about recreating the textual and scenic components of the original theatrical event, and more about focusing our energies on recreating a similar sense of the original production's spirit in reception. In this proposal the event will occupy the former H-Block of the prison, which was not due for destruction until the final stages of the demolition in late 2007/ early 2008. In 2003 artist Jai Redmann built a replica of Guantanamo Bay in Manchester,[14] where nine volunteers agreed to be held under the same circumstances as those detainees who were being held in Camp X-Ray at that time.[15] Redmann's provocative model gives us a starting position. In April of 2005 John Reed in his 'defence of the indefensible' suggested the British public should be 'a little slower to condemn and a lot quicker to understand ... [the] unprecedented challenges' faced by British soldiers who had been video taped beating Iraqi civilians at Amara ('Reed Urging Sympathy for Troops,' n.p.). These arguments are all too depressingly familiar, and as excuses they serve to remind us of the necessity for counter-narratives. Both the experiences of policing in Northern Ireland throughout the 1970s and 1980s and the words of Kofi Annan underline the inherent dangers of such 'special' practices and aptly rebuke Reed's claim for 'understanding':

Human rights law makes ample provision for strong counter-terrorist action, even in the most exceptional circumstances. But compromising human rights cannot serve the struggle against terrorism. On the contrary, it facilitates achievement of the terrorist's objective – by ceding to him the moral high ground, and

---

[13] The proposed site for the museum, the hospital wing where Hunger Strike prisoners died, is proving a contentious political issue and the exact nature of the museum's form, content, and symbolic purpose is far from agreed as yet. For a full account of the 'master plan' for the redevelopment of the Maze site see:
http://www.ofmdfmni.gov.uk/masterplan.pdf .

[14] This project can be viewed online at:
http://clearerchannel.org/media/page.php?id=1156&prefix=video

[15] The nine volunteers were chosen to represent each of the nine real British detainees then being held at X-Ray.

provoking tension, hatred and mistrust of government among precisely those parts of the population where he is most likely to find recruits. Upholding human rights is not merely compatible with a successful counter-terrorism strategy. It is an essential element in it. (Kofi Annan, qtd. in Amnesty International, 'United Kingdom Human Rights: a Broken Promise,' n.p.)

In just over five years, over two hundred extraordinary (that word again) rendition flights are thought to have passed through the United Kingdom's airspace: flights which seem like an almost perfect inversion of Foucault's 'all-space' metaphor: flights designed by inventive military strategists and slippery legal advisers to exist in a 'no space' beyond the obligations of international law. Irene Khan, Secretary-General of Amnesty International, suggests: 'Nothing so aptly portrays the globalization of human rights violations as the US government's programme of 'extraordinary renditions' ('Freedom from Fear', n.p.). The severity of such actions should not be understated:

> 'rendition' usually involves multiple human rights violations, including abduction, arbitrary arrest, detention and unlawful transfer without due process of law. Most victims of 'rendition' were arrested and detained illegally in the first place: some were abducted: others were refused access to any legal process. 'Rendition' also violates a number of other fair trial guarantees – for example, victims of 'rendition' have no possibility of challenging their detention, or the arbitrary decision of being transferred from one country to another (Amnesty International, 'United Kingdom Human Rights: a Broken Promise', n.p.).

Although there had been considerable media speculation surrounding the issue of rendition flights, and groups such as Amnesty International have been claiming the practice has existed for a number of years, it was only in September 2006 that the Bush administration finally admitted to the practice, and in February 2008 that British Foreign Secretary Peter Miliband admitted that two such flights had landed in Britain in 2002. Also in 2006 Swiss Senator Dick Marty published the findings of his report for the Council of Europe's Parliamentary Assembly into European member states' collusion in the illegal transport of detainees. Marty's report names 14 European states, including Ireland and the United Kingdom, believed to have acted with complicity in facilitating rendition flights:[16] the report names both Shannon Airport in southern Ireland and Prestwick Airport in the United Kingdom as locations where rendition flights have landed for unknown reasons. The Irish Anti-War Campaign has published a petition in response to the revelations surrounding Shannon Airport's involvement in rendition, charging the Irish government with complicity:

> in the criminal actions and warmongering of the US military and government in Iraq by allowing over 500,000 US troops through Shannon Airport since the beginning of 2003, an act in flagrant violation of Irish neutrality. In addition the government's decision to facilitate US aircraft involved in the CIA 'renditions' programme, and its refusal to search these aircraft, implicates Ireland in serious violations of International law and seriously questions its human rights obligations as a signatory of the Geneva and Hague Conventions. ('Say No to War and Occupation. US Military Out of Shannon. Statement and Appeal to the Irish Government on the Third Anniversary of the US-led Invasion of Iraq' n.p.)

The key point here is, of course, 'torture flights' are in breach of International Human Rights Law. Moreover, facilitating these flights by permitting them access to British and Irish airspace and providing secure locations for re-fuelling puts both the British and Irish governments equally in breach of International Human Rights conventions:

> Under international law, states are obliged to prohibit the transfer of an individual to another state where that person faces a real risk of serious human rights violations, including enforced 'disappearances', torture or other ill-treatment, arbitrary detention or flagrant denial of their right to a fair trial. States are also obliged to prevent, criminalize, investigate and punish all of those acts, including conspiring and aiding and abetting them. (Amnesty International, 'United Kingdom Human Rights: a Broken Promise' n.p.)

In the North of Ireland, what is essentially a new city that is to be built on the site of the Maze Prison – the first city of a nearly 'agreed Ireland'[17] – has been heralded as emblematic of our newly enabled

---

[16] The full report is available at:
  http://assembly.coe.int/ASP/APFeaturesManager/defaultArtSiteView.asp?ArtId=474
[17] 'Agreed Ireland' seems to have emerged and gained prominence as the latest addition to the lexicon of the Peace Process since the outcomes of the St Andrews' Agreement in October 2006.

state's tolerance, our plurality, and our democratic accountability. Staging *Fogarty* at the Maze, in whatever form, throws such claims into crisis. By occupying the site we ironize policies rich in contradictions. We seize a local moment and cast it outward to expose internationally relevant contradictions. We work the fault line. The 'extraordinary' measures 'haven't gone away you know'. They are still in place: in places. Foucault suggests there are two forms of heterotopic spaces: the heterotopia of crisis, locations where the individual in crisis will seek out solace and a place to act out (parks, military service, brothels): and heterotopias of deviation such as asylums and prisons, for example, places to accommodate and contain personal crisis. The final dramaturgical approach to *Fogarty* holds out the interesting possibility of reversing the heterotopias of deviation. The possibility of creating sites to stage heterotopic crisis as the contradictions materialize. Spectators might then cast their gaze simultaneously locally and internationally. Critically alert spectatorships in crisis and aware of it. Ideally, panoptic spectatorships.

Bibliography

Amnesty International. 'United Kingdom Human Rights: a Broken Promise.' 9 July 2007 http://web.amnesty.org/library/Index/ENGEUR450042006.

Burvill, Tom, 'Playing the Fault Lines: Two Political Theater Interventions in the Australian Bicentenary Year 1988', Colleran and Spencer, 229 – 246.

Byrne, Ophelia, ed., *State of Play: The Theatre and Cultural Identity in Twentieth Century Ulster* (Belfast: Linen Hall Library, 2001).

Colleran, M, and Jenny S. Spencer, eds, *Staging Resistance: Essays in Political Theater* (Michigan: U of Michigan P, 1998).

Foucault, Michel 'Of Other Spaces, Heterotopias' http://foucault.info/documents/heteroTopia/foucault.heteroTopia.en. html. Last accessed 27 Feb. 2007.

---, Power/Knowledge: Selected Interviews and Other Writings, 1972 – 1977 (New York: London: Harvester Wheatsheaf, 1980).

Khan, Irene 'Freedom from Fear', Amnesty International Report 2007: the State of the *World's Human Rights* http://thereport.amnesty.org/eng/Freedom-from-fear. Last accessed 23 March 2009.

Lynch, Martin *Three Plays* (Belfast: Lagan Press, 1996).

McVeigh, Robbie, *It's Part of Life Here: the Security Forces and Harassment in Northern Ireland* (Belfast: Committee on the Administration of Justice, 1994).

Mills, Sara, *Michel Foucault* (London and New York: Routledge, 2003)

Press, Eyal. 'Tortured Logic: Thumbscrewing International Law'
Amnesty Magazine
http://www.amnestyusa.org/amnestynow/tortured.html. Last
accessed 27 February 2007.

'Reed Urging Sympathy for Troops' BBC
http://news.bbc.co.uk/1/hi/uk/4730966.stm. Last accessed 20 Feb
2007.

Reinelt, Janelle 'Notes for a Radical Democratic Theater' Colleran and
Spencer, 283 – 300.

'Say No To War and Occupation US Military Out of Shannon. Statement
and Appeal to the Irish Government on the Third Anniversary of
Iraq.'
http://www.irishantiwar.org/news/item.tcl?news_item_id=101829.
Last accessed 14 July 2007.

Soja, Edward, *Thirdspace: Journeys to Los Angeles and Other Real-
And-Imagined Places* (Oxford: Blackwell, 1996).

12 | The Utopian Performative in Post-Ceasefire Northern Irish Theatre

Lisa Fitzpatrick

This essay considers ways in which theatre in Northern Ireland has been engaging with experiences of trauma, violence and grief as the post-Ceasefire society continues to take shape. Drawing upon Dolan's work on the 'utopian performative' (2005, 5), and incorporating the work of Laub and Carlson amongst others, I will be analyzing theatrical performance as a process that can aestheticize violent loss and trauma in order to explore the potential for transcendence and open hopeful possibilities for the future. The essay references a number of recent touring productions, including *Family Plot* (2005), *Puckoon* (2009), *The History of the Troubles (According to my Da)* (2003 and 2009), and *Chronicles of Long Kesh* (2009), but three performances from 2006-7 provide the main primary material: *The Waiting Room*, *Macbeth* (both of which are site-specific), and *Bog People*. These three plays have been chosen because of their rootedness in specific, haunted sites and landscapes, which engages them with local histories and memories, potentially offering new possibilities for healing and reconciliation.

Since the Good Friday Agreement in April 1998, a range of measures have been put in place to move Northern Ireland beyond its history of sectarian prejudice and violence, and to inaugurate a new period of peace and, ultimately, reconciliation. The report *Future Policies for the Past* from the think-tank Democratic Dialogue published the proceedings of a round-table discussion staged in September 2000 to address issues of peace and reconciliation (Report 13, www.cain.ulst.ac.uk/dd). The report notes that 'Enduring personal grief is compounded by adversarial political argument, with little willingness to assume responsibility for what has taken place in the past and not much clarity about what approach should be adopted in the future' (Report 13, online). It identifies 'an underlying theme of grief and resentment' from the victims or survivors of the period, and notes that this broad category could controversially include all those who have grown up since 1969: '*all* have suffered because of the conflict' (*Introduction*, online). Almost a decade later, the recent report from the Consultative Group on the Past (CGP), published in January 2009, reiterates many of the same points. The CGP report notes that between 1969 and 2001, in addition to the 3,523 violent deaths attributable to the conflict, 47,000 people were injured in 16,200 bombings and 37,000 shooting incidents, and there were '22,500 armed robberies, 2,200 arson attacks and some 19,600 people were imprisoned for scheduled offenses' (2009, 60-2). The report recognizes that victims and survivors 'are now faced with the challenge of a society that wants to move on' (62) even as it identifies the conflict as continuing in another form: 'while we have left the violence behind us, we have found new ways to continue the conflict. This is evidenced by the contention around the language used when describing the conflict and those who played a role in it' (66). Despite aspirations for a 'new Northern Ireland where toleration, respect for cultural and religious diversity, equality and justice are the foundations of our relationships', there is continuing sectarianism, fuelled by segregation, even in the generation who have grown up post-Ceasefire. The report notes for example that there are 'a greater number of so-called 'peace' walls now than existed throughout the conflict' (75). Tim Miles's essay in this collection notes the grim statistics.

Both reports emphasize the importance of addressing victims' needs through public acknowledgement of their suffering, if reconciliation and forgiveness are to be achieved. *Future Policies for the Past* eschews the romanticization of forgiveness, recognizes its limitations, and agrees the value of narrowly pragmatic definitions of reconciliation as preferable to outright conflict. Nonetheless in the section entitled *Forgiveness and Reconciliation*, Duncan Morrow likens political reconciliation to forgiveness in personal relationships, and argues that 'forgiveness [is] so burning in Northern Ireland ... [because] so many of the injuries are understood as the grief not only of individuals but of whole communities. Injury can thus make political demands and seek political action ...

The decision to forgive ... becomes of importance to everyone – because without it the political stability of the whole system is endangered' (online). The CGP report emphasizes the benefits of remembering the conflict formally and publicly as offering opportunities to people to 'reflect openly on the past and come to terms with its impact upon their life' (96), to celebrate and honour the dead, to comfort the bereaved and to rebuild for a different future. 'As the past only exists now in memory, in order for us and future generations to truly understand ... and move towards a shared and reconciled future, all of society ... should be encouraged to remember' (96). Storytelling – both speaking and listening – is identified in the report as a particularly important method of sharing memories and commemorating (99).

The importance of communal reconciliation identified by both reports, which depends in part on a public recognition of the grief and injury to the community as well as the individual, presents an opportunity to theatre and performance. Historically, theatre has provided a forum for the investigation and debate of pressing public concerns and traumatic social upheaval. It may provide a space for communal explorations of grief, while, through the medium of mimetic representation, distancing the spectator from the immediacy of loss, allowing an emotional and critical distance from which to view what has happened. The public nature of theatre also lends itself to what LaCapra describes as 'socially engaged memory work': a ritualized, performatively relived version of the past done for secondary witnesses who will respond with 'empathetic un-settlement' (1999, 713). It can offer a space to 'mourn the dead and bear witness' (Moss, online). Paul Connerton defines 'social memory', as a process by which members of a community come to know each other 'by asking for accounts, by giving accounts, by believing or disbelieving stories about each other's pasts and identities' (1999, 21). In the context of Northern Ireland, with shared or public storytelling already an acknowledged pathway to reconciliation and forgiveness, theatre plays a potentially powerful role in accessing and nurturing such memory.

The productions under discussion here engage with shared memory in a range of ways. One technique used increasingly commonly in Northern Irish theatre is to neutralize traumas of the past through laughter, as in Big Telly's new production of *Puckoon*, where the creation of the Border is at the centre of the comedy: in recent depoliticized productions such as that of Martin Lynch's *The*

Interrogation of Ambrose Fogarty, which was a serious and controversial drama when it was first staged at the Lyric Theatre in 1982, and in new work such as *The History of the Troubles* and *Chronicles of Long Kesh*, both also by Lynch. *The History of the Troubles*, according to its advance publicity, will 'bring out the best of the Troubles' in a 'laugh-a-minute gallop through 30-odd years of civil unrest'. *Chronicles* similarly incorporates comedy skilfully into the characterization and the vignettes of prison life, while juxtaposing them with quieter, more sombre moments that recognize the various ways in which prison officers, their families and the families of the inmates were all also prisoners of that place and time. In plays like *Carnival* (2008) by Lucy Caldwell, the plight of travelling Roma circus performers and their tales of former glory evoke a sense of dispossession and disorientation which arguably represents the plight of the Loyalist community in post-Ceasefire Northern Ireland. Daragh Carville's *Family Plot* (2005) similarly uses metaphor to explore the role of forgiveness and self-reflection in the process of moving forward. Carville presents the scarred and embattled, dead members of the Kerr family, who must make peace with each other if they are to escape Purgatory. Noticeably, in response to this performance the audience seemed to laugh both at the comic and at the more serious scenes, with spectators at Coleraine's Riverside Theatre laughing at the husband's references to beating his wife. The apparent desire to laugh at representations of violence, coupled with a tendency by artists to minimize the shock and sense of threat in performance through the blocking and set design, suggests that laughter's ability to alleviate tension and to create a transient sense of togetherness through the shared joke is one function of post-Ceasefire theatre. Bergson argues that 'laughter appears to stand in need of an echo ... Our laughter is always the laughter of a group' (1980, 64). Thus the laughter in the theatre as events that were in their time traumatic and divisive are enacted or recalled on stage, may function to ease tension and unite the spectators into one cohesive group.

This effect is particularly noticeable in the 2007 touring production of *Ambrose Fogarty*. While Maguire (37) describes the 'vicious beating' of Fogarty and the audience response at the premiere production, the post-Ceasefire production showed little explicit violence enacted, on a theatrical set that evoked none of the claustrophobic sense of threat of the original performance, or of the written text. The laughter with which the text was received, however, arguably demonstrated both the audience's reluctance to be drawn into potential disagreements about the roles of the police in interrogating Fogarty, and another of Bergson's observations of laughter: that it reflects a resistance to emotion, and is characterized by 'the *absence of feeling*' (original italics) (63). Such a response, however, depoliticizes the violence and trauma associated with the Troubles and conceives of peace only by refusing to acknowledge the problems of the past. The ongoing political relevance of this play – for example as a response to events in the Middle East, as Paul Devlin's essay explores – is similarly neutralized by this approach to interpretation.The depoliticization of the violence, and the nostalgic rendering of the Troubles that often accompanies it, is only one characteristic of contemporary Northern Irish theatre. Even plays that are largely comic, like *The Chronicles of Long Kesh*, include scenes of remembrance that engage the audience in momentary reflections of grief and loss. In *Chronicles*, a moving sequence commemorates the Hunger Strikers, with the recitation of their names against a rendition of Sam Cooke's Civil Rights anthem, *A Change is Gonna Come*. But this is followed by Freddie Gillespie's monologue address to the audience, lamenting the terrible loss of life and the paucity of the gains of thirty-seven years of civil unrest. Shouting, 'Fuck the Hunger Strikers', Gillespie reminds the audience that 67 people died in the rioting surrounding their deaths. He names some of the forgotten victims in a moment of shared grief and pity, an opportunity for reflection and recognition of the indiscriminate nature of suffering.

The moments of grief and appeals to reflection in these productions is situated and sited in the three productions discussed below: *The Waiting Room* by Kabosh, performed at the Ebrington Barracks in Derry: *Macbeth* by Replay Productions, performed at the Crumlin Road Gaol, and *Bog People* by Big Telly Theatre Company, which told a series of stories that centred on that ubiquitous Irish landscape, the bog. In the latter, designed by Stuart Marshall, the series of short plays was performed on a set composed of enlarged photographs of people, textured with peat, thereby drawing attention to the landscape setting, the history of bodies preserved in the bog, and the tragedy of the disappeared whose absence is marked on stage through the visual signifiers of the photographs, and through the stories the characters tell about bodies found and lost in the bogs. This performative representation of the local landscape as haunted by death and loss is given a different form of expression in the productions by Kabosh and Replay. These were performed in 'haunted' sites, to borrow Carlson's term: the spaces were something else before they were interpellated into theatre spaces, and therefore have the potential of 'bleeding through' (133) in the process of reception. Both sites engage with the recent history of the conflict in Northern Ireland, evoking memories of military control, state power, community privilege or marginalization: loss of liberty, loss of life, or loss of that power and control: and political and paramilitary resistance. Significantly, both sites were disused and their status as performance spaces was also transitional: since Kabosh's production much of the Ebrington site, including the building where the performance was staged, has been demolished. The sites themselves, therefore, slide out of being, are ephemeral, and are transformed by the processes of peace building as it continues around them.

The Waiting Room was a 2006 bilingual (French and English) devised piece of physical theatre that referenced the contemporary films *Amélie* in content and *Dogville* in aesthetics of staging. There was no programme for the show and little advance information was provided. The audience gathered at a designated place, the Waterside Theatre, and were taken from there by bus to a secret location: Ebrington Barracks. On the bus the director distributed letters from different characters to the spectators, which provided some exposition since the letters were addressed to loved ones away at war or to the President bewailing the plight of the village. Unknown to the audience the actors were also on the bus, though this was only evident when the performance began with individuals stepping forward from within the crowd to speak the opening lines. The play tells the story of a small French village where the men have been away at war for twenty-one years: the set and costumes suggest the mid-twentieth century but this is never explicitly addressed. With the exception of an ancient bomb disposal expert named Napoleon Blownaparte, the villagers were all women. Each had developed a nervous or eccentric habit in her anxiety and loneliness. This unhappy situation was disrupted by the abrupt arrival of Albert, a balloonist who fell from the sky, and whose presence acted as a catalyst for transformation. In the final magical scenes, scraps of paper fell from the sky/ceiling bearing the message that the war was lost. Together with the airman, the villagers created a gigantic hot air balloon, and left the village forever.

The barracks where the play was performed was a space very much like a village surrounded by high metal fencing and backing onto the river on Derry's East bank, and the performance took place in the former assembly hall. It has since been radically altered, and many of the buildings have been razed to prepare the way for a new, civilian development with residential, commercial, and cultural quarters. The performance was staged on the floor of the hall, where the street and the different houses were marked out with white rehearsal tape. These spaces were dressed with props and furniture to create the characters' homes and gardens: the audience were guided around the hall to watch the story unfold, and were sometimes also broken into small groups for more intimate discussions with the characters. The storytelling structure brought spectators into a character's 'home' to hear their personal stories of loss and desire. The audience was also encouraged at particular points to speak, to vote, and to dance with the characters, building a transitive sense of community in the empty barracks, and a sense of intimacy and connection.

The relationship of the space with the plot created a melancholic atmosphere, made manifest in the abandoned buildings surrounding the playing area and the eerie sense of a ghost-town or Famine village. The characters, like ghosts from another time, inhabited the spectators' present for the short performance, before disappearing in Albert's balloon. The play ended with the announcement that the villagers had 'lost the war', a moment that allowed for a shared sense of grief that potentially transcended political identity by marking the ending of an historical period in the life of the community: but the transformations wrought by Albert's arrival have also demanded meaningful personal change from each of the characters: a willingness to relinquish old attachments and to attempt something new. The final scene, in which the villagers rise out of their previous existence, is an optimistic image of transcendence while the narrative gently ruminates on grief and loss.

Macbeth was staged by Replay Productions in Belfast's Crumlin Road Gaol, also a disused building at a point of transformation. The gaol opened in 1846 and was closed in 1996, and like Ebrington is being developed as a symbol of community regeneration and, possibly, commemoration. Over the decades, its prisoners included Eamon De Valera, Gusty Spence, Ian Paisley and Gerry Adams Snr, father of the Sinn Féin leader, and, like Ebrington, it is a site that already means something, and not only for the contemporary community. Both buildings have been part of the history of their surrounding communities, and have been players in the history of the Troubles in Northern Ireland's two main cities. Now disused and transformed briefly into sites of performance, the prison and the barracks become open, public spaces, permeable and accessible to ordinary civilians. As sites for theatre, their history is set aside – albeit perhaps briefly – and they take on a new significance and are shaped by new memories and experiences.

Prior to the performance the spectators queued outside the locked gates of the prison, while faceless figures in long, black hooded robes appeared from inside the gaol to usher them through huge doors into the vaulted entrance gateway, to face a second metal door. These mysterious robed figures recalled images from childhood nightmares, and were suggestive of the closed, foreboding presence of the gaol and the invisible but no doubt widely discussed experiences of the inmates. As one door slammed shut behind the spectators they were left in the dark, while moans and shrieks rang out over the sound system followed by the lines from scene 1. The first scene with the witches was performed entirely through sound, making its function as a prologue clear as it managed the transition of the audience from the bustle of the street to the closed dark performance space beyond the gates. The liminal nature of this threshold space reiterated the audience's movement from the everyday world to the dramatic world.

Macbeth's first encounter with the witches significantly took place in a wasteland exterior which had been the burial ground for executed prisoners. There the witches dressed in white bloodstained shifts emerged shrieking from the gloom, reanimated bodies of the dead twisting the actions of the characters in the present. As a potent image of the violent invasion of the present by the past, these figures functioned as memorials to the executed and the martyred, and to the culture of martyrdom and vengeance that has disfigured Northern Ireland's recent political and civic life. As the action moved into the main building and the audience pursued Macbeth deeper into the harsh labyrinth, the set began to function almost as an expressionistic backdrop to the action, so that the character was both imprisoned by, and punished for, the terrible tragedy that had spun far beyond his control. The play was not adapted to address the Troubles, but certain scenes resonate – such as the murder of Macduff's young son and the attack on his wife (Act IV, scene ii).

In these two productions – *The Waiting Room* and *Macbeth* – 'already written texts are placed in locations outside conventional theatres that are expected to provide appropriate ghostings in the mind of the audience' (Carlson, 134). He quotes Gatti's comment that the performance space in site-specific work is 'not [located] in some kind of Utopian place, but in a historic place, a place with a history' (Carlson, p.134). Gatti's use of the term 'Utopian' suggests that performances in purpose-built theatres take place in utopia in the literal sense of a nowhere: site-specific performances in contrast take place in 'a place with a history'. Certainly the barracks and the gaol have histories that situate the performances and the play-texts within the histories and discourses of the host communities, and in doing so they gather layers of meaning and create meanings beyond the boundaries of the performance by creating new memories and new embodied experiences of the sites. The spectators have entered the barracks or the gaol, have engaged imaginatively with an enacted story of grief, loss, death, and war, have stood in the cold exercise yard, walked through the cells, and touched the iron bars. In doing so, the spectator changes the site and in turn is changed by it.

Bog People was a collection of short plays staged as an evening of performance and linked by the physical setting of the bog and the recurring motifs of grief and love. The work was inspired by Seamus Heaney's poetry collection of the same name. Director Zoe Seaton describes the poems as 'incredibly evocative' of the current situation, raising questions of 'justice, revenge, grief, life and death, the tragedy of the Troubles and the challenge of moving beyond them'. None of the plays directly cites the history of the Troubles: instead stories of ancient bodies found in the bog, a man's tale of his wife's desertion, and an old woman's memory of dancing with an African-American soldier who was then lynched by her community, are allowed to resonate with the shared experience of the theatre audience. Arriving at a set for such apparently disparate texts was difficult, Seaton notes, until the designer pointed out that the plays are about love, and about 'how you feel about somebody who is gone'. The design for the play was ultimately based on cut-up photographs of people, enlarged, covering both the walls and floor of the set, and textured with peat to blend the human with the land, and to create a set that was deeply connected to the landscape. For Seaton, it reminds us that the ground beneath our feet is haunted by those who have lived and died before us. And despite the sadness inherent in the subject matter, the play celebrates life and the human capacity to survive and be happy.

Jill Dolan argues that

> live performance provides a place where people come together, embodied and passionate, to share experience of meaning making and imagination that can describe or capture fleeting intimations of a better world.

Defining her concept of the 'utopian performative', she rejects the idea that it necessarily involves the representation of a utopia on the stage, or that it is a form of activist theatre. Rather, she sees it as an aesthetic that can

> lead to both affective and effective feelings and expressions of hope and love ... for other people, for a more abstracted notion of 'community', or for an even more intangible idea of 'humankind'.

It is a 'small but profound' moment in which performance 'lifts everyone slightly above the present'. In relation to post-ceasefire theatre, therefore, it is not about representing peaceful cooperation or visions of a future, better Northern Ireland: it is about moments of intersubjective, heightened connectedness that allow the possibility of such cooperation to exist, affectively, for a short time.

The emphasis in the Consultative Group on the Past (CGP) report (2009) on reflection and remembering resonates with these productions. Their content engages allusively, rather than explicitly, with the Troubles, which allows the audience to distance the events on stage from the local conflict, and offers space for reflection. These plays can be understood independently of Northern Ireland's recent history, yet they offer an affective engagement with the emotional landscape of post-Ceasefire reconciliation. Each play in its different way recognizes that the war is over, although none proposes that the way forward is clear: and each offers an empathetic opportunity for the sharing of sorrow, grief, and regret through the actions and losses endured by the characters. In *Bog People* the old woman's sorrow for the young African-American soldier echoes countless similar stories of impossible loves: the violence enacted on him warns the whole community of the dangers of exogamy, and her silence about his death speaks of her own complicity with his killers. In another of the *Bog People* plays an old man grieves for the wife he loved, who has long since vanished: he has never found out what happened to her or why she left him. His grief, and the pain of not

knowing, echoes the real life testimonies of the families of the disappeared. The storytelling structure of a number of the pieces, and
the characters' narratives of their various losses, create testimonies
of grief in which the audience may find their own sorrow mirrored
and acknowledged.

The evocation of the 'pastness' of the conflict is a feature of
Macbeth and *The Waiting Room* in particular: in *Bog People* it is
only implicit in the historical distance between the present moment
of performance and the deaths and disappearances represented on
stage. However, *Macbeth* concludes with the vanquishing of the
eponymous (anti)hero, whose violent lust for power has almost
destroyed Scotland: MacDuff, who kills him off-stage, declares
'behold, where stands / The usurper's cursed head' (Act V, viii). The
war is over, and the gaol that represents Macbeth's increasing
alienation and loss of self within the brutal labyrinth of his own
ambition is emptied of spectators and actors, the characters and the
memories of the performance lingering as ghostly memories that
shape the future public perception and experiences of the space. *The
Waiting Room* ends with the end of the war, and the characters'
transcendence of their former lives. The haunted sites add to the
sense of 'pastness': by uniting the audience through their shared
memories of the public space, and creating the opportunity for
personal memory to overlap with community memory and with
remembered public speech about the original functions of the sites.
Spectators therefore engage with both the site itself and with the site
transformed for performance. The abandoned barracks at Ebrington
is haunted by local memories of its role in the conflict and its
historical status within the city: it is also haunted as any abandoned
village is, by the memories and remnants of those who once
inhabited it, and finally it is haunted by the theatrical text, which
speaks directly to the site as a space that the men have left, and that
will be emptied (and demolished) with the ending of the war. The
performance therefore, on one level, engages with and celebrates the
history and final destruction of its site though actions accomplished
in the actual social world.

The integration at moments of all or some of the audience into
the action – a technique which was used more extensively in *The
Waiting Room* than in *Macbeth*, aids in the creation of a sense of
shared experience. By speaking intimately to the spectators, engaging them in the democratic processes of the village, dancing with
them, and speaking directly to them, *The Waiting Room* created a

sense of an ephemeral community of performers and spectators. To a lesser extent, *Macbeth* engaged the audience through the use of the promenade form, involving the spectators physically in the progression of the performance. As the actors moved deeper into the gaol, the audience were compelled to follow, and to linger uneasily by the darkened cell doors and in the various nooks and crannies of the Victorian building. Meanwhile, the ending of both productions with the proclamation that the war is over may reiterate the recent history of Northern Ireland, while admitting that the horrors and grief of the war are not easily dispelled.

Amy Hungerford writes that in order to receive traumatic experience, the spectator must feel an identification with the victim, and willingly immerse him/herself in the literature of testimony (p.3). In the case of Northern Ireland, however, the trauma is a shared, lived experience that affects the entire community, and is subsumed into everyday life within the region. Most – though not all – of these performances and productions concern themselves with the expression of shared experience of the Troubles and the questions of reflection, grief, and the traumatic stress of living in a violent environment, rather than with the intensity of trauma experienced by the smaller proportion of the population who were maimed or bereaved, by paramilitaries or by agents of the state. In this sense, all who have grown up since 1969 are witnesses, as the *Future Policies for the Past* report argues.

This process of witnessing is both giving voice to experience and listening to the experiences of others. It is important therefore to the concept of the utopian performative, with its moments of affective togetherness, and sense of audience cohesion. Similarly the shared laughter at the performances of Lynch's plays, for example, or shared moments of silence in the face of sorrowful or traumatic memory, unite the audience into one, if only briefly. Dori Laub notes the importance of silence to the process of bearing witness:

> speakers about trauma on some level prefer silence so as to protect themselves from the fear of being listened to – and of listening to themselves ... while silence is defeat, it serves them both as a sanctuary and a place of bondage (Laub, 58).

The inexpressible nature of some experiences also plays a part here: words may be inadequate to convey the intensity of emotion: silence may at times be the more eloquent response.

Significantly, these productions do not offer a catharsis: they are not structured to lead the audiences through the horror and grief to the purgation of those emotions. The sense of horror and grief remain, but are recognized and granted dignity. Jane Moss, writing of post-conflict theatre in Quebec, notes examples of plays that may 're-enact violence, memorialize the victims, and perform mourning work in order to renew our shattered faith in humanity' (online). In these moments in Northern Irish theatre of utopian performativity, where the audience are briefly united in an intersubjective experience of togetherness, and where a possible future is glimpsed, theatre engages in a process of aestheticizing loss and transcending the brutality of the past.

Bibliography

ARK Northern Ireland, *Conflict Archive on the Internet (CAIN)* http://cain.ulst.ac.uk/ ©1996-2008. Last accessed 20/2/2009

Assman, Jan, 'Collective Memory and Cultural Identity' *New German Critique* 65, 1995: 125-133.

Bell, V, *Culture & Performance* (Oxford, New York: Berg, 2007).

Bergson, Henri, 'Laughter' *in Comedy,* ed. Wylie Sypher (Baltimore & London: The Johns Hopkins University Press, 1980).

Carlson, Marvin, *The Haunted Stage: The Theatre as Memory Machine* (Ann Arbor: University of Michigan Press: 2003).

Caruth, Cathy, ed., *Trauma: Explorations in Memory* (Baltimore: The Johns Hopkins University Press: 1995).

Connerton, Paul, *How Societies Remember* (Cambridge: Cambridge University Press, 1989).

Consultative Group on the Past, 2009. *Report of the Consultative Group on the Past.* Available online at www.cgpni.org. Last accessed 20/2/2009.

Democratic Dialogue, 2000 *Future Policies for the Past* available online at http://cain.ulst.ac.uk/dd/report13/report13.htm. Last accessed 20/2/2009.

Dolan, Jill, *Utopia in Performance* (Ann Arbor: University of Michigan Press, 2005).

Hamber, Brandon, D. Kulle, R. Wilson, eds, *Future Policies for the Past*, Report No. 13 (Belfast: Democratic Dialogue, 2001). Available online at www.cain.ulster.ac.uk. Last accessed January 23, 2009.

Hungerford, Amy, *The Holocaust of Texts: genocide, literature, and personification* (Chicago: London: University of Chicago Press, 2003).

LaCapra, Dominick, 'Trauma, Absence, Loss', *Critical Enquiry* 25:4, 1999: 696-727.

Maguire, Tom, *Making Theatre in Northern Ireland* (Exeter: University of Exeter Press 2006).

Morrow, Duncan, 'Forgiveness and Reconciliation' in *Future Policies for the Past*, Report No. 13 (Belfast: Democratic Dialogue, 2001). Available online at www.cain.ulster.ac.uk. Last accessed January 23, 2009.

Moss, Jane, 'The Drama of Survival: Staging Post-traumatic Memory in Plays by Lebanese-Quebecois Playwrights' *Theatre Research in Canada* 22:2, Fall/Automne 2001. Available online at http://www.lib.unb.ca/Texts/TRIC/ Last accessed February 20, 2009.

Oliver, Kelly, *Witnessing: beyond recognition* (Minneapolis & London: University of Minnesota Press, 2001).

Phelan, Peggy, *Unmarked: The Politics of Performance* (London & New York: Routledge, 1993).

Žižek, Slavoj, *Violence* (London: Profile Books, 2008).

13 | Performance and potentiality: Violence, procession, and space.

Jonathan Harden

> No-one ever seems prepared to accept that the simple act of
> massing large numbers of people on the streets can lead only to
> violence in the fevered atmosphere of Northern Ireland.
>
> (Former British MP, Harold Jackson, quoted in, 'No march –
> 13 would be alive', *News Letter*, 02.02.1972).

In September 1968, The Northern Ireland Civil Rights Association
(NICRA) and the Derry Housing Action Committee (DHAC)
organized the first civil rights march to be held in Derry, for 5th
October 1968. It was, in many ways, to be a rehearsal for the events
of 30th January 1972, a day recalled in local and international
memory as Northern Ireland's 'Bloody Sunday'.

Right from the first planning meeting in September '68, in which
the largely Belfast-resident NICRA committee visited Derry, signs
were not good. The NICRA representatives who met with Eamonn
McCann and the Derry organizers were dangerously unfamiliar with
the geography of the city and agreed to a route which started in the
Protestant Waterside and proceeded across the Craigavon Bridge
(via more Protestant areas) to the walled centre:

> It was immediately clear that the CRA knew nothing of Derry.
> We had resolved to press for a route which would take the
> march into the walled city centre and expected opposition from
> the moderate members of the CRA. But there was none. No one
> ... understood that it was unheard of for a non-Unionist

procession to enter that area (Eamonn McCann, qtd. Purdie 138-9).

The centre of the 'maiden city', so-called since the successful resistance to the motley Jacobite forces in its heroic but slightly bizarre siege of 1689, was a symbolic haven of British unionism. Indeed, Paul Kingsley (179) records that Deputy Inspector-General of the RUC, Graham Shillington told Scarman, in the inquiry into the riots and shooting of summer 1969, 'If anyone in authority could give an undertaking to the RUC that the crowd had no intention of breaking out into the city centre, he would withdraw police'. The potential for trouble was exacerbated when it became clear that a parade by the strongly loyalist Apprentice Boys, following a similar trajectory, had been planned for the same date some months in advance. The situation that faced the Northern Ireland government was one of potential chaos, and, consequently, under the terms of the 1951 Public Order Act, William Craig, Minister of Home Affairs, banned all parades on both sides of the Foyle on that day. When retrospectively challenged about the decision, Craig claimed that, 'The civil rights march was banned because they were proposing to march through areas that would provoke a serious riot'. In Derry, he added, 'down through the years, it had been established that Loyalists could parade in certain places, Republicans in certain places' (Purdie 147).

When civil rights marchers gathered in Duke Street on 5th October in an attempt to defy the ban, along with some British Labour Party MPs and a young John Hume, proceedings were opened with a simple march as far as the police line. Betty Sinclair, the NICRA secretary, climbed on a chair and advised people to go home, concluding ominously, 'There must be no violence' (Kingsley 148). Bob Purdie summarizes subsequent events as follows:

> [M]archers set off along Duke Street, trying to find another way onto the bridge. The police hastily threw a cordon across the end of Duke Street and here the first clashes occurred. During these first scuffles the blue civil rights banner was seized and ripped by police ... the police, with batons drawn, advanced on the crowd ... The police carried on down Duke Street, clearing the crowd in front of them as demonstrators screamed hysterically. Detachments of police went after individuals and, when the street was nearly clear, water cannons were brought in (Purdie 1990: 141-142)

In this essay, I will suggest that all acts of procession, parade and marching contain the potential to be re-drafted as acts of violence. While only some may be interpreted as violent acts in their formal, unruptured form, *all* may, if circumstances dictate, turn to chaos and riot. As a distinct genre of the processional canon, the civil rights march is a performance of violence even before it breaks out of its own normative boundaries: a momentary, symbolic re-presentation of other forms of violence being done against the protestors and those they represent. The riot, born out of an interrupted performance of rights – either established and historically unchallenged (in the case of the Orange Order for example) or denied and aspirational (in that of the civil rights movement) – is thus in all cases a performance of frustrations: social, political, economic, spatial. 'The performance of violence' suggests anthropologist David Riches, 'is inherently liable to be contested on the question of legitimacy' (11). If the march is a technology of the dominant ideology, the riot accepts that legitimacy has either been threatened, overthrown and/or replaced, or that it has not and may not ever be achieved. It is both a performance of violence done, and a live, improvised act of counter-violence.

Performing Violence / Violence Performing

In *The Anthropology of Violence*, Riches proposes the 'performer' as one of three necessary elements in his 'triangle of violence' (11). Like Peter Brook's famous lone body walking across the 'empty space' of a 'bare stage', the aggressive act too requires 'someone else ... watching', what Riches terms the 'witness'. The sole difference between Brook's model for 'a piece of theatre', and Riches' for a violent performance is that the anthropologist replaces the space of performance with a second performer, or 'victim'. To paraphrase Brook (11): this is all that is needed for an act of violence to be engaged. Can Brook's space function as Riches' victim? If we allow Riche's triangle to be thus skewed, can the act of walking – chosen by Brook for its everydayness – be interpreted as a performance of violence against the now victimized space? How does the act of walking come to perform past and present violence? How does this simple physical gesture become a potential starting point for an explosion of improvisatory agency, resulting in violence against the city, its streets and its buildings?

The first problem one encounters with Riches' 'triangle of violence', when attempting to extend its performative application, is in the blurring of an essentially transactional model. In *Violence: Theory and Ethnography*, Pamela Stewart and Andrew Strathern begin to complicate Riches' use of performance terminology:

> Performer, victim and witness may be pluralities rather than singular actors. And especially since witnesses may be diverse and may also be directly or indirectly involved in the issues at stake, the category of witness is potentially extremely complex. Further, witnesses, depending on their reactions or positions, may themselves turn into performers or victims, or both (4).

Riches does not account for a witness who may function also as a performer of kinds, either assisting the primary performer by adding to the violent aggression of the victim, or in the more complex (but morally basic) assumption that if a witness fails to intervene to halt or suppress the act of violence, they become 'performers' by association, simply by the fact of their passivity: they collaborate with the violent act unless they engage as a performer in counter-action. By contrast, any action that resists the violence of oppression is by definition a performance of counter-violence, regardless of its nature. Victims and witnesses of oppression, control, discipline and punishment either accept or resist their situation, both in themselves roles in the performance of violence that go beyond Riches' performer-victim-witness model.

Similar considerations apply in Northern Ireland, where the contexts of struggle are different, but the various witnesses of violence are not just passive spectators of it, in large part because when violent acts are common and diffused through the populace, all witnesses are also potential victims and everyone may be suspected of being in some sense a performer, causing Riches' triangle to implode on itself (Stewart & Strathern 37).

The implosion of Riches' triangle does not, however, collapse the argument for using a glossary of terms borrowed from the field of performance studies. How else do we begin to name and so accommodate the subtleties of violent improvisation but with the expansion of 'actor' to include concepts of re-acting, active spectating or indeed performing as part of an ensemble? Violence, Riches later suggests, is both a practical (instrumental) *and* symbolic (expressive) phenomenon, transforming the social environment and dramatizing the importance of key social ideas (Riches 1986: 11). Thus, violence performs more than just the anger or aggression of a single performer. In it are expressed, symbolized or theatricalized previous actions to which the performer may have been witness or victim and which have given rise to the necessity for reproduction. All violence has a history. It is enacted and re-enacted: there is, to paraphrase Schechner, no such thing as once-performed violence. For the purposes of this chapter then, violence is considered to be at its most basic an action that violates performative norms. At the opposite end of the scale, it can be a mass form of symbolic and ritualized political protest, the exercise of state power against the individual or the disproportionate terror imposed by one or a few upon the state and its people.

The Role of Space: performer, witness and victim

> Our daily environment is assailed by representations of violence: ... a manifest delinquency observed on the streets ... Our imagination is fed with images of threatening sites (Body-Gendrot 214).

Michel Foucault has argued that space is fundamental to the exercise of power, that space has an agency of its own. It is not merely 'a product of social relations which are most likely conflicting and unequal' (Massey 152), 'but also a producer and cause of [unequal, conflicting] social relations' (Shirlow & Murtagh 20). In other words, as Doreen Massey concludes, space 'change[s] us [... it is] an arena where negotiation is forced upon us' (154). The architecture of the city, therefore, impedes the agency of individuals, and in so doing, further invites violence directed against its control. Its ordering of individuals not only defines itself against, but implies the resistance and ultimate revolution of those same individuals.

Space, to extend Foucault's assertion, is central to the exercise of dissent. Indeed, such a position would begin to explain why architecture, understood by Foucault 'as a function of the aims and techniques of governments of societies', often acts as the victim of violence against state authority and its past and present manifestations (2000: 349). Indeed, power is expressed through the monopolization of such 'governmental' spaces by 'legitimate' social groups and the exclusion of certain weaker, 'illegitimate' groups to the margins. The built environment, reaching its ultimate expression in the city, is to space what the timetable is to time: its underlying ordering principle implies its negative alternative: disorder, chaos, and freedom (1991 149-54). 'Large modern cities'

says Hepburn 'are relatively volatile congregations of humanity [...
where] incidents can develop quickly, and resistant populations are
hard to control' (89). Thus, acts of violence performed against the
modern city have been concerned with a 'politics of inclusion – the
claims of visible minorities and other marginalized groups to
cultural recognition and political enfranchisement' (Ley and Mills
372).

Such conditionally occupied 'social' spaces, are in themselves
products of their patron government and society, and so naturally
reflect and uphold its contingent structures and hierarchies. It is
thus that 'the model of the city', as recounted by Foucault, 'became
the matrix for the regulations that apply to a whole state' (2000:
351). The city is not just the city: it can be seen to serve as a
metonym for the state at large, representing its power and its
achievements, reflecting its failings and aspirations and bearing
witness to its problems at street level. Indeed, a more complex
metonymic lineage may be drawn, in which within the urban
context, certain significant architectural loci come to represent the
surrounding city and by extension the nation of which that city
forms part. Violence against a monument, wall or building is rarely
based in aesthetics or anarchy, but is a performance of larger social
issues with a distinctly symbolic function, 'an endurable "aide-
memoire" of harm done and of threat unstated ... condens[ing] the
performance of violence into distinct space' (Shirlow & Murtagh 8-
9). The landmark *is* the city, the city *is* the state. There is, therefore,
no city issue that is not at the same time a state issue, no larger state
issue which is not evidenced on the city streets. This is the place in
which to both express and contest hegemony, to perform and to
counter-attack the violence of its control.

These demonstrations and counter-demonstrations are marked
in the memory of space. In their various performances, imaginations
and re-imaginations, the city offers histories of itself to both
champion and challenger. 'There is no place' offers Michel de
Certeau (108), 'that is not haunted by many different spirits hidden
there in silence, spirits one can "invoke" or not'. In Northern
Ireland, this spectral cache has been increased by hundreds of years
of political and religious difference, thirty years of province-wide
terrorism, and the geographical polarization that has resulted. While
all phenomena are, of course, temporal, and without doubt conflict
in Northern Ireland is infused with history, it also has a series of
geographical dimensions. Here, suggest Shirlow and Murtagh,

'residents transform daily occurrences and emotions into a symbolic system of territorial attachment' (14-18). The history of Northern Ireland's urban centres in the late twentieth century is bounded by high walls and barbed-wire, government-enforced urban segregation and community-built barricades: and littered with the wreckage of landmarks lost through the conflict. In Belfast's recent troubled past, the sorry catalogue of architectural atrocities – events in which the place survives as sole named casualty in spite of numerous human fatalities – still resound with chilling power: the burning of Bombay Street, the bombing of the Abercorn Restaurant, Oxford Street Bus Station and McGurk's Bar, to name a few. Such acts of spatialized violence have left long-lasting scars on the built fabric of Northern Ireland's towns and cities. Unlike the lesions made by motorway building, or the cosmetic augmentations of the ongoing project for urban regeneration, these are the stigmata of vicarious suffering made distinct in the living memory of people and given eternal life in the chronicles of local history.

Steps to conflict: how (and where) is walking violent?

> [V]iolence – as distinct from power, force or strength – always needs *implements* (as Engels pointed out long ago). (Arendt 4)

The procession, parade and march may not be as readily interpreted as implements of violence as the more literal arsenal of personal props Arendt appears to conjure. Brook's imagined walk across the empty space of performance is hardly a violent act. But the urban space, as we have seen, is not an empty one. Walking into, across or through the city is then a rather more significant action, yet it is not simply the setting that defines the meaning of the performance. The action, decontextualized, is not without meaning.

At once strictly timetabled and spatially mapped, procession is a performative form embedded with martial imagery and significance, and so with an easily sustainable connection to violence. It is, in its purest form – the march – a highly ordered and ordering act. In *Discipline and Punish*, Foucault notes the detail and precision with which eighteenth-century French military manuals deconstruct and standardize the various manoeuvres undertaken by a soldier:

> The act is broken down into its elements: the position of the body, limbs, articulations is defined: to each movement are assigned a direction, an aptitude, a duration: their order of

succession is prescribed. Time penetrates the body and with it all the meticulous controls of power (1991, 152).

Montgomery's *La Milice française*, and '*Ordonnance du 1er janvier 1766, pour régler l'exercice de l'infanterie*', both quoted by Foucault in his further exploration of the subject, prescribe a precise ritual of practice for the seemingly simple, natural act of walking that is akin to that of handling and deploying a firearm. In procession, however, the violent act is that of passage itself: procession is dangerous even if the 'trigger' is never pulled. Invasion as a concept, as and of itself, does not need other types of violence to be deemed an aggressive, and hence violent, act: when 'Napoleon marches on Italy', 'Hitler invades Germany' or 'Saddam storms Kuwait', we are in no doubt as to the violent ramifications of the act of passage from one space into another.

Even in the everyday practices of marginalized, dissident and disappeared subcultures, one may observe a disregard for the authoritative programmes of urban space and therein a comparable attempt to appropriate space for themselves. Here, violence *takes* place. The potentiality of the simple act of walking where one is not supposed to becomes a weapon to be used against the space in which it finds itself. This is a confrontation of human and environmental agency, the violence of the individual against the power of architecture, the claim of the outsider to share or wrest a space that is not yet their own. Procession rehearses violence against the control of built environment. It is the embodiment of spatial agency, of claims to rightful habitation of exclusive spaces. It is, in effect, what Ronnie David (1966) might call, 'Guerilla Theatre', in that it 'is symbolic action [of which] some of its structures have been adopted from guerilla warfare – simplicity of tactics, mobility, small bands, pressure at the points of greatest weakness, surprise' (Schechner 163). As such, it demands and so often precipitates violent counter-action. Following a performance of a version of guerilla theatre piece *Kent State Massacre* (first performed on La Guardia Place NYC) in Washington on May 9 1970, in which Richard Schechner and others threw gallons of animal blood over themselves and on the street, Schechner records a police officer declaring 'People who mess up the public streets should be shot' (164). In Northern Ireland, the absence of an obvious theatrical frame and the limited self-awareness of the performers involved in similarly processional 'acts' of guerilla theatre often engendered exactly this 'actual' violent response. It is worth noting, in this context, that President Nixon's telegram to the families of those murdered in the Kent State Massacre suggested that 'violent dissent leads to tragedy' (qtd. Schechner 166). In a Northern Irish context, there is no more potent qualification of this assertion than in the events of Bloody Sunday. As in Schechner's performance of *Kent State Massacre*, the violence levelled against the Northern Irish state on Sunday 30 January 1972 was largely spatial and so symbolic: the ill-fated civil rights march intended to terminate at Derry's Guildhall, an architectural icon of British and Protestant power in Northern Ireland. Held back by British troops, the ultimate expression of Nixon's statement was realized when 13 civilians were shot dead by the pursuing soldiers in the ghettoized space beyond the walls of Protestant 'Londonderry'. Declared by its Catholic inhabitants as 'Free Derry', the liberated space arguably became the fourteenth casualty of the day when compromised both literally and symbolically by the violent invasion of British troops. But what of the performances that led to such an event?

The Northern Ireland Civil Rights Association (NICRA) was founded on 29 January 1967 at a public meeting in the International Hotel, Belfast. From the outset, their agenda encompassed multiple goals, including several with a spatial connection, notably an end to the gerrymandering of local electoral districts and to discrimination in the awarding of local authority housing. Interestingly, however, there were no street protests during the association's first year. The first civil rights march in Northern Ireland was not held until 24 August 1968. In a conscious imitation of tactics used by the American Civil Rights Movement, the new organization subsequently held marches, pickets, sit-ins and protests to pressure the government of Northern Ireland to grant these demands. In its symbolic political performances, 'the civil rights movement had started to hold demonstrations that penetrated the centres of the cities and towns in Northern Ireland, centres viewed as Protestant' (Bryan 2003 251). Feldman, however, highlights the problems inherent with transporting this policy across the Atlantic:

> In Northern Ireland the adoption of American civil rights tactics collided with the dubious historical status of civil space in that province. Unlike the United States with its constitutional enshrinement of civil space, there were no significant juridical or experimental counterpoints to sectarian space that could relativize this construct and offer alternative cultural models (22).

While like those of their American brothers, NICRA's marches were in principle demanding rights within the state, it was more precisely the issue of so-called 'civil space' that was being contested on the streets of Northern Ireland. For Catholics in the province, the ability to exercise the right to parade had in recent times varied from space to space (Jarman and Bryan 20). In violating performative norms of interaction between marginalized groups and public spaces of authority, the civil rights marches were imbued with the potential for violent outbursts against those spaces.

Feldman proposes that:

> [T]hey were questioning the hegemonic position of Unionism. This was not only true in the wider political sense but also in a symbolic, territorial sense. The civil rights demonstrations took routes where, for over forty years, only the Protestant Orange Order had marched. Albeit that the territory under question was the center of Belfast, Derry and other towns, this nevertheless created a new political dynamic (qtd. Bryan 2003: 255).

This 'new dynamic' was nowhere more sharply illustrated than in the question of a movement's 'freedom to march', which was not recognized by a substantial number of the unionists.

The discontent around which the different strands of the civil rights movement coalesced were the inequalities in housing, employment and political representation, but one of the most prominent ways in which discontent was manifested was through demonstrations. The result was that the area of inequality that was most directly challenged was over rights of public political expression. It was difficult to directly challenge housing policy and employment practice but the right to march could be physically contested (Jarman and Bryan 59)

In both Derry and Belfast, parades considered to be of an Irish nationalist character had been excluded from the city centre dating as far back as 1870 (Bryan 2003: 254). In a more recent context, the forces of the state in Northern Ireland allowed public political displays by constitutional nationalists on condition that they did not 'transgress into areas perceived as Protestant' (Jarman and Bryan 48). The two main cities, being at least symbolically Protestant, were therefore, officially off-limits to civil rights demonstrations.

The 1951 Public Order Act gave police power to re-route or impose conditions on a parade wherever there appeared to be the possibility of serious disorder, or if the situation required, allowing the Minister for Home Affairs to ban parades in an area for up to three months, but unlike legislation in other regions of the United Kingdom, the Northern Ireland Act required the police to be given forty-eight hours notification of a parade unless the procession was 'customarily held along a particular route'. In practice, this exempted the Apprentice Boys, Orange and other loyal orders from giving notification. As there were no longer any 'traditional' parades by Catholics in the centre of Belfast or Derry because they had historically been opposed by loyalists, by the state and by the police, the civil rights marches, perceived as nationalist, were required to give notice (Jarman and Bryan 53).

If the calendrical organization of traditional parades channelled ethnic violence into specific formats and times, the fact that the NICRA marches occurred outside of established calendrical order meant that they were more closely related to the spaces in which they operated than the dates of their performance. The well established, structured, formulaic processions enacted by the loyal orders were inclined towards a scripted realization and were subsequently refined through annual and seasonal repetition that traced its history back through almost three hundred years: Civil Rights marches, by contrast, tended to be relatively impromptu, ad-hoc, and so potentially improvisatory performances. By definition then, the latter were characterized by the empowerment and agency of individuals, were more prone to the intervention of the unpredictable and were always in danger of descent into the chaotic. If architecture impedes the agency of individuals, the improvisation of riot enables it.

Looking back over the five-year gestation period of political violence in Northern Ireland, Bew, Gibbon, and Patterson (171) state in reference to the civil rights demonstrations during the years 1966-1971:

> Marches in particular meant, and still mean, the assertion of territorial sectarian claims. To march in or through an area is to lay claim to it. When so many districts are invested with confessional significance by one bloc, or another, undertaking a secular march creates the conditions of territorial transgressions [... such demonstrations] inevitably had a further tendency to involve involuntarily the unskilled working class, possibly in submission to arbitrary violence' (qtd. Feldman 21).

The civil rights movement's policy of 'non-violence', defined as it is in negative terms (i.e. it 'is not' *violence* rather than 'is' pacifism) implies the attempted containment of its alternative. An established, if less frequently achieved tactic of disenfranchised, marginalized and arguably powerless groups, non-violence is thus inclined to result in the outbreak of its own 'monster within'. If, as Arendt proposes, 'Power and violence are opposites: where one rules absolutely, the other is absent', then in the vacuum left by the absence of power, violence finds its place (Arendt 56).

Often such violent acts were both directed against the built environment and commandeered the surrounding architecture into their arsenal: 'public buildings including those owned by the Electricity Board, Ulsterbus, and the Post Office were smashed up and set on fire': 'At Dungiven the RUC station was also attacked with stones and petrol bombs and the Orange Hall and Courthouse were burnt down': while in Derry, 'children were ripping up paving stones, breaking them, putting them in wheel barrows and transporting them to where the main confrontation was' (Kingsley 179-181). If as Robert Fogelson (81) contends, looting can be considered a political act because it is a direct attack upon the concept of private property right, as 'a bid for the redistribution of property' (Upton 196) and by extension a performance born out of the violence of economic disenfranchisement, then attacks on spaces synonymous with political control – police stations, Orange halls and courthouses – can be seen as a direct assault upon the legitimacy of territorial power, of violent performances born out of the violence of exclusion from such spaces.

For Performative violence to remain theatrical, there must be some sort of distance between the audience and the spectacle. For the violence to retain its materiality, to avoid sinking into discursive space and becoming an image of itself, it must move in some way to rupture the frame within which it is viewed (Graver 1995: 51).

Pictures of the Northern Ireland Civil Rights Association march of 5th October 1968 taken by an RTÉ cameraman, were broadcast to shocked viewers across the globe. To this audience, removed from the performance and able to observe its theatricality without fear of being asked to participate, it put Derry and the civil rights movement on the map, highlighting the perceived injustices against which they were protesting in a way that was comparable to the familiar pictures of race riots and anti-war demonstrations in the United States. 'The civil rights marches questioned the state's control of public space and the forces of the state reacted violently' (Jarman and Bryan 61). It was hardly the Kent State Massacre: that day would come in January 1972, but the genre was the same and its influences were easily identifiable in the adapted script. The two days following the blockaded march bore witness to rioting in nationalist areas of Derry in which the limits of police control were highlighted and surpassed. On 22nd November, in an attempt to prevent repeat performances and improvised versions around the theme, Prime Minister of Northern Ireland Terence O'Neill announced a series of reforms, including promises to make changes in the local government franchise and the allocation of local government housing. Following a televised appeal for calm by O'Neill on 9th December, the more moderate civil rights associations declared a month-long halt to marches. It was thus that 1969, for many the most significant year in the Troubles timeline, was welcomed in with the previously packed street-stage eerily empty of performers.

The New Year brought changes in the nationalist agenda of spatial inclusion. They began for the first time to question the rights of Protestants to hold the parades that went through or near predominantly Catholic areas in a manner that would have previously stood in some contradiction to the campaign for equal civil rights. After persistent clashes between the police and members of predominantly Catholic areas there was a greater emphasis within the Catholic community to try and assert control over the areas in which they lived, particularly in the Bogside, where there was a concerted attempt to exclude the security forces and the area was proclaimed 'Free Derry' (Jarman and Bryan 57). It was in this revised atmosphere of reception that a processional performance by The Apprentice Boys in Derry on 12th August 1969, according to popular versions of history, finally precipitated the Troubles (Bryan 2000: 86), rupturing the frame of both its live performance and televised re-enactment as tension and discontent that had been building throughout the day quickly spread to Armagh, Coalisland, Dungannon, Dungiven, Lurgan and inevitably to Belfast:

> The police became unable to deal with the situation ... Houses were wrecked and hundreds of families forced to move out. Eventually on 15 August, it was decided to call in the troops ... In July and August 1969 ten people died, nearly 1,000 were injured and 170 homes were destroyed and 417 damaged (Bryan 2000: 86).

The government's first response was to finally place a ban on marches and demonstrations (Bryan 2000: 86). Catholic nationalists, however, soon continued to violate performative norms and take temporary possession of city spaces to which many felt they had no claim. Procession, it could be argued, rehearsed violence against the control of built environment, functioning as the embodiment of spatial agency, of claims to rightful habitation of exclusive spaces. '[T]he essential drama' suggests Marvin Carlson, is 'in *transformation* – in how people use theater as a way to experiment with, act out, and ratify change' (191). In violating established modes of interaction between marginalized groups and public spaces of authority, civil rights marches were imbued with the potential for violent outbursts against those spaces. The violence of 5th October 1968, 12th August 1969 and of 30th January 1972, did 'not promote causes, neither history nor revolution, neither progress nor reaction', rather 'serve[d] to dramatize grievances and bring them to public attention' (Arendt 79).

> [T]he real tragedy of it all is the over-use of the streets as a method of protest, the use of them for meetings and marches at every excuse has meant that our most powerful weapon – the streets – has been destroyed in places like Derry because it would be today irresponsible in a place like Derry to bring people through the streets as violence would be inevitable unless there would be superhuman effort of organization and discipline (John Hume, 'Why violence is not the answer' NIO Press Cuttings – Civil Rights).

When restricted, halted or cancelled then, the processional performance is robbed of its projected narrative structure and scripted dramaturgical trajectory. It thus becomes no more than a frustrated mob possessing a gaseous, expansive energy that demands release through improvisatory and so potentially chaotic means: the show must go on. The act of breaking with its own rigid form, rooted in the state-manufactured violence of militarism and its imposition on the physical agency of the individual, becomes an act of violence against these universal ordering, disciplining principles, and against the oppressive architectural forms that symbolically attempt to contain it. Like the procession from which it has burst forth, this is a transient, symbolic, theatrical performance representative of other forms of violence being done against the protesters and their like – 'the violence of unemployment, exploitation, bad housing, compulsory emigration and the denial of human dignity' ('Non-violence is the only way to achieve justice', *Irish News*, 5 April 1971). Here, space can act as victim, as performer, as witness, or indeed as an implement in the violent act: its agency can be magnified, subverted or entirely removed. The indisputable multi-dimensionality of space swells Riches' triangle to a pyramid in which each point has multiple facets. While the fixed, two-dimensional model does not allow for potential improvisation or the renegotiation of roles, the pyramid bends, shifts and skews in the turbulence of external forces and the heat of internal tensions. Space is unstable. Violence is explosive.

> I, Augusto Boal, want the spectator to take on the role of actor and invade the Character and the Stage ... This invasion is a symbolic trespass. It symbolizes all the acts of trespass we have to commit in order to free ourselves from what oppresses us ... If we do not go beyond ... the limits imposed upon us, even the law itself ... if we do not trespass we can never be free (Boal 2000: xxi).

Bibliography

Arendt, Hannah, *On Violence* (San Diego, New York & London: Harvest, 2000).

Boal, Augusto, *Theatre of the Oppressed* (London: Pluto, 2000).

Body-Gendrot, Sophie, 'Violently divided cities: a new theme in political science', *Managing Divided Cities*, ed. Seamus Dunne (Keele: Keele University Press, 1994): 214-227.

Bollens, Scott, *Urban Peace-Building in Divided Societies* (Boulder: Westview Press, 1998).

Brook, Peter, *The Empty Space* (London: McGibbon & Kee, 1968).

Bryan, Dominic, 'Belfast: Urban Space: "Policing" and Sectarian Polarization', *Wounded Cities: Destruction and Reconstruction in a Globalized World* ed. Jane Schneider and Ida Susser (Oxford & New York: Berg, 2003).

---, *Orange Parades: The Politics of Ritual, Tradition and Control* (London: Pluto Press, 2000).

Carlson, Marvin, 2003 *Performance* (New York: Routledge, 2003).

Certeau, Michel, *The Practice of Everyday Life* (Berkeley: University of California Press, 1984).

Dawe, Gerald, *The Rest Is History* (Newry: Abbey Press, 1998).

Dean, Tacita and Jeremy Millar, *Place* (London: Thames and Hudson, 2005).

Feldman, Allan, *Formations of Violence: The Narrative of the Body and Political Terror in Northern Ireland* (Chicago and London: University of Chicago Press 1991).

Foucault, Michel, *Discipline and Punish* (London: Penguin, 1991).

---, *Power*, ed. James D. Faubion (London: Penguin, 2000).

Graver, David, 'Violent Theatricality: Displayed Enactments of Aggression and Pain', *Theatre Journal*, Vol. 47 No. 1, March 1995, 43-64.

Hepburn, A.C.H., 'Long division and ethnic conflict: the experience of Belfast'. *Managing Divided Cities*, ed. Seamus Dunne (Keele: Keele University Press, 1994).

Jarman, Neil and Dominic Bryan, *From Riots to Rights* (Coleraine: University of Ulster Press, 1998).

Kingsley, Paul, *Londonderry Revisited* (Belfast: Belfast Publications, 1989).

Ley, David and Caroline Mills, 2000 'Can there be Postmodernism of Resistance in the Urban Landscape', *The Spaces of Postmodernity: Readings in Human Geography* ed. Michael J. Dear and Steven Flusty, (Oxford: Blackwell, 2000).

Massey, Doreen, *For Space* (Thousand Oaks: Sage Publications, 2005).

Purdie, Bob, *Politics in the Streets: Origins of the Civil Rights Movement in Northern Ireland* (Belfast: Blackstaff Press, 1990).

Riches, David, 'The Phenomenon of Violence', *Anthropology of Violence* (London: Blackwell, 1986) 1-27.

Schechner, Richard, 'Guerilla Theatre: May 1970', *Tulane Drama Review* Vol. 14, May 1970. 163-68.

Shields, Rob, *Places on the Margin* (New York: Routledge, 1991).

Shirlow, Peter and Brendan Murtagh, *Belfast: Segregation, Violence and the City* (London: Pluto Press, 2006).

Stewart, Pamela J. and Andrew Strathern, *Violence: Theory and Ethnography* (London & New York: Continuum, 2002).

Upton, James N., 'A culture of violence'. *Managing Divided Cities*, ed. Seamus Dunne (Keele: Keele University Press, 1994): 191-213.

14 | Parading Memory: Producing Commemoration in the Irish Republic's Celebrations of 1916

Holly A. Maples

On the 16 April 2006, the government of the Irish Republic held a military parade in Dublin City in celebration of the 90th Anniversary of the Easter Rising. In June of 2006 another event occurred that further transformed the context of commemoration, and acted to align the past with the present political moment: the 90th Anniversary of the Battle of the Somme. Throughout the twentieth century these two events have symbolized opposing ideologies in Irish commemorative practice. Diverse communities in both Northern and Southern Ireland have used key historical events to express current political and cultural ideologies. The 2006 celebrations of both events in the Republic give witness to the radical economic and cultural transformations of contemporary Ireland and can be viewed together as commemorations of that State's future rather than its past. However, as this essay argues, the power of collective nostalgia in the Irish context also offers the community slippage from present concerns to past triumphs.

The 2006 Easter parade began at Dublin Castle and concluded at the Garden of Remembrance. This was the first official commemoration since the summer of 1969, when the parade was suspended because of its perceived connections with the Provisional Irish Republican Army, and in response to the outbreak of violence during celebrations of the Rising in the North.[1] While the 1966

---

[1]For a study of the history of commemoration of the Easter Rising in Ireland see Máirín Ni Dhonnchadha and Theo Dorgan, eds, *Revising the Rising* (Derry: Field Day, 1991).

commemoration had been an optimistic pageant – much like the 2006 parade – intervening remembrances of the Rising became charged with political controversy. The re-instatement of the parade in 2006 was a celebratory affair which reflects both the continuing peace process in Northern Ireland and the current prosperity found in the Republic of the 'Celtic Tiger'.

While the re-emergence of the Easter Rising parade in 2006 is an expression of the significant political and economic changes on the island as a whole, the commemoration of the Battle of the Somme in the same year emphasizes the Republic's increasing interests in Continental Europe and the rise of the European Union. For the first time, the Irish Republic joined in to honour the Irish dead in an international ceremony that included representatives from both sides of the war, commemorating an event that had been excised from Irish history and transformed into something purely British, or Unionist. Therefore, this was more than just a celebration of Ireland's European present and future: the Irish Republic's presence in the European Remembrance ceremonies for the Somme re-wrote the country's own commemorative past.

As Fintan O'Toole suggested in the *Irish Times' Supplement to the Easter Rising*, when we speak of the Rising we are speaking of two things: the myth, and the event (March 2006). I would argue, however, that all commemorations have three main components: the myth, the selective event that is being portrayed, and most importantly, the contemporary community who are enacting that commemoration. The 2006 celebrations of the Rising exploited nostalgia for the past to highlight the current prosperity and peace of Celtic Tiger Ireland, while the commemoration of the Battle of the Somme emphasized the Republic's inclusion in the European Union against the backdrop of the sacrifices and atrocities of World War One. However, by reclaiming the Republic's commemorative celebrations of the Easter Rising, as well as their part in the Battle of the Somme, the Republic of Ireland assisted in the transformation of these events for their own aims. The Irish reclamations of the Easter Rising and Battle of the Somme are symbolic constructions of the country's 'Road ahead' as well as the one behind.

Easter Rising and Battle of the Somme: A History of Surrogation

On 1 July 1916, the battle began which had been expected to be the turning point in the First World War, but in fact would drag on for months and become one of the biggest disasters of European military history. During the first morning alone over 20,000 British, Scottish, Welsh and Irish soldiers were killed by German firepower with 35,000 wounded and 8,000 German dead: by the end, over a million soldiers from both sides were killed or wounded. However, it was not merely the extent of the casualties which gave the Battle of the Somme its notorious reputation, but the fact that, though it lasted from July to November, it gained only six miles of land for the Allied Forces. Over the course of five months, the battle line generally remained static with the soldiers burrowing deeper into the trenches. In fact, during World War I, twice as many soldiers died from infection and disease caused by conditions in the trenches than from wounds received in any battle[2] In the numerous memoirs, songs, poems or performances of the time, the Somme only has to be mentioned to evoke mass slaughter, military debacle, and tragedy for both sides. In England, memory of all that went wrong with trench warfare is caught up in the sites of specific battles such as the Somme, Gallipoli, Verdun, Dunkirk, and other such locations of human tragedy. As the *The Irish Times* commented in a special report:

For many, the standard, iconic images of the Somme, Verdun and Ypres are those of the war itself: the mud-soaked battlefields, the moonscapes of craters, the bare shapeless tree trunks jutting forlornly from the ground, the indistinguishable grey faces trudging in procession to their deaths (Ruadhán Mac Cormaic, 4 December 2006).

The landscape of battle became a symbolic location of tragic loss for a generation: poignant battlefields of memory and sites of commemoration for years to come.

As the literature of the war has testified – works by the poets Siegfried Sassoon, Wilfred Owen, David Jones, Isaac Rosenberg and

---

[2] For detailed research on the history of the Battle of the Somme see: Peter Liddle, *The Battle of the Somme: A Reappraisal* (L. Cooper: London, 1992), and Stewart Ross, *The Battle of the Somme* (Raintree Press, Chicago, 2004). For contemporary accounts of the battle, see: John Buchan & George H. Casamajor, *The Battle of the Somme: The First Phase* (T. Nelson & Sons, New York: 1916).

Robert Graves, novels like Erich Maria Remarque's *All's Quiet on the Western Front*, or the memoirs by writers like the nurse Vera Brittan – the cultural memory of World War One in post-war England, France and Germany is one of tragedy. The image of young soldiers destroyed in their thousands in careless campaigns waged by elderly generals is evocative of the more general victimization of the population by the ruling class. David Jones of the Welsh Fusiliers described his foray into Mametz Wood at the Battle of the Somme:

> Across upon this undulated board of verdure chequered
> Bright
> When you look to left and right
> Small, drab, bundled pawns severally make effort
> Moved in tenuous line
> And if you looked behind – the next wave came slowly, as
> successive surfs creep in to dissipate on flat shoe
> and to your front, stretched long laterally,
> and receded deeply
> the dark wood (165).

This epic modernist poem, *In Parenthesis*, is a gripping journey of a soldier's experience throughout the war. Jones suffered from severe Post Traumatic Stress Disorder, known at the time as 'shell shock', which greatly altered the rest of his life. Such representations established the conflict as an enduring symbol of the blatant madness of war. Unlike the ideologically 'necessary' World War Two, the construction of collective memory for post-war culture transformed the First World War battles into an icon of the unnecessary, and a signifier of the destructive carnage of Empire upon its people for both sides of the conflict.

Despite the common view of the Great War as a site of botched battles and ineffective nineteenth-century military strategy with the destructive power of twentieth-century technology, in Ireland the Somme transformed from a site of tragic remembrance into a symbol of British solidarity for the Ulster Unionist Protestant community. This image has continued throughout the years and transformed the battles of 1914-1918 into appropriated sites for loyalty to the Unionist cause on Irish shores. The marching season in Northern Ireland coincides with the Somme Remembrance Day and has often been seen by both Nationalist and Unionist communities alike as a commemoration owned by the Unionist side in this sectarian conflict. Like the Battle of the Somme, the Easter Rising has also been appropriated into a narrative of previous and future struggles for independence and heroic Republican national histories. Joseph Roach describes the appropriation of the past found in both the Easter Rising and Battle of the Somme as a process of surrogation:

> culture reproduces and re-creates itself by a process that can be best described by the word surrogation. In the life of a community, the process of surrogation does not begin or end but continues as actual or perceived vacancies occur in the network of relations that constitutes the social fabric. Into the cavities created by loss through death or other forms of departure, I hypothesize, survivors attempt to fit satisfactory alternates (2).

According to Roach, culture is in a constant process of surrogation of memories, events and individuals. The Irish use of surrogates to reflect the networks of culture and identity power structures offers a highly charged playing ground for Roach's understanding of the phenomenon. The symbolic battles over memorial and historical terrain between the Irish Republic, and the Orange Order, and Republican parades, gives witness to how the battle of the Somme, the Easter Rising, and other Irish commemorative sites, are surrogated by communities on both sides of the Border.

The Unionist appropriation of the battle of the Somme is just as active a surrogation of collective memory as the Irish Republic's erasure of it. With regard to Joseph Roach's definition of surrogation, the Unionist appropriation of the battle of the Somme is in itself an act of violent forgetting. Fintan O'Toole elaborates upon this ironic surrogation of history:

> In some ways, the Somme posed as many challenges to Unionist as it did to nationalist orthodoxy. In order to re-member the battle as a glorious sacrifice (contrasted to the stab-in-the-back of treacherous Catholics in the Easter Rising), it was necessary to forget its essential obscenity. In order to use the memory of the Somme to bolster obedience to authority, it was necessary to forget that the courage and self-sacrifice of the troops was betrayed by the folly of their leaders. In order to use the Somme as a marker of Protestant character, it was necessary to forget, not merely the presence of Catholic nationalist divisions, but also the fact that the Ulster Division had fought in what was seen as a typically 'Irish' way. It lost so many men because those men ran with reckless zeal into the German lines, and were then forced to beat a bloody retreat (*The Irish Times* 4 December 2006).

No matter how the Ulster Unionists strategically misinterpreted the battle, their appropriation of the Somme became an act of surrogation, a claiming of sectarian ownership over a uniform commemoration of suffering which affected both communities.

The Unionist surrogation of the Somme began with the commencement of battle being delayed by a day. Due to an act of fate, the battle, which was supposed to have begun at the end of June, started on the same day as the Battle of the Boyne. As early as 1917, only a year later, the commemoration of the Belfast Twelfth focused on the Somme's coincidence with traditional Ulster victories. Dominic Bryan describes this fusion of the Somme with the Ulster Unionist cause in his book *Orange Parades: The Politics of Ritual, Tradition and Control*:

> On 1 July 1916 it was the 36th (Ulster) Division that spearheaded the attack at the Battle of the Somme. Within two days 5,500 men were killed or wounded (Bardon 1992: 455), and back in Belfast press reports of the glorious push were soon joined by the lists of the casualties. Orangeism had a blood sacrifice and renewed military and political legitimacy ... Colonel Wallace spoke of the new 'glorious first of July' since it coincidentally took place on the same date as the Battle of the Boyne using the old calendar. He recounted that men had 'sashes over their shoulders' and drove the enemy before them 'on the banks of the Somme, as their fathers had done 226 years before on the banks of the Boyne' (55-6).

From a devastating battle of diverse Allied military companies to a concentrated act of triumphant Protestant might, the surrogation of the Somme was so successfully realized that the Irish Catholic contribution to the entire war was erased, by both Unionist and Republican communities. While the nationalist World War One soldiers were forgotten, the Ulster soldiers' battles turned victims into victors, and transformed the war in a desire to create Protestant heroes for the struggle against Irish independence. Whereas the English recorded mass casualties in the 'War to End All Wars,' the Irish Unionists commemorated the triumph of Ulster courage and their noble sacrifice for the Motherland. The Somme commemorations in Northern Ireland have been so separated from the historic events that, according to Fran Brearton:

> The stereotype of the martial Irishman – valiant, aggressive, heroic, with a daredevil spirit – is seemingly remote from the stereotype of the Ulster Unionist – entrenched, defensive, immovable (cited O'Toole, 4/12/2006).

However, Brearton goes on to describe the 'inadequacies of those stereotypes' revealed by the actual events of the Battle of the Somme, where on the first of July the Ulster troops charged valiantly ahead of their comrades during the battle and were tragically caught in between the two lines, so that many of their numbers were gunned down by Allied rather than Axis forces (cited Fintan O'Toole, 4 December 2006).

While the Unionists expanded their part in the battle, the Irish nationalist historical narrative erased the Battle of the Somme, as Declan Kiberd states:

> For decades after independence, the 150,000 Irish who fought in the Great War (for the rights of small nations and for Home Rule after the cessation of hostilities, as many of them believed) had been officially extirpated from the record. No government representative attended their annual commemoration ceremonies in Christ Church: and none publicly sported a poppy (239).

By the 1990s, however, the Irish Republic began to re-examine the part played by Irish soldiers in the battles of the Somme and other campaigns of the Great War. With the development of the European Union and increasing globalization, the search began for collective historic experiences which drew Ireland and the Irish population into the fold of the greater European community. The forgotten history of World War One perhaps began to seem as problematic as its memory had earlier done during the formation of the Republic. The Irish contribution of the Battle of the Somme now offered a possible representation of Ireland's contribution to this collective European tragedy. While Ireland remained neutral during the Second World War and could not take part in the wide-scale international D-Day commemorations of 1994, the Battle of the Somme was a perfect place to insert itself into the embrace of the European Union. During the media attention surrounding the 2006 celebrations, Fintan O'Toole illustrates the danger of this oversight in *The Irish Times*:

> Because it had such a huge impact on human self-understanding, the Somme ought to have been a part of Irish official memory, even if not a single Irish soldier had taken part. That in fact Irish involvement in the Somme was at least as prominent in proportional terms as that of any of the other combatant nations ought to have assured it a prominent place in our sense of our collective past. Yet, for at least 70 years, the memory of the Somme gave way to other battles of remem-

brance, as competing versions of Irish history dug their own trenches (4 December 2006).

The Irish erasure of its contribution to the First World War may have been a response to a combination of the Republic's discomfort with its own imperialist past, and the Ulster Unionists' appropriation of the massacre as part of its narrative of loyalty to the Crown. However, no matter what occurred during the past ninety years, as O'Toole and others argued in 2006, the new climate of Irish commemorative history and its contribution to the European community has returned the focus to the Somme and the Irish contribution to a wide scale European tragedy.

Commemoration for a New Era

Many cultures offer commemorations of past individuals and events. However, at times, societies develop particular climates for commemoration, moments in history when the need to celebrate the past forms a significant part of the national practice. The climate of commemoration may be due to shifting values in a society, or moments of radical change, events which create the need to re-affirm a culture's past or future due to the fear of losing that history altogether. Due to the globalization of its economy, the current wave of immigration and the recent increase of wealth into the country, the Republic of Ireland has been witness to multiple trans-formations of its community and landscape, and to its very identity. These transformations have caused a significant re-evaluation of the Irish nation and, indeed, what it means to be 'Irish' in all areas of the country's social, political and economic spheres. During this transitional period, centennial and commemorative celebrations have occurred in every aspect of Irish life. These celebrations have encapsulated political events like that of the Easter Rising and the Battle of the Somme, the bicentennial of the 1798 Rebellion, the births and deaths of historical figures, like the Beckett Centenary – for which the Fianna Fáil government paid €800,000 – and, even those of fictional occurrences as with *Bloomsday*, a centennial celebration in honour of James Joyce's *Ulysses*.

As the wave of commemorations hit the nation, we must pause to ask, who are these celebrations for? What is the purpose of com-memorations and whom does it benefit? In essence, what is being commemorated: macro or micro history, or a nostalgic longing for less complex struggles and a retreat back to a time with more consistent understandings of 'Ireland' and 'Irishness'? In the following examination of the recent Irish commemorative events of the 90th Anniversary of the Easter Rising and the Battle of the Somme, this essay illustrates that no matter how diverse commemorative events may be, they all reveal the anxieties of their own contemporary identities and the desire, through commemorative rites, to manipulate the past into a palatable form for present imaginings of a community's historical legacy. Commemorative events aim to establish an understanding – or affirmation – of a community's own identity.

The act of commemoration can be read as an analysis of contemporary social and political aims and mentalities. By focusing on the act of commemoration itself and the current Irish Republic's commemorative history, I argue that the commemorative parades in the Republic of the Easter Rising and the Battle of the Somme are performances of contemporary economic, political and social power over the country's own past. The Irish Republic's memorial history of the Battle of the Somme and the Easter Rising illustrate how commemorations function as performative *acts* of both collective cultural identity and pastness. A national commemoration is not only the celebration of past events and past cultures, but a deliberate construction of the past for present and future communities, cultures, politics and policies.

Commemoration and National Memory: Politics of A Chosen Past

Memory is what binds a community together: it is through mnemonic triggers that a group of individuals finds a common heritage, a common past. For a community whose identity is under threat, it is 'the possession in common of a rich legacy of memories' (52-54) according to Ernest Renan, which helps to form or create a nation. In this way, popular memory is an essential part of the formation of the nation. Commemorative events – such as centennials, monuments, parades, or festivals – all play active roles in that formation through the building of collective memory. According to Ian McBride, '[m]emories are constantly being described, narrated, illustrated and commemorated in order to inscribe them upon the public memory. These evocations of popular memory are not simply important but, rather, necessary for the formation of a society' (1-42). Moreover, the commemorations of public memory are platforms for a community to enact that memory and, by doing so, make the public subscribe to the official (or on the other hand, counter-) memory being created. Thus the community can perform not only their position within collective history, but also their place within a society. A commemoration is a complicit *act* of a people towards its community.

However, a commemoration, like any organized event, is constructed. The commemoration is deliberately planned to fulfil a certain agenda for its orchestrators. According to Pierre Nora, such events replace the loss of ritual in society: they are the *lieux de mémoire* (sites of memory) which 'mark the rituals of a society without ritual' (12), creating simulacra of a forgotten past which manipulate the plastic form of history into palatable forms for the current society:

> *Lieux de mémoire* originate with the sense that there is no spontaneous memory, that we must deliberately create archives, maintain anniversaries, organize celebrations, pronounce eulogies, and notarize bills because such activities no longer occur naturally (12).

Commemorative celebrations offer a space for such sites of memory to be offered to a public not only lacking such sites of nostalgia, but longing for them. These 'ritualized' performances offer an authenticating ritual for the construction of collective memory. The *lieux de mémoire* allows historical events to become mythic, transformed from a moment of history into a site of collective ontological belonging.

The performance aspect of a commemoration, like a parade or rally, is developed not only by the event organizers but by its audience as well. The audience participates within the event (i.e. through singing and dancing, applause, cheering or other activities) playing an active role in the performative aspect of commemoration. Thus the people are demonstrating their solidarity within the national structure through their very presence and participation in the event.[3] Anthropologist Kelly Askew describes this duologue

---

[3] In his account of the celebrations surrounding the American Revolution, Waldstreicher spoke of these performative events as: 'Celebrations were no afterthoughts to independence, nor were they mere symbolizations of accumulated oedipal anxieties. They were anticipated, deliberate, necessary responses to the Declaration of Independence.' David Waldstreicher, 'Rites of Rebellion, Rites of Assent: Celebrations, Print

which occurs between a people and its country in civic celebrations and commemorative displays. In her study of public events and traditional music in Tanzania, Askew writes of how, upon arrival in Tanga, the president of Tanzania reinforced his 'political and social superiority' while 'the youths and musicians had performed their loyalty to the state' through the presentation of a festive display of allegiance and power by the witnesses and participators of the event (4-5). Through the 'festive display' all participants and witnesses tacitly present their loyalty (or dissent) to the state by the very nature of the commemoration. Askew's study of Tanzania is strangely apposite to commemoration in the Irish context. The Irish Republic constructs parades or commemorative events to display the nation to the populace: however, the populace also perform their own place within the nation through civic performances. Commemorative performance practices fuse the public sense of 'nation-hood' to the State itself. Even by their very presence, the audience, willing or not, presents a national body for the national event. Through verbal and physical acts at a commemorative event, the audience becomes integrated into the celebration and performs its own role, or multiple roles, within it. The physical body of the audience becomes transformed into a national formation of identity, a symbol of the nation within these commemorations by its mass form. In *How Societies Remember,* Paul Connerton describes how memory becomes embodied in these performances through the performative acts of community: 'In habitual memory, the past is, as it were, sedimented in the body' (24). The recurring rituals of commemorative performance do not merely re-instate accepted memory in the audience's mind, but rather inscribe the memory upon the bodies of the audience. Commemorative performance, through audience applause and consensual participation, creates the embodiment of living memory. Through these commemorative acts, the audience is transformed from passive watcher into active participant in the political struggle towards nationhood.

Commemorative performances keep alive past events while, at the same time, dictating which events of the past will be continued in the future. Consequently, the past is malleable material constantly shifting and being shifted by contemporary society and the individuals that make up that society. Through commemoration and revisionist history, the past becomes a substance to be shaped and formed according to what is needed within it. The past is not only 'chosen' but formed and transformed into a substance necessary for contemporary consumption. The past is constructed in order to fit in with the designs of the commemoration organizers and, at the same time, that of the public imagination.

The Climate of Commemoration

The elaborate Easter Rising parade in 1966 appeared to be a celebration of the economic expansion seen by the Irish Republic in the mid-sixties. The celebration was framed by the press to honour not only the 1916 martyrs, but also the significant changes to Ireland during the radical decade of the 1960s. However, the increasing tension in Northern Ireland caused the Rev. Ian Paisley and the Ulster Constitution Defence Committee to have a train of parade participants from the South be barred from entering Northern Ireland (Bryan, 80). By the spring of 1967, the rising violence in the North transformed the 1916 events into a symbol of Northern Irish Republican protest. On 29 March 1970 an Easter parade in Derry culminated in violence with several parade participants injured (ibid., 87). Commemorations of the Easter Rising became so connected to 'The Troubles' in Northern Ireland that during the subdued memorial marking its 75th anniversary, Taoiseach, Charles J. Haughey was asked by members of the press why he was holding the ceremony at all (Kiberd, 1991). Haughey's commemoration was a small, hushed affair, consisting of speeches from a few veterans and the placement of flowers around the General Post Office in Dublin, a focal point of resistance during the Rising. However, public hostility to the event, as a result of the ongoing violence of the IRA, was such that even these minor commemoration activities appeared a dangerous threat to the Irish Republic and the island as a whole.

Due to such a politically-charged history, the reinstatement of the march in 2006 and the surrounding activities in honour of the Easter Rising was cause for celebration by the Republic, according to the Fianna Fáil government, as a powerful statement of the successful peace process in the North. Bertie Ahern, the Irish Taoiseach, demonstrated his faith in the development of peace in Northern Ireland by declaring that the commemoration would be an opportunity for 'Remembrance, reconciliation and renewal' (BBC News 16/4/2006). However, as Mary McAleese, the Irish president asserted, in the post-Celtic Tiger Republic, the 1916 Rising was an event that goes beyond the conflict in Northern Ireland, or the birth of the Republic: 'We rightly look back on our past with pride at the men and women who lived in very different times from ours, and who made sacrifices of their lives so that we would enjoy these good times' (ibid.) In essence, McAleese declared that the parade of the Easter Rising was a demonstration of today's prosperity as well as yesterday's sacrifice. Although these statements were criticized in the Irish press as attempts by the Fianna Fáil party to use the commemorations to boost their support in upcoming elections for Dublin in 2006, the commemorations of the 1916 Rising were a celebration of the future's predestined victory over its past.

With such extreme changes in the population and topography, there were many areas within the abundance of Celtic Tiger Ireland that were not emphasized by the Fianna Fáil government. The disparity between rich and poor, the abuse of drugs and alcohol and the rising racism in Ireland show a different side to the newly prosperous country so lauded by Mary McAleese during the Easter Rising commemoration ceremony. The conflicting view of Celtic Tiger Ireland is one of prosperity and poverty, globalization and increasing racial and cultural tensions. In his criticism of much of the confident rhetoric around the prosperous and seemingly changing ideologies of the Irish landscape, Luke Gibbons describes this ironic contradiction in the country:

> The dramatic shift from being a country impaired by chronic unemployment and emigration until the 1980s to being a host-culture for immigration in the 1990s is accordingly welcomed as a sign of growing multiculturalism in which Ireland can at last take leave of its troubled past. However, as we have seen, the suffering bound up with historical injustice and sustained cultural loss does not lend itself to overnight cures, and it may well be the process of disavowal, the surface optimism of a culture in self-denial, which poses the greatest problem to a genuine engagement with cultural difference (105).

Gibbons posits that the Irish culture should confront its history before it can truly engage in a critical interrogation of its current culture beyond the surface of economic and social prosperity. However, his assertions that the Irish are not willing to engage in a study of their past and only look to the future ignores the continuous examinations of the past found in contemporary Irish cinema, literature, theatre and commemorative practice. Moreover, his belief that it is through the examination of the Irish colonial past that an understanding of multiculturalism and modernity will occur in contemporary Irish society denies the possibility that the past can also offer a place for escape from the present: a nostalgic journey into a history with events that can both justify existing displays of identity, and help to inculcate that identity into an intractable, adherent force. In essence, the construction of collective memory aids in the formation of a barricade against change.

In the current community of an evolving Ireland, where the understanding of 'Irishness' is in flux, commemorative celebrations become a way to venerate not only the past, but also to re-affirm traditional understandings of Irishness. Commemorations are more necessary when a community is in transition and its identity is under threat. Ernest Renan describes how the past and representations of the past help to bind a community together through the remembrance of collective sacrifice. The nation is formed and reformed through contemporary representations of the past.

A nation is therefore a large-scale solidarity, constituted by the feeling of the sacrifices that one has made in the past and of those that one is prepared to make in the future. It presupposes a past: it is summarized, however, in the present by a tangible fact, namely, consent, the clearly expressed desire to continue a common life (52-4).

As seen with Fianna Fáil's manipulation of the Easter Rising for its own governmental propaganda, commemoration events and centennials are powerful because, according to Linda Hutcheon, the intangibility of the past makes it an ideal platform on which to raise present issues. The nebulous construction of collective national memory creates an emotional tie to an imagined past that holds a powerful grip over a community. Hutcheon describes this as manufacturing a feeling of nostalgia through contemporary commemorative events. 'It is the very pastness of the past,' Hutcheon suggests, 'its inaccessibility, that likely accounts for a large part of nostalgia's power' (Hutcheon, cited Glazer, 37). The malleability of the past to reconstitute itself into the image of present belief systems makes it the ideal source for current tensions to play themselves out. While twenty-first century Ireland encompasses multivalent communities of diverse cultures, races and religions, commemorations and centennial events of the past century help to create a comforting nostalgia for the public by celebrating the Ireland of the early twentieth century with its supposedly homogenous identity and traditional struggles between the colonized and the colonizer. With England as the colonial 'other,' turn-of-the-century Ireland is perceived by many in the present to have had a common enemy and a firm commitment to shaping its own sense of 'Irishness,' an identity that is now perceived as under threat in a more visibly global Ireland.

The late nineteenth and early twentieth century in Ireland was a period of active cultural and political productivity and major change in the country, a time of admirable achievements to commemorate in any era. However, the study and commemoration of these achievements can not be looked at outside of their current cultural context. It is not the past that changes, but contemporary culture's relationship to it. In P.J. Mathews's work on the Celtic Revival, published in 2003, he comments that 'At a time when the homogenizing pressures of globalization on local cultures have registered as a major concern with cultural criticism, the achievements, as well as the failures, of the Irish revival may have much to teach us about the cultural dynamics of Ireland in the twenty-first century' (148). As Mathews argues, a new and vigorous understanding of the past may help Ireland, or any culture, to throw light upon current changes, or current cultural transformations. If Ireland at the turn of the millennium is witnessing vast transformations of its landscapes and communities, it can be no more radical a transformation than that seen at the turn of the previous century. In this way, the celebration of a centenary event remains a powerful victory of past achievement and of established change for a society looking for answers to its current evolution by acknowledging those in its history. Commemorative practice in the Irish Republic transforms history for contemporary national and communal agendas. Through the fostering of collective nostalgia, the present and the past can be placed in opposition with one another to highlight, or alleviate, anxieties over radical trans-formations of the community and the nation.

During the 90th Anniversary celebration, the Republic of Ireland's decision to join in the European commemoration of the Battle of the Somme remains a part of its contemporary emphasis on inclusion in the European Union. By reclaiming their own part of this particular battle, and in World War One as a whole, the Republic of Ireland assisted in the transformation of a commemorative event for its own aims. The need to memorialize this tragic event now, ninety years after it happened, is significant in that

it goes beyond an individual level (with most, if not all, of the soldiers who witnessed this battle being dead, and therefore unaffected
by the commemoration) to a communal, or inter-communal event.
As the first Irish minister to participate in a Somme Commemoration, Mary Hanafin, the Minister of Education, clarifies: 'It's
not so much that we are interested in history for the sake of
remembering, but in history for what we can learn from it, and how
we can move forward from it.' (*The Irish Times* 4/12/2006). The
Irish participation in the memorial event became symbolic of the
contemporary political climate in both Northern and Southern
Ireland. 'For the Irish people to commemorate that is hugely
significant,' Hanafin explained. 'It shows the improved relations
between North and South, and between England and Ireland' (ibid.).
In the commemoration of an event from the 'long past,' the
tragedies of World War One had lost their grip on the European
community: the Irish reclamation of the Battle of the Somme is a
symbolic construction of the country's place within the European
community of the early twenty-first rather than twentieth century.

The 90th Anniversary of the Battle of the Somme was emphasized
as an 'act of healing' between the former Allies and Axis powers,
(Germany was delighted to participate in the commemorative activities alongside Britain and France), between the Irish and British,
and Northern and Southern Ireland. Nevertheless, despite the noble
rhetoric surrounding the ceremonies, some old conflicts arose. Ian
Paisley denied that the commemoration had anything to do with
finding similarities between Ulstermen and the IRA, while Britain
offended Ireland with Prince Charles's oversight in forgetting to
acknowledge Ireland as one of the countries that experienced
overwhelming losses during the war.[4]

The commemoration in Ireland of the Battle of the Somme
absorbed the event within the greater legacy of Irish
commemorations. The Irish contribution to the First World War
was swiftly transformed from a British commemorative activity to a
distinctly Irish one. Bertie Ahern was quick to liken the Irish acts of
heroism in the Somme to that of the Easter Rising, and thus
transform Irish fighting for Imperialist 'King and Country' into an
act of Irish national heroism and sacrifice. As the Taoiseach

---

[4] Charles mentioned Canada, Australia, New Zealand and India but did not
mention Ireland at all. Later his press secretary assured *The Irish Times*
that Prince Charles did not deliberately leave out Ireland, but the
oversight rankled none-the-less. See *The Irish Times*, 4 July 2006.

declared, 'More than 5,000 men of the 36th Ulster Division fell in
the first two days in July 1916. They fought alongside 200,000 Irish
men from every county of Ireland. Their bravery was no less than
that shown by the insurgents of Easter Week' (*The Irish Times*
29/6/2006). By making clear connections between the two battles of
1916, Ahern, among other members of the Fianna Fáil government
and the Irish media, attempted to justify their shift in Irish
commemorative history and transform the public's understanding of
the significance of the Battle of the Somme as an *Irish* conflict on a
par with that of the Easter Rising. While on the first of July 2006,
the Irish government became part of the European Somme
commemoration activities in France, in Ireland they continued
memorial activities and honoured the event. Bertie Ahern emphasized that the Irish commemoration of the Battle of the Somme
and the reinstatement of the Easter Rising parade were both acts of
re-appropriation:

> [The Easter Rising Commemoration] Televised live, the
> ceremony had been abandoned with the outbreak of the
> modern Troubles in the North. However, the ruling Fianna Fail
> party, which Mr Ahern leads, judged that it was a propitious
> moment to 'reclaim' a part of the state's history, which had
> been 'colonized' by Sinn Fein, the Provisional IRA's political
> wing. Last week Mr Ahern unveiled a postage stamp
> commemorating the Battle of the Somme, in a very public
> acknowledgement of Ireland's British military history (*The
> Irish Times* 29/6/2006).

Both of these commemorative events were, as Bertie Ahern
argued, the re-appropriation of colonized history (one by the IRA
and the other, fittingly, by the Ulster Unionists). The act of re-
surrecting history became, for the Fianna Fáil government, yet
another triumph of Ireland's future over its past. Moreover, the
triumph was not only over a terrible battle in history, but over the
rights of commemoration itself. The Irish Republic's appropriation
of what has long been considered a Unionist memorial is also an act
of defiance against the Northern Irish conflict's binary of historical
events and commemoration practice.

Commemorating the Future

Commemoration acts to bind communities together through the
imagined past. These imaginings are created, not solely through
print culture as previously noted in Benedict Anderson's work, but

also through rituals of performance. Collective memory is important because it is what reinforces our understanding of ourselves and our community. Individual memory may not be reinforced as it is both unpredictable and constantly shifting. It is through collective imaginings that our world takes on solid, concrete form: as Ian McBride notes, the past becomes 'stabilized'[5] through this collective process.

The recent commemorations of the Battle of the Somme and the Easter Rising reflect contemporary societal change in the Irish Republic's attitude to its past. While the 2006 Battle of the Somme commemorations act as a celebration of Ireland's participation within the greater European community, the recent anniversary of the Easter Rising represents the triumphant prosperity of the new economy over past struggles and economic deprivation. Moreover, both of these events influence the way the Irish community perceives its future and its past, and instigate, perhaps, other social movements of revisionist history and memorial healing within the community itself.

Bibliography

BBC News, 16 April 2006.

Askew, Kelly, *Performing the Nation* (Chicago: University of Chicago, 2002).

Bryan, Dominic, *Orange Parades: The Politics of Ritual, Tradition and Control* (London: Pluto Press, 2000).

Buchan, John & Casamajor, George H., *The Battle of the Somme: The First Phase* (T. Nelson & Sons, New York: 1916).

Connerton, Paul, *How Societies Remember* (Cambridge: Cambridge University Press, 1989).

Cronin, Michael, Kirby, Peadar & Gibbons, Luke, eds, *Reinventing Ireland: Culture, Society and the Global Economy* (London: Pluto Press, 2002).

Cormaic, Ruadhán Mac, 'Soldiers Songs' *The Irish Times*, 4 July 2006.

Dorgan, Theo and Ni Dhonnchadha, Máirín eds. *Revising the Rising* (Derry: Field Day, 1991).

Dungan, Myles, 'Fighting Amnesia' *The Irish Times*, 4 July 2006.

'Easter Rising Supplement' *The Irish Times*, March 2006.

---

[5] 'When we recall the past, then, we do so as members of our groups – a family, a local community, a workforce, a political movement, a church or a trade union.' Ian McBride, 'Memory and National Identity in Modern Ireland', in *History and Memory in Modern Ireland*, ed. Ian McBride (Cambridge: Cambridge University Press, 2001): 6.

Glazer, Peter, *Radical Nostalgia: Spanish Civil War Commemoration in America* (Rochester: University of Rochester Press, 2005).

Jones, David, *In Parenthesis* (New York: New York Review Press, 1937). Reprinted (New York: New York Review Press: 2003).

Kiberd, Declan, *Inventing Ireland: The Literature of the Modern Nation* (London: Vintage Press, 1996).

Liddle, Peter, *The Battle of the Somme: A Reappraisal* (L.Cooper: London, 1992).

Mathews, P.J., *Revival: The Abbey Theatre, Sinn Fein, the Gaelic League and the Co-Operative Movement* (Cork: Cork University Press, 2003).

McBride, Ian, ed., *History and Memory in Modern Ireland* (Cambridge: Cambridge University Press, 2001).

Nora, Pierre, 'Between Memory and History: Les Lieux de mémoire', *Representations* No. 26, Special Issue: *Memory and Counter-Memory* (1989): 7-24.

O'Toole, Fintan, 'Why We Remember' *The Irish Times,* 4 July 2006.

Renan, Ernest, 'What Is a Nation?' *Becoming National: A Reader*, Ely, Geoff & Ronald Grigor Suny, (New York & Oxford: Oxford University Press, 1996): 41-55.

Roach, Joseph, *Cities of the Dead: Circum-Atlantic Performance* (New York: Columbia University Press, 1996).

Ross, Stewart, *The Battle of the Somme* (Raintree Press, Chicago, 2004).

Strinati, Dominic, *An Introduction to Theories of Popular Culture* (London & New York: Routlege, 2004).

Waldstreicher, David, 'Rites of Rebellion, Rites of Assent: Celebrations, Print Culture, and the Origins of American Nationalism' *The Journal of American History* 82, no. 1 (1995): 37-61.

Williams, Raymond, *Marxism and Literature, Marxist Introductions* (Oxford: Oxford Press, 1977).

15 |Performing Provisionalism: Republican Commemorative Practice as Political Performance

Kris Brown and Elisabetta Viggiani

Provisional Irish Republicanism, whether in its political form as Sinn Féin, or its military wing, the Provisional Irish Republican Army, was for decades seen as the vanguard Irish Republican community within the disputed territory of Northern Ireland, struggling to secure British withdrawal from the six north eastern counties of Ireland and their unification with the rest of the island. It was a conflict which produced over three and a half thousand dead, of which almost 1800 were attributable to killings by the Provisional IRA (McKittrick et al, 153). Members of this organization, and its political surrogate, Sinn Féin, made up 364 of the casualties (Tírghrá Committee, 2002). Republicans were rigorous in memorializing their dead throughout the conflict, with commemorative parades and militarized, politicized funerals: similarly, the material culture of remembrance – wall murals, plaques and monuments – dots the urban and rural landscape of Republican areas. Commemoration and memorialization represent mourning, and it is quite true that part of Provisional Republican commemorative activity involves the unvarnished remembrance of friends, neighbours, relatives and comrades-in-arms: but this essay focuses on the performance of remembrance, commemoration and memorialization in terms of Provisional Republicanism as a political movement and project. This Provisional performance is an amalgam, peppered with emotional content and appeals, binding together ritual display, blunt symbolic communication, and public projection of political messages and historic tropes and narratives.

Provisionalism represents the hegemonic force within Republicanism, and crucially, despite a number of violent and bloody interruptions, has been a most active participant in the peace process, calling ceasefires, participating in political negotiations and declaiming the need to move to a new peaceful environment. During this protracted period there seemed a clear political will emergent within the Provisional Republican leadership, observable from the first ceasefire of 1994, but particularly clear since the 1998 Belfast Agreement, to slip between the old ideological shibboleths of Irish Republicanism, using symbolism, much of it traditional, as political cover. Abrupt iconoclasm was shunned, but the substance of traditional Republican dogma could be eroded just as the public performance of traditionalist symbols was maintained, even accelerated.

Many Republican memorials sprang up in the years following the first ceasefire with some of the largest appearing since 2000.[1] In the same period, memorial sites have served as public stages for the performance of politics, acting as focal points in time and space around which group members gather to convey a common sense of social identification and belonging. Memorial sites do not simply play a part as a framing space for rituals, they also act as props and enriching scenery, providing a supplementary repertoire of symbols with which spectators and protagonists can augment the projected narrative. Commemorative activity remains a significant and ever present part of the Provisional Republican calendar, though one scarcely reported in mainstream media. In seeking to unpick the importance of commemorative display, that need to maintain a projection of heroes and historical narratives onto public highways, we might first examine the need commemorative performance fulfils for Provisionalism in general terms, before examining its performance of commemorative practice in detail.

---

[1] For information on the growth of memorialization in Belfast in recent years see Elisabetta Viggiani's introduction and database 'Public Forms of Memorialization to the Victims of the Northern Irish 'Troubles' in the City of Belfast' at http://cain.ulst.ac.uk./viggiani/index.html. Accessed January 2007.

A Nexus for Performance: National Identity, Conflict and Remembrance

The Provisional IRA is a paramilitary group, an illegal 'secret army' composed of civilians organized along quasi-military lines. It has couched its political programme and justification of its activities in terms of communal defence, patriotism, national allegiance and the maximization of national independence. According to its training manual, the Green Book,[2] it even regarded itself as a shadow Republic, the legitimate sovereign body on the island of Ireland. This claim may seem the apotheosis of a dogmatic Republican theology, but regardless of how sincerely or not this traditionalist tenet was maintained, it reminds us of an assertion nestled at the core of Provisional Republicanism, that it reserves the right to use force, a right jealously guarded by the state, whether Irish or British. In a sense, the Provisional Republican movement projected two political facets more usually projected by a state: the latter's assertion that it alone commands national allegiance and the need to legitimize its monopoly of force. War commemoration and memorialization is a powerful connecting strand between national allegiance and national identity, and the legitimation of force. Benedict Anderson observes that the ghostly imaginings of war commemoration are at the hub of a process where a national community feels an identification with its dead, thus weaving an imagined continuity through time. Tombs of the Unknown Soldier are the most evocative examples of this, graphically perpetuating the emotive appeal that states make in persuading their citizens to die for them. War commemoration is thus a crucial rite in interpolating members of a particular group as part of an imagined community that transcends, and ultimately, cheats time and death (Anderson, 16-7).

If a shared history of struggle produces tropes of continuity and attachment within a national community, then memorialization and commemoration can be seen as playing a part in underwriting social cohesion, particularly in times of peace. This conception of nationalism as founded on a history of shared conflict and sacrifice, is undoubtedly contentious in a wider sense, bypassing as it does other forms of attachment based on culture and civic involvement, but it

---

[2] Tim Pat Coogan, *The IRA* (London: HarperCollins, 1995): 544-545, 549. See also Brendan O'Brien, *The Long War – The IRA and Sinn Féin* (Dublin: O'Brien Press, 1999): 401-402.

has a resonance when applied to a political movement which proclaims patriotism, has condoned the use of force, and which has
existed through a protracted crisis in which it killed approximately
1800 people and suffered hundreds of casualties itself. Communal
violence has amplified the sentiment of national identification, and
collapses it to a sub state level based around a community's local
area, which goes some way to explaining commemorative acts
undertaken by Republicans in the streets of Northern Ireland. As
Appadurai explains 'such violence ... invariably intensifies the sac-
ralization and nationalization of streets, houses and neighbour-
hoods and other aspects of ordinary life' (Appadurai, 139). Over the
decades of conflict, Provisional Republicans have become embedded
in their local communities, not simply through a shared political
identity, but also through a shared sense of threat, social and
cultural activity, and simple kinship. Commemorative display does
not take place in these areas simply through the will of a local
politico-military elite, to a substantial degree it reinforces and
reflects a feeling of attachment, which although not hegemonic, can
be widely held.

The Importance of Death, Ritual and Memory in Provisional Republicanism

The anthropologists Huntington and Metcalf have argued that the
examination of customs and rituals which communities use to deal
with death, can serve to unpack wider cultural and social issues. In
many societies:

> the issue of death throws into relief the most important cultural
> values by which people live their lives and evaluate their
> experiences. Life becomes transparent against the background
> of death, and fundamental social and cultural issues are
> revealed (Huntington and Metcalf, 2).

This is certainly true of Provisional Republicanism, a movement
which places high importance on keeping and transmitting the
memory of the dead. One of the largest categories of content within
the pages of the movement's newspaper *An Phoblacht/Republican
News* is that of commemoration (Picard, 98), whilst some see in the
commemorative diligence of Republicanism, a kind of civil religious
aspect, in which commemorative piety plays an important part in
explaining the movement's durability (O'Doherty, 22).

The basic integrity of the ideology is thus bound up with ensuring that the community of the faithful is aware of the need to remember, and the projection of that memory periodically in ritual acts. This mixing of political beliefs with a somewhat religious display and practice, is not a parochial appendage unique to a movement grounded in Catholic Ireland, but is similar to what Mosse, in his study of the commemoration of the dead of the First World War, has called the 'cult of the fallen soldier' (Mosse, chapter 6). Rituals of death could be political tools and weapons too: Mettress and Metress in an examination of pre-ceasefire Republican funerary practice underline its utility in the psychological theatre of war, noting how it was used to fashion solidarity within the Nationalist and Republican community, and was a site of ideological, and even physical, conflict between Republicans and state forces (1993). Ritual performance was politics, and could also be another front in the 'war'.

The issues of solidarity and the transmission of memory are crucial within Provisional Republicanism, whether the backdrop is a pre-ceasefire militarized society, or purely political conflict. Martin McGuinness has written of 'the importance of remembering and periodically renewing the memory process as a way of reaffirming, acknowledging and making a valuable contribution to advancing the Republican cause', and in elaboration compares the Republican community in some depth to that of an extended family, at the centre of which beats the heart of remembrance (McGuinness, 2).

This reveals two crucial strands within the Republican commemorative tradition: the importance of the transmission of memory as a means of underlining historical continuity, and the building of a sense of solidarity, of fictive kinship, presenting the community as a united political clan sharing the same values and memory. Both serve as a means of projecting legitimacy. This is of great importance in reassuring grassroots supporters and potential doubters that despite the pressures and political weaving of the peace process, Provisional Republicanism is aware of its origins and remains true to them.

This remembrance does not happen automatically, but is the result of conscious, directed activity, one which fully understands the power of publicly performed ritual. Indeed, Republican thinking on the growing importance of publicly performed political ritual is in part shaped by British commemoration of its war dead. A British model of spectacle and community involvement is to be emulated, not attacked as the jingoistic waving of the butcher's apron. As McGuinness enthused:

> Down the years I've marvelled at how the British government do this when important commemorations and anniversaries come round ... they know how to do it and they can involve everyone within society and I think a lot of lessons could be learned here. All of us are struck, every November, at the way in which the British go about honouring their war dead, and I think that they're better at it than the Irish. Now, I'm not saying that that's an argument for doing it in the same way as the British do it. What I'm talking about is the effort that's put into it and sometimes the imagination that's supplied to it.[3]

There should be little surprise at this enthusiasm for commemorative performance. Indeed as Kertzer has noted, revolutionary, radical or anti-state groups may find the public performance of ritual even more useful than established sources of authority would. Performed rites provide a basis for communication, common identification, the delegitimizing of existing power relations, a redefinition of possible power relations in the political future, create strong emotive resistance to the state, and can even allow movement leaderships to emerge or replenish themselves.[4] Commemorative ritual, rather than being an obscurantist embellishment, appears instead to provide a useful, rational set of tools with which to build and reinforce a political movement.

Commemorative performance involves a high degree of symbolism: in disciplined or stylized action, backdrop, or the flags, banners, insignia and other impedimenta carried by participants. It is this rich, thickened symbolism which provides a particularly effective means of communication along two axes: the symbolism may be replete with 'condensation symbols', values and ideas saturated with emotion, whose simplicity and forcefulness makes them ideal mnemonics, readily propagating the projected message amongst the audience of followers and participants. As Cohen argues, symbols of the past, infused with timelessness and narratives of struggle or martyrdom, have exactly this role and are particularly effective during periods of intense political or social

---

3 Interview with Martin McGuinness, broadcast on Good Morning Ulster, BBC Radio Ulster 11 April 2006. Transcript in possession of author.
4 David Kerzer, *Ritual, Politics & Power* (New Haven: Yale University Press, 1988): 160, 169-172: references to this work are hereafter in the text: (RP, page).

change, allowing communities to 'drop their heaviest cultural anchors' and minimize the potential damage of transformation. Thus the political message is broadly propagated with the intention of having a soothing or supportive effect (Cohen, 101-2). Along the second axis, symbolism is fundamentally ambiguous, perhaps its greatest strength. No meaning is carried inherently, and even if the form of the ritual performance is relatively rigid, the content of the meaning can undergo significant transformation: in short they are malleable, and allow those who are using or observing them to supply part of their meaning. Thus their employment in ritual commemorative performance is effective in fostering a sense of solidarity even when consensus is lacking. Any dissonance may be more readily corralled and controlled when widely accepted symbolic screens are used as ring fences. The obfuscation of potentially damaging political actions by the careful use of unifying symbols is a powerful tool.[5]

Of course, some of the most potent symbols in areas of political conflict, around whom the most emotive rituals may be performed, are victims, war heroes, and the martyred dead. One view is that commemorative activity relating to the dead and their perceived sacrifice, acts as a contributory factor to the intractability of conflict, hardening public antipathy towards the enemy, and urging followers to avoid cheapening martyrdom by engaging in compromise or sell out (Bar-Tal, 89-92). But a countervailing view exists, in which commemorative performance has a transformative utility. The anthropologist Katherine Verdery has written of the political use of the exhumation and re-burial of national heroes and war casualties in post socialist Eastern Europe. In her interpretation, the dead, as political symbols, are 'effective in moments of system transformation' (125) their great advantage as symbols derives from one salient fact:

> they don't talk much on their own ... Words can be put into their mouths – often quite ambiguous words – or their own words can be ambiguated by quoting them out of context. It is thus easier to rewrite history with dead people than with other kinds of symbol which are speechless.

They thus provide an 'excellent means for accumulating something essential to political transformation: symbolic capital' (29: 33).

---

[5] Ibid., pp.14-15, 53: see also (RP, 69-71).

Performing Provisionalism: Two Case Studies of Provisional Republican Commemorative Performance[6]

Until That Certain Day: The Commemoration of Tom Williams

Tom Williams was a young member of the IRA, who was hanged for his part in the killing of a member of the Royal Ulster Constabulary at Easter 1942. Although all six members of his captured IRA unit were initially sentenced to death, Williams, as leader, took sole responsibility and was executed in September 1942, his body being interred in an unmarked grave in Crumlin Road Gaol. For almost six decades, Republicans had campaigned to have his remains exhumed and re-interred in the Republican Plot in Milltown cemetery in west Belfast, as per Williams's wishes. On 19 January 2000, Williams's remains were finally laid to rest in Milltown, but at the family's insistence he was buried in a private ceremony, in the family grave, and not in the politically sacral Republican plot. The funeral was a moving and well attended affair, as thousands followed or watched the cortege pass on its journey from the funeral mass to the cemetery. Many Provisional Republicans were in attendance, and participated in funereal rites, but this was not their main day for commemorating the death of Williams, a notable Republican martyr. The family, after all, had preferred his grave to be with his real, as opposed to fictive, Republican kin. The following Sunday, 23rd of January was scheduled for an organized parade and commemoration of Williams, as organized by the Belfast National Graves Association, a group headed by figures associated with Provisional Republicanism such as Joe Cahill (a former comrade of Williams) and Liam Shannon.

The commemorative parade and display was well organized and attended – the number of spectators was variously estimated at 50,000 by Republican paper *An Phoblacht/Republican News*, and over 10,000 by the unionist leaning *Belfast Newsletter*. [7] The commemorative performance began with a wreath laying ceremony at the site of Williams's family home in Bombay Street: a colour party dressed in uniform black leather jackets and black berets and carrying national and provincial flags of Ireland, and Republican

---

[6] Information on the case studies is derived from participant observation, video recordings and newspaper reports of the time.

[7] '50,000 Honour Williams', *An Phoblacht/Republican News*, 27 January 2000: 'Campbell attack on marching Ministers', *Belfast News Letter*, 24 January 2000.

banners, laid floral tributes and dipped flags, as a piper played a lament. The colour party is clearly designed to represent the military aspect of Republican struggle, and its parade orders are given in Irish, and performed in a semblance of military step. This perhaps, reflects not only William's own role as an IRA volunteer, but also the site of the ceremony in Bombay Street. This street is especially 'sacred' to Provisional Republicans, being the site of the initial anti-Catholic pogrom of 1969 which directly fed into the founding of the Provisional IRA. This street, in many ways, is the figurative origin point of Provisionalism, and underlining Williams's links to the locality by way of public performance, is an impressive way of stressing modern Republicanism's continuity with the martyrs of the past. This ceremony is however, merely a precursor. The main parade forms at Clonard Street on the Falls Road, in preparation for the march to Milltown. The colour party is swollen by between 30 and 40 Republicans, male and female, and many in their teens, who form up in ranks of 3, led by pipers. It is common practice for Provisionals to involve, or showcase, younger Republicans at these events, presumably to represent the re-generation of the cause and its connection with all sections of its constituency: these youths wear black berets, black jackets and Irish tricolour armbands, again in emulation of military dress. Sinn Féin political figures follow behind, and following them in the parade are women Republicans, bearing wreaths and the commemorative military symbols of black beret, black gloves, and folded Irish tricolour, representing Williams's IRA activity.

In Republican commemorative parades there is often an informal air, and the line between spectators and participants is often permeable. Thousands of spectators, of all ages, fall in behind the main body of the parade, and are organized into three ranks by the many stewards: this participation in the ritual performance creates and projects a strong sense of solidarity and communal affiliation, underscoring claims of legitimacy. As Jarman has noted, Republican commemorative parades often follow this 'funereal' processional style, whilst Loyalists favour a more militarized and formal model with a sharper definition between spectator and participant (198).[8] But Republicans also include a strongly militarized component as evidenced by their colour parties and use of Republican marching

---

[8] Neil Jarman, 'Commemorating 1916 Celebrating Difference: Parading and Painting in Belfast' in *The Art of Forgetting*, eds Adrian Forty and Susan Kuchler (Oxford: Berg, 1997): 198.

bands. In Williams's commemoration, one Republican band displayed a highly ritualized military performance: their march was formal and as one white gloved hand and arm swung boldly, the other was held rigidly behind the back. The march was silent, the drum was shrouded in black cloth.

The parade terminated at the County Antrim Republican memorial in Milltown, but the political theatre continued. The artefacts of performance, the wreaths, beret, tricolour and gloves were laid on the grave: a bugler sounded the last post as the colour party dipped their flags, only to raise them again as he played reveille, a performative representation of the cycle of death and rebirth. Speeches were made by Joe Cahill and Gerry Adams in which certain key messages and tropes were declaimed: the need for the Republican community to re-dedicate itself to the struggle for Irish unity and independence, the importance of heroic figures as role models for Republican behaviour, and the need to counter the demonization of Republicans by stressing the legitimacy of their struggle and the equivalence of their grief. For Adams, the attempt to ignore or vilify Republican loss and suffering in the recent conflict was simply a 'part of British counter-insurgency strategy', and the political content of the commemoration is in large part the public performance of the perceived historical continuity of Republican struggle and its legitimacy. Williams, a tragic figure with an emotional appeal amplified by his youth and the drawn out drama of his death, serves as a powerful condensation symbol around which the faithful can rally at a time of political transformation. As a martyr he can no longer speak for himself, but he can be used as a symbol by the living. In the oration Williams's name is linked to that of Provisional Republican martyrs of the 1981 Hunger Strike, and all are set in the continuum of sacrifice stretching from 1916 to the modern generation. The message by word and deed is that the modern Provisional movement remains the legitimate, dominant expression of Republicanism, fully secure in its lineage, never forgetting where it has come from.

Williams was a representative of the military face of Republicanism, at a time when Republicanism was a marginalized force. But in the performance and display of his commemoration, and the invocation of his name, he becomes a useful symbol as the movement grows and the peace process develops, shattering any prospect of marginalization and tipping the centre of gravity within Provisionalism forever towards the political and away from the military. Reverence to an iconic figure is used to show adherence to traditional Republican values whilst the sentiments declaimed at his commemoration are that the struggle has 'moved on'. The language of military opposition to Britain, more familiar to Williams, is long replaced in an oration peppered with phrases such as 'new dispensation', 'conflict resolution' and 'healing processes' (*An Phoblacht* 27/1/2000). The performed memory of violence and sacrifice underwrites a transformed politics.

The 25th Hunger Strike Anniversary Commemoration

The commemorations of the 25th anniversary of the 1981 hunger strike, a prison protest in which 10 Republican prisoners fasted to death, were organized by the National Hunger Strike Commemoration Committee, a grouping composed largely of figures associated with the dominant Provisional strand of Republicanism. The Committee organized a large parade and rally at Casement Park in West Belfast, on 13 August 2006, marking the high point of the island wide Republican commemorations.[9] Crucially, the 25th Anniversary fell in the same year as the 90th Anniversary of the Easter Rising: the spirit of the Easter Rising was invoked and attached to the modern phase of Republicanism in a most fundamental manner. The guardianship of national identity was to be passed baton-like in a relay from the well recognized heroes of 1916, the founding fathers of the Irish state, to the Provisional martyrs of the most recent conflict. Jim McVeigh of the National Hunger Strike Commemoration Committee claimed that the Hunger Strikers were essentially a modern incarnation of the Easter pantheon, and the committee would be 'drawing clear parallels between the two events' (*An Phoblacht* 9/3/2006).

The commemorative parade and rally numbered many thousands and followed normal Provisional commemorative practice in terms of colour parties, bands, spectator participation and involvement of youth. What was also evident was an increased use of spectacle, costume and theatricality. Dozens of activists marched in formation dressed as blanket men and women, giving clenched fist salutes, evoking the protesting Republican prisoners who refused to wear

---

[9] For the range and number of commemorative events running from February to October 2006, see *Cuimhníonn Glúin – 25th Anniversary Commemorative Programme of Events* (Belfast: National Hunger Strike Commemoration Committee, 2006).

prison uniform. Others dressed as eighteenth century United Irishmen, carrying facsimile pikes, in an assertion of the historic continuity of Republican struggle. Colour was also supplied by the many visiting cumainn (party branches) of Sinn Féin. They carried large colourful banners, graphically linking the political and military sides of Republicanism: portraits of fallen Provisional volunteers feature heavily on the banners, as do images of armed, masked and uniformed IRA men, often pictured in action in a figurative rural landscape, replete with Celtic and Republican symbolism. The banners serve as mnemonic stage props, reminding spectators of the roots of Republican activity: whiffs of cordite that trigger memories of continuity with past struggles, even as Sinn Féin strides away from militant struggle. This commemorative display of 'violence' is repackaged as a comforting glance backwards, rather than a propagandistic support for armed struggle. A series of street theatre enactments and tableaux dotted the route of the parade, each depicting events from the Hunger Strike period familiar to members of the Republican community, in a variety of moods and tones. In one tableau, the aftermath of a security force raid is depicted: on one side of the makeshift stage a woman, clad only in dressing gown, sits in her parlour weeping, while on the other side of the stage two police detectives barrack her husband in an interrogation room. On another platform, the criminal justice system, represented by 'Lord Diplock' is satirized. 'Diplock', an actor outfitted with an outsize Judge's wig, gloves, and gavel, loudly parrots abuse at the spectators informing them that their struggle is 'an abomination' and that the current parade is an 'illegal assembly'. Wire puppet strings snake upwards from his arms.

Thousands attended the concluding rally in Casement Park which was equipped with a professional PA system, video screen and proper stage: Republican ex-prisoners marched in, and to much handclapping and cheering, formed a military style column in the middle of the field. Eulogies for the Hunger Strikers were made, songs were sung from the stage and spectators spontaneously joined in and applauded. The keynote speech was made by Sinn Féin President Gerry Adams, and it was a speech which succinctly drew together the themes of Republican continuity and transformation. A knowing nod of appreciation was given to the Provisional IRA, which Adams modishly referred to as the 'wind that shook the barley' and he reminded the spectators that the IRA remained threaded through the Republican constituency: they were 'the people sitting close to you'. But militarism was absent from the tone of the speech. Quotes from Bobby Sands were used to underline the need for 'strategic compromises' in the future: strategic thinking and political movement being recurrent themes of the speech. The Hunger Strikers became paragons of political analysis, strategic manoeuvring, the need for unity and 'magnanimity', and were thus beacons for the transformation of Republican politics, whilst simultaneously their sacrifice echoed the martyrdom of others in the historic Republican pantheon. History thus served as a prop to future re-orientation. The memory of Sands, and other fallen Republicans, was directly invoked and imagined by Adams, as attendant, omnipresent spirits guiding Sinn Féin's hand in negotiations, and even in Downing Street, 'keeping us [Sinn Féin] right'. As malleable, potent, but voiceless symbols, the Republican dead can serve to buttress Republican transformation and compromise.

Memorial Sites: Actors or Backdrops?

The performance of commemorative rituals and the process of memorialization by means of monuments and statues both arise from the same social need for collective groups to express their shared identity and to reinforce their present values and assumptions through their representation of the past. However, they are often seen as parallel and independent manifestations of it, differing in form and somewhat in nature.

Rituals are actions to be carried out and they fulfil their very essence by conjuring up and releasing movement, be it the actual physical marching of the participants in a parade or the emotional involvement stirred in the hearts of the audience at a burial speech. Rituals are living, and they partake of memory's fluidity and flexibility; giving the impression of an immutability of form to meet the demand of tradition, they constantly reshape themselves in meaning, adapting to the varying circumstances in which they are performed. Being paradoxically 'at once unchanging and yet ever changeable' (Jarman, 10), they defeat time through their reenactment over and over again.

Memorials, on the contrary, share rigidity with the dead they commemorate and definitiveness with death itself. Carved in stone, once erected in a particular defined place, they are left in their fixity and durability as permanent reifications of a society's collective memory at a precise moment in time. Most importantly, they function as temporal markers, drawing a line between past and present and defining by their very existence, respectively, what can be commemorated and what can be experienced or performed.

Thus, the relation between rituals and memorials might seem one between two differing and interchangeable ways of commemorating: on the one hand, an active, vibrant, participatory performance that actualizes memory: on the other hand, a manifestation of memory that freezes it in a static and passive illusion of eternity. However, we believe that rituals and memorials are better interpreted in their coexistence, their relation defined not as dichotomous, but as mutual and inter-reliant. Although often in the past ignored by cultural geographers and anthropologists, the nature of this relation is worth considering in order to investigate how both forms of memorialization are enabled and at the same time constrained by their interdependency.

At a primary level, this relation can be understood as one of form and content: the morphology of the territory delineates the spatial limits of human action, whilst the latter entrusts 'meaning' onto its geographical location. On the one hand, the physical configuration of the memorial site demarcates both the spatial boundaries and the agencies of the ritual action. By enclosing a certain area within fences or boundary walls, thus singling it out as the appropriate and publicly recognized locus for the unfolding of the ceremonial performance, memorials function as theatrical stages towards which everybody's gaze is directed and onto which everyone's physical and emotional activity concentrates. Moreover, they define who is allowed inside and who is left outside, who is the actor and who the spectator of the ritual action. As Jay Winter observes in relation to First War World memorials, 'in many ... there is a fence, doorway, or border clearly marking the distinction between an area adjacent to the monument ... [This] border described the space set aside for mourners, either family members, veterans, or officials, speaking for the community, who were present during annual commemorative ceremonies' (Winter, 96).

On the other hand, on these special occasions the spotlights are turned on the otherwise 'unlit' memorials and they 'acquire with meanings through the rituals and ceremonies performed in their space' (89). In daily routine, if we exclude sporadic tourists on black-taxi tours, memorial sites are deserted and almost overlooked by passers-by; however, they become protagonists of the estate's life every time they are used as sites for commemorations, and the cold still stone is revived and restored to importance by the ceremonial movement that takes place around it. Thus, at a primary level, memorial sites seem to simply function as theatrical backdrops for the ritual performance, defining its spatial boundaries and agencies. In return, the ceremonial action shares with them the limelight, 'turning them on' with meaning.

Following a recent trend in the social sciences that moves away from considering the mere '"localization" and "topography"'...of remembrance in monuments and historic sites',[10] memorial space is now understood and investigated as 'a medium rather than a container for action, something that is involved in action and cannot be divorced from it' (Tilley, 10). Far from functioning exclusively as a backdrop, it is 'not just a spatial parameter, and physical environment, in which interaction occurs', but 'it is these elements mobilized as part of the interaction' (19). Memorial sites, therefore, become 'locales', 'places created and known through common experiences, symbols and meanings' (18). If collective groups express and reinforce through memorialization their political ideologies and social identities, memorials play an important role in reifying and symbolizing these feelings. They not only define the spatial boundaries of the ritual action through which these sentiments are conveyed, but they *actively* contribute to their expression and reinforcement.

An analysis of the physical configuration of Republican memorial sites in Northern Ireland illustrates how this originates from a structural level. In Milltown Cemetery in Belfast, for example, out of the numerous communal plots erected by different groups within the Republican movement, two in particular might best illustrate how memorials underpin political beliefs: the IRA County Antrim Roll of Honour memorial and the Provisional IRA communal plot. The IRA County Antrim Roll of Honour[11] consists of a limestone monument built in a cruciform shape rising from a black base in the form of a cross. Circularly along the cross's arms are enlisted all IRA Volunteers from County Antrim who died from 1797 to the present.

---

[10] Michael Mayerfeld Bell, 'The Ghosts of Place,' *Theory and Society* 26, 6 (1997): 814.

[11] See 'Milltown Cemetery – IRA County Antrim Roll of Honour' (West Belfast, memorials) in Elisabetta Viggiani, 'Public Forms of Memorialization to the Victims of the Northern Irish "Troubles" in the City of Belfast,' <http://cain.ulst.ac.uk/viggiani/west_memorial.html#136>.

In all probability, names were originally inscribed in chronological order, but new clusters have been subsequently added where empty spaces were left, thus creating a swirling web of letters and numbers, a hypnotizing sequence where names and years chase each other, finally coalescing in an undifferentiated panoply of death.

Against a counter-productive hypothetical 're-ordering', the IRA County Antrim monument thus mirrors and reinforces at a material level, by means of its physical structure, the political capital gained by Republicans in their use of the past. By remembering through the same memorial 'martyrs' of different eras in an unbroken line of resistance to the British state until the present day, the contemporary Republican movement claims and reaffirms its legitimacy as the direct and only inheritor of this glorious tradition of struggle that dates back to the 1798 United Irishmen Rebellion.

A similar device to stress continuity with the past as a warrant of legitimacy is employed in the case of the Provisional IRA communal plot.[12] The plot's interesting and somewhat unusual design presents two distinct enclosed blocks of light brown stone, merging one into the other. The central monument features a black granite plaque inscribed with the 1916 Proclamation of Independence and it is shaped as a semi-circle that overlooks the entire site from the back. Its boundary wall is built as an ascending triangle and an Irish tricolour stands at its highest vertex. It is preceded by a second lower structure: a long corridor converging into the central semi-circle on either side of which are entombed deceased members of the Provisional Irish Republican Army and Provisional Sinn Féin.

The visitor is invited to enter the corridor and walk to the central monument. Thus, he or she is accompanied on this journey towards the 'cause' by all the heroes who in different times have sacrificed their lives in the struggle for Irish freedom. Whilst their names are listed singly, thus acknowledging the importance of each individual death, their 'joint' entombment in a series of identical shared graves merges them into an undifferentiated group united by the commonality of their shared cause. An independent Ireland receives and embraces its dead, as the image of Erin holding in her arms – Pietà-like – the body of a dying volunteer found on many other Repub-

---

[12] See 'Milltown Cemetery – PIRA Communal Plot' (West Belfast, memorials) in ibid.
<http://cain.ulst.ac.uk/viggiani/west_memorial.html#133>.

lican memorials illustrates.[13] Its key importance in Republican ideology is reinforced by placing its tangible outcome – the 1916 Proclamation – at the centre of the monument, poignantly adorned by the presence of an Irish tricolour.

Similarly to the case of the IRA County Antrim memorial, the underlying assumption is that the legacy of resistance and valour that has been sown during the years is reaped by the contemporary movement that, despite major shifts in strategy of action, is still devoted to pursuing the same goal as its illustrious ancestors. Commemorating fallen volunteers of different eras is a common feature of Republican forms of memorialization, as witnessed by a vast number of monuments where the deceased from the local communities are remembered together with the hunger strikers, the 1798 and 1916 rebels, and the deceased who participated in the IRA pre-1970s campaigns, thus emphasizing a temporal continuum of 'subjection ... struggle [and] heroic defeat' (McBride, 15). The Republican 'mode of memory', therefore, can be described as an accretive one, where 'the episodic history of republicanism, focused on successive waves of insurgency, has generated a more innovative pattern of commemoration as each generation of icons has subsumed its predecessors' (26).

Evoking iconic figures from different eras in a single place creates what Mikhail Bakhtin has termed a 'chronotope', a unique fusion of time and space where 'time, as it were, thickens, takes on flesh, becomes artistically visible: likewise, space becomes charged and responsive to the movements of time, plot and history' (Bakhtin, 84). Ben-Amos pointed out with regard to the French Third Republic's state funerals, 'the chronotope of these ceremonies brought together the national past, embedded in the sacred monuments, the individual past of the deceased, and the republican present', all concentrated in a single geographical site (48). The same could be said of the reburial of Tom Williams. By fusing landscape with 'sacred history', memorial sites make the latter 'visible and therefore tangible', 'they conflate history and geography and weave historical memory into the spatial configuration of nationhood' (Azaryahu and Kellerman, 111).

In summary, as the case of Republican memorials clearly shows, commemorative sites provide not only an appropriate and publicly

---

[13] See for example fountain in 'PIRA, A Company, 2nd Battalion, Belfast Brigade' (West Belfast, memorials) in ibid.
<http://cain.ulst.ac.uk/viggiani/west_memorial.html#160>.

recognized locus for the unfolding of the ritual action, but most importantly partake of and reinforce the cultural values and socio-political beliefs that are asserted through it. They 'are not merely the material backdrop from which a story is told, but the spaces themselves constitute the meaning by becoming both a physical location and a sight-line of interpretation' (Johnston, 293).

Memorial Sites as Extra-Ordinary Places

According to Shils, every society is governed by a central zone of values and belief, drawing on which the ruling authorities affirm and maintain their political power. Whilst he postulates that this centre 'has ... nothing to do with geometry and little with geography' (3), being exclusively of a metaphorical/ideological nature, Geertz rightly goes further in affirming that this centre should be understood as well in a literal sense, translated onto the spatial dimension (28-9). Reification and localization of primary constituents of social identity, this centre necessarily holds symbolic importance and partakes of what Émile Durkheim has termed the 'sacred', that toward which men feel respect, thus becoming 'sacred space'.

According to the definition given in Eliade's *Encyclopedia of Religion*, a sacred space is 'a defined place, a space distinguished from other spaces. The rituals that a people either practise at a place or direct toward it mark its sacredness and differentiate it from other defined spaces' (Brereton, 526). At sacred spaces, 'the sacred values of the community are brought into focus and become tangible through a set of symbols and rituals and ... the communication of society with these sacred values occurs' (29).

As seen above, memorial sites are usually demarcated by fences and boundary walls: thus, a portion of space is singled out and its 'difference' from the surrounding area stressed. They fulfill their function and acquire meaning through the ritual action that is performed around them. Moreover, at these locations collective groups both express their 'attitudes and values ... toward those persons and deeds that are memorialized' (Barber, 65) and reinforce their *present* cultural, social and political attitudes and values through what they choose to remember and what to forget. Therefore, memorial sites can be properly deemed 'sacred spaces' in modern society. Considering this assertion, it is worth investigating how Republican memorials possess both distinctive attributes of sacred spaces: spatial centrality and extraordinariness.

A careful look at the landscape of commemoration in the city of Belfast shows how memorial sites all stand in a similar spatial relation to the communities to which they pertain: with less than ten memorials built along arterial routes, the majority of them are enclosed within the estates in side-streets far off the main commercial roads, symbolic hearts of the community hidden from strangers' sight and protected from external attacks. This inherent centrality, moreover, is reaffirmed in ritual performances. Ben-Amos has noted with reference to royal processions in the French Third Republic that 'these mobile phenomena always related to an immobile centre from which they departed and to which they returned' (29) and that this centre was symbolically brought into play for the consolidation of political power.

Similarly, Republican commemorative marches and ceremonies in contemporary Northern Ireland pivot around permanent forms of memorialization: they either depart from or travel to pre-existent memorial sites or culminate in the unveiling of new ones: moreover, these locations act as public platforms for delivering ideological speeches and orations on pressing political issues. As for their extra-ordinariness, we have already illustrated how the structural con-figuration of memorial sites helps to differentiate a portion of space from the surrounding area, separating it from the functional settings of everyday human activities and singling out its 'special status'. However, it is the decorative element that above all provides 'a theatrical quality that [transforms] familiar spaces into an extra-ordinary environment, distinguishing them from the other parts of the city' (40).

Republican commemorations, like many other examples of street theatre around the world, make extensive use of both temporary and permanent decorative elements. Whilst they all contribute to reinforce the visual resonance of the event, their specific functions differ, depending on their location and durability. Amongst temporary decorations, those erected along the route of marches and processions – such as Irish tricolours, green-white-and-orange pennants and banners on lampposts[14] – act primarily as stage scenery, both framing the itinerary along which the ritual performance will take place and embellishing it.

---

[14] For example, plastic banners portraying the 1981 hunger strikers could be seen in many Catholic areas throughout summer 2006, during the numerous marches that marked the 25th anniversary of the strike.

At memorial sites, instead, colourful flags replace habitually empty flag poles and flowers and candles adorn the surrounding area: by changing the original form and view of the monuments, these decorative elements 'activate' the extraordinary function of these locations, indicating that it is time to interpret and use the memorial site as sacred space. Sombre exteriors are thus animated and adorned to highlight the difference with the other non-sacred parts of the city. Whilst the stage is cleared and all backdrop cardboards and fabrics dismantled when the curtains are drawn at the end of a play, these temporary ornaments are instead left to decay after the ritual performance has taken place until the last shred or petal is carried away by the wind. On the other hand, permanent decorative elements are granted a more enduring and significant position since they provide protagonists and spectators with a supplementary repertoire of symbols which augment the projected narratives of victimhood and resistance.

A survey of the symbols engraved on memorial stones and plaques shows how they are persistently drawn from the traditional imagery of Irish Republicanism's history: the golden harp, emblem of the 1798 United Irishmen rebellion; the phoenix rising from the ashes, originally used by the Irish Republican Brotherhood (the Fenians) in the 1860s; the Starry Plough, symbol of the Irish Citizen Army; the Easter Lily, worn to this day in remembrance of the 1916 Easter Rising; the orange sunburst, repeatedly used from the 1870s and now official emblem of the Fianna Éireann; the four shields of the pre-partition provinces of Ireland; the lark in barbed wire, evoking Bobby Sands and the hunger strikers (236-9). Collating symbols linked to different seminal events of Republican history at the same memorial site – often carved on adjacent plaques – is another recurrent device that concurs, together with the structural configuration of the monuments and the narratives conveyed through the ritual performance, to stress continuity with the past as a warrant of legitimacy.

In conclusion, memorial sites can be rightly considered 'sacred spaces' in modern society, presenting both distinctive features of spatial centrality and extraordinariness. Spatial centrality is intrinsic in their location at the heart of community estates and it is reinforced every time that they are used as departure or arrival points for commemorative marches and ceremonies. As for their extra-ordinariness, although primarily achieved by means of the enclosed nature of their physical configuration, it is enhanced by a vast use of symbolic elements, carrying out differing functions depending on their nature and durability, most importantly the expression and reinforcement of projected political and ideological narratives.

Conclusion

Republican commemorative practice has served as a strategy of mediating political messages to its wider constituency in the period after the signing of the Belfast Agreement of 1998. The Republican culture of commemoration represents something more than mourning or the recognition of loss: it can be seen essentially as the representation of a living continuity with the past and the expression of historical legitimacy, linking new forms of political engagement with older forms of violent resistance. In a post conflict setting which has seen swingeing ideological compromises by Provisional Republicanism ranging from disarmament to the acceptance of state institutions, and a shifting of the strategic locus away from the use of military violence, the political performance of commemoration serves as a valuable strategy in reassuring base support and providing insulation from criticism: a strategy which also serves to facilitate the rededication and reinvigoration of the political project and maintains the cohesion of identity within the wider Republican constituency. This performance of politics allows the projection of crucial narratives and symbols of victimhood and resistance via the means of participatory parades, rallies and street theatre: memorial sites play an important role in providing an appropriate locus for the unfolding of this political drama. 'Sacred spaces' for modern society, they do not function exclusively as a backdrop for the ceremonial action, but also reinforce, by means of their physical configuration and the use of a vast repertoire of decorative elements and symbols, the cultural values and political beliefs expressed through that commemorative performance.

Bibliography

'50,000 Honour Williams' *An Phoblacht/Republican News*, 27 January 2000.

Anderson, Benedict, *Imagined Communities. Reflections on the Origin and Spread of Nationalism* (London: Verso, 1983).

Antrim's Patriot Dead. 1797-1953 (Belfast: Belfast National Graves Association, n.d.).

Appadurai, Arjun, 'The Grounds of the Nation-State – Identity, Violence and Territory', in Goldmann, Kjell, Ulf Hannerz, & Charles Westin, *Nationalism and Internationalism in the Post-Cold War Era* (London: Routledge, 2000).

Ashplant, Timothy G., Dawson, Graham & Roper, Michael, *The Politics of War Memory and Commemoration* (London: Routledge, 2000).

Azaryahu, Maoz & Kellerman, Aharon, 'Symbolic Places of National History and Revival: A Study in Zionist Mythical Geography', *Transactions of the Institute of British Geographers* 24,1 (1999): 109-123.

Bakhtin, Mikhail, 'Forms of Time of the Chronotope in the Novel', in Holquist, Michael, *The Dialogic Imagination: Four Essays* (Austin: University of Texas Press, 1981).

Barber, Bernard, 'Place, Symbol, and Utilitarian Function in War Memorials', *Social Forces* 28,1 (1949): 64-68.

Bell, Michael Mayerfeld, 'The Ghosts of Place', *Theory and Society* 26,6 (1997): 813-836.

Ben-Amos, Avner, 'The Sacred Centre of Power: Paris and Republican State Funerals', *Journal of Interdisciplinary History* 22,1 (1991): 27-48.

Brereton, Joel P., 'Sacred Space', in Eliade, Mircea, *The Encyclopaedia of Religion. Vol. 12* (London: Macmillan, 1987): 526-535.

Cairns, Ed & Roe, Mícheál D., *The Role of Memory in Ethnic Conflict* (Basingstoke: Palgrave, 2002). Reprinted (Basingstoke: Palgrave Macmillan, 2003).

'Campbell Attack on Marching Ministers' *Belfast News Letter*, 24 January 2000.

Cohen, Anthony P., *The Symbolic Construction of Community* (Chichester: Ellis Horwood, 1985). Reprinted (London: Routledge, 1992).

Coogan, Tim Pat, *The I.R.A.* (Oxford: Pall Mall, 1970). Reprinted (London: Harper Collins, 1993).

Cuimhníonn Glúin. 25th Anniversary Commemorative Programme of Events (Belfast: National Hunger Strike Commemoration Committee, 2006).

Durkheim, Émile, *The Elementary Forms of the Religious Life* (London: George Allen & Unwin, 1915). Reprinted (New York: Free Press, 1995).

Geertz, Clifford, Local Knowledge: Further Essays in Interpretive Anthropology (London: Fontana, 1983).

'The Hunger Strikers – This Generation's 1916' *An Phoblacht/Republican News*, 9 March 2006.

Huntington, Richard & Metcalf, Peter, *Celebrations of Death: The Anthropology of Mortuary Ritual* (Cambridge: Cambridge University Press, 1979).

Jarman, Neil, *Material Conflicts. Parades and Visual Displays in Northern Ireland* (Oxford: Berg, 1997).

Jarman, Neil, 'Commemorating 1916 Celebrating Difference: Parading and Painting in Belfast', in Forty, Adrian & Küchler, Susanne, *The Art of Forgetting* (Oxford: Berg, 1999).

Johnson, Nuala C., 'Sculpting Heroic Histories: Celebrating the Centenary of the 1798 Rebellion in Ireland', *Transactions of the Institute of British Geographers* 19,1 (1994): 78-93.

---, 'Cast in Stone: Monuments, Geography, and Nationalism', *Environment and Planning D* 13 (1995): 51-65.

---, 'Mapping Monuments: The Shaping of Public Space and Cultural Identities', *Visual Communication* 1,3 (2002): 293-298.

Kertzer, David I., *Ritual, Politics, and Power* (New Haven: Yale University Press, 1988).

Leonard, Jane, *Memorials to the Casualties of Conflict. Northern Ireland 1969 to 1997* (Belfast: Northern Ireland Community Relations Council, 1997).

Low, Setha M. & Lawrence-Zúñiga, Denise, *The Anthropology of Space and Place. Locating Culture* (Malden: Blackwell, 2003).

Mayo, James M., 'War Memorials as Political Memory', *Geographical Review* 78,1 (1988): 62-75.

McBride, Ian, *History and Memory in Modern Ireland* (Cambridge: Cambridge University Press, 2001).

McGuinness, Martin, 'Introduction', in *Unforgotten Sacrifice. A Tribute to Fallen Comrades* (Belfast: Twinbrook and Poleglass Commemoration Committee, 1999).

McKittrick, David, Kelters, Seamus, Feeney, Brian, Thornton, Chris & McVea, David, *Lost Lives. The Stories of the Men, Women and Children who Died as a Result of the Northern Ireland Troubles* (Edinburgh: Mainstream Publishing, 1999). Reprinted (Edinburgh: Mainstream Publishing, 2004).

Metress, Seamus & Metress, Eileen, *The Communal Significance of the Irish Republican Army Funeral Ritual* (Unpublished Paper, 1993). Linenhall Library, Belfast.

Mosse, George L., *Fallen Soldiers. Reshaping the Memory of the World Wars* (New York: Oxford University Press, 1990).

O'Brien, Brendan, *The Long War: The IRA and Sinn Féin* (Dublin: O'Brien Press, 1993). Reprinted (Dublin: O'Brien Press, 1999).

O'Doherty, Malachi, *The Trouble with Guns. Republican Strategy and the Provisional IRA* (Belfast: Blackstaff Press, 1998).

Picard, Robert G., 'How Violence is Justified: Sinn Féin's An Phoblacht', *Journal of Communication* 41, 4 (Autumn 1991): 92-103.

Shils, Edward A., *Center and Periphery: Essays in Macrosociology* (London: University of Chicago Press, 1975).

Tilley, Christopher, *A Phenomenology of Landscape: Places, Paths and Monuments* (Oxford: Berg, 1994).

Tírghrá Committee, *Tírghrá. Ireland's Patriot Dead* (Dublin: Tírghrá Committee, 2002).

Verdery, Katherine, *The Political Lives of Dead Bodies: Reburial and Post Socialist Change* (New York: Columbia University Press, 1999).

Viggiani, Elisabetta, 'Public Forms of Memorialization to the Victims of the Northern Irish "Troubles" in the City of Belfast', *CAIN* (November 2006). Accessed (January 2006): <http://cain.ulst.ac.uk/viggiani/index.html>.

Winter, Jay M., *Sites of Memory, Sites of Mourning: The Great War in European Cultural History* (Cambridge: Cambridge University Press, 1995).

Notes on Contributors

Kris Brown is a Post Doctoral Fellow at the Transitional Justice Institute, University of Ulster. His research interests focus on commemoration, memory and memorialization in post conflict Northern Ireland, especially themes relating to victimhood, the nature of the conflict, relations with the state, the use of political symbols, and national identities. Internationally comparative approaches deepen aspects of this work. Other research interests include political developments within Ulster Loyalism, modern Irish Republicanism, and arms decommissioning.

Paul Devlin is a lecturer in Drama at the University of Ulster's School of Creative Arts. His research interests include: Irish theatre, with an emphasis on theatre produced in the north of Ireland, workers' theatre movements, political theatre, theatrical efficacy, and theories of popular culture. His doctoral research was on working-class theatre in Ulster.

Danine Farquharson is Associate Professor of Irish Literature at Memorial University, St. John's, Newfoundland. She has published on contemporary Irish fiction and film in the *Canadian Journal of Irish Studies* and *New Hibernia Review* and has contributed to and co-edited *Shadows of the Gunmen: Culture and Violence in Modern Ireland* (Cork U.P.).

Lisa Fitzpatrick received her PhD from the University of Toronto, where her research was on the emergence of a postnationalist aesthetic in contemporary Irish theatre. Her research interests are in contemporary performance in Ireland, the performance of rape, and women's writing for theatre. She lectures in Drama at the School of Creative Arts at the University of Ulster.

David Grant has enjoyed a varied career in theatre throughout Ireland as director, critic and teacher. He has been Managing Editor of *Theatre Ireland* magazine, Programme Director of the Dublin Theatre Festival, and Artistic Director of the Lyric Theatre, Belfast. He is currently Head of Drama Studies at Queen's University, Belfast, where his main research focus is in Applied Drama.

Kyna Hamill is a Lecturer in the Core Curriculum Humanities programme at Boston University. She received her PhD in Theatre History from Tufts University. Her research areas include violence as entertainment, the early Italian Commedia dell'arte and inter-sections of comedy and violence. She is the editor of *They Fight: Classical to Contemporary Stage Fight Scenes* (Smith & Kraus, 2003).

Jonathan Harden lectures in Drama at Queen's University Belfast.

Tom Maguire is a Senior Lecturer in Drama at the University of Ulster. He teaches in the areas of contemporary British and Irish drama, applied theatre, theatre practice and storytelling. He has published and presented conference papers internationally on British and Irish theatre, including in the journals *Kunapipi, Modern Drama, Performance Research, Postcolonial Text* and *Theatre Research International*. His monograph *Making Theatre in Northern Ireland Through and Beyond the Troubles* was published by University of Exeter Press in 2006. He is Chair of SCUDD, the UK subject association for Drama and a member of the Advisory Board for PALATINE, the Higher Education Academy's subject centre for Dance, Drama and Music. He is Chair of Big Telly Theatre Company.

Holly Maples is a Lecturer in Drama at the University of East Anglia. She is also a professional actress and director and, most recently, directed projects for the Festival of World Cultures in Dublin and the Actor's Company Theatre Royal in the United Kingdom. She has also worked as a facilitator with community groups and asylum seekers in Ireland and throughout the world. She trained as an actress at the Central School of Speech and Drama in London, and has her Ph.D. in Drama from Trinity College Dublin. Her publications include contributions in *The Encyclopedia of Modern Drama* (Columbia University Press), *Memory and Ireland* (Syracuse University Press), *Performing at the Crossroads: Critical Essays on Performance Studies and Irish Culture* (Palgrave

Macmillan), and *Redefinitions of Irish Identity in the Twenty-First Century: A Postnationalist Approach* (Peter Lang).

Tim Miles is writing a PhD on the work of Gary Mitchell at Royal Holloway, University of London. His essay 'Understanding Loyalty: The English Response to the Plays of Gary Mitchell' is published in *Irish Theatre in England* (edited by Ben Levitas and Richard Cave, Dublin: Carysfort Press, 2008). He has lectured at Royal Holloway and Manchester Metropolitan University.

Paul Moore is head of The School of Creative Arts at the University of Ulster's Magee campus, in Derry. His main research areas are sound art, the digital arts and, in particular, the relationship between sonic experience and identity. He is a member of the UK Soundscape Assocation and the Sonic Arts Network. Most recently his research work has become more exhibition-based, and recent examples include *Landscope*, a collaborative installation with Jem Finer, and *Remembering the Gaumont*, a sound exhibition at Lancaster Gallery in Coventry. He is an Honorary Research Fellow at Coventry University and a visiting professor at City/Varsity University in Capetown.

Cormac Newark has held research positions at Trinity Hall, Cambridge, and the Università degli Studi di Ferrara (funded by the Leverhulme Trust): his published work includes articles on French and Italian nineteenth-century opera and literature (for example in the *Cambridge Opera Journal*, the *Journal of the Royal Musical Association*, and the *Guardian*) and contributions to various collections of essays. He currently lectures at the University of Ulster.

Eugene O'Brien is senior lecturer, Head of the Department of English Language and Literature and director of the MIC Irish Studies Centre in Mary Immaculate College, Limerick. His publications include: *The Question of Irish Identity in the Writings of William Butler Yeats and James Joyce* (1998): *Examining Irish Nationalism in the Context of Literature, Culture and Religion: A Study of the Epistemological Structure of Nationalism* (2002): *Seamus Heaney – Creating Irelands of the Mind* (2002): *Seamus Heaney and the Place of Writing* (2003): *Seamus Heaney: Searches for Answers* (2003). He co-edited: *La France et la Mondialisation/France and the Struggle against Globalization* (2007): *Reinventing Ireland through a French Prism* (2007) and *Modernity and*

Postmodernity in a Franco-Irish Context (2008). His current book, *'Kicking Bishop Brennan Up the Arse': Negotiating Texts and Contexts in Contemporary Irish Studies,* will be published by Peter Lang in 2009.

Catherine Rees is a lecturer in Drama at Loughborough University. Her major research interest is the plays of Martin McDonagh as well as other contemporary Irish and 20th Century British dramatists, specifically plays focusing on questions of nationalism, gender, postcolonialism and postmodernity. She is also interested in the interdisciplinary connections between Theatre Studies and Cultural Geography, particularly in relation to representations of place on the stage and site-specific performance. Other research interest areas include theatrical protest and censorship, trauma studies and dark tourism as well as the protest murals of Northern Ireland.

Elisabetta Viggiani is a graduate of La Sapienza University, Rome, where she studied English language and literature. After completing an MA in Irish Studies, working on public forms of memorialisation for the victims of the Troubles, she is currently undertaking a PhD at Queen's University, Belfast on the politics of commemoration in Northern Ireland.

Index

Carysfort Press was formed in the summer of 1998. It receives annual funding from the Arts Council.

The directors believe that drama is playing an ever-increasing role in today's society and that enjoyment of the theatre, both professional and amateur, currently plays a central part in Irish culture.

The Press aims to produce high quality publications which, though written and/or edited by academics, will be made accessible to a general readership. The organisation would also like to provide a forum for critical thinking in the Arts in Ireland, again keeping the needs and interests of the general public in view.

The company publishes contemporary Irish writing for and about the theatre.

Editorial and publishing inquiries to:
Carysfort Press Ltd., 58 Woodfield, Scholarstown Road, Rathfarnham, Dublin 16, Republic of Ireland.

T (353 1) 493 7383
F (353 1) 406 9815
e: info@carysfortpress.com
www.carysfortpress.com

HOW TO ORDER

TRADE ORDERS DIRECTLY TO:
CMD/BookSource
55A Spruce Avenue,
Stillorgan Industrial Park
Blackrock,
Co. Dublin

T: (353 1) 294 2560
F: (353 1) 294 2564
E: cmd@columba.ie

INDIVIDUAL ORDERS DIRECTLY TO:
eprint Ltd.
35 Coolmine Industrial Estate,
Blanchardstown, Dublin 15.

T: (353 1) 827 8860
F: (353 1) 827 8804
Order online @ www.carysfortpress.com

FOR SALES IN NORTH AMERICA AND CANADA:
Dufour Editions Inc.,
124 Byers Road, PO Box 7,
Chester Springs, PA 19425,
USA

T: 1-610-458-5005
F: 1-610-458-7103

Ireland's Economic Crisis - Time to Act
Essays from over 40 leading Irish thinkers at the MacGill Summer School 2009

Eds. Joe Mulholland and Finbarr Bradley

Ireland's economic crisis requires a radical transformation in policymaking. In this volume, political, industrial, academic, trade union and business leaders and commentators tell the story of the Irish economy and its rise and fall. Contributions at Glenties range from policy, vision and context to practical suggestions on how the country can emerge from its crisis.

ISBN 978-1-904505-43-3 (2009) €20

Deviant Acts: Essays on Queer Performance

Ed. David Cregan

This book contains an exciting collection of essays focusing on a variety of alternative performances happening in contemporary Ireland. While it highlights the particular representations of gay and lesbian identity it also brings to light how diversity has always been a part of Irish culture and is, in fact, shaping what it means to be Irish today.

ISBN 978-1-904505-42-6 (2009) €20

Seán Keating in Context: Responses to Culture and Politics in Post-Civil War Ireland

Compiled, edited, and introduced by Éimear O'Connor

Irish artist Seán Keating has been judged by his critics as the personification of old-fashioned traditionalist values. This book presents a different view. The story reveals Keating's early determination to attain government support for the visual arts. It also illustrates his socialist leanings, his disappointment with capitalism, and his attitude to cultural snobbery, to art critics, and to the Academy. Given the national and global circumstances nowadays, Keating's critical and wry observations are prophetic – and highly amusing.

ISBN   978-1-904505-41-9   €25

Dialogue of the Ancients of Ireland: A new translation of Acallam na Senorach

Translated with introduction and notes by Maurice Harmon

One of Ireland's greatest collections of stories and poems, The Dialogue of the Ancients of Ireland is a new translation by Maurice Harmon of the 12th century *Acallam na Senorach*. Retold in a refreshing modern idiom, the *Dialogue* is an extraordinary account of journeys to the four provinces by St. Patrick and the pagan Cailte, one of the surviving Fian. Within the frame story are over 200 other stories reflecting many genres – wonder tales, sea journeys, romances, stories of revenge, tales of monsters and magic. The poems are equally varied – lyrics, nature poems, eulogies, prophecies, laments, genealogical poems. After the *Tain Bo Cuailnge*, the *Acallam* is the largest surviving prose work in Old and Middle Irish.

ISBN: 978-1-904505-39-6 (2009)   €20

Literary and Cultural Relations between Ireland and Hungary and Central and Eastern Europe

Ed. Maria Kurdi

This lively, informative and incisive collection of essays sheds fascinating new light on the literary interrelations between Ireland, Hungary, Poland, Romania and the Czech Republic. It charts a hitherto under-explored history of the reception of modern Irish culture in Central and Eastern Europe and also investigates how key authors have been translated, performed and adapted. The revealing explorations undertaken in this volume of a wide array of Irish dramatic and literary texts, ranging from *Gulliver's Travels* to *Translations* and *The Pillowman*, tease out the subtly altered nuances that they acquire in a Central European context.

ISBN: 978-1-904505-40-2 (2009)   €20

Plays and Controversies: Abbey Theatre Diaries 2000-2005

by Ben Barnes

In diaries covering the period of his artistic directorship of the Abbey, Ben Barnes offers a frank, honest, and probing account of a much commented upon and controversial period in the history of the national theatre. These diaries also provide fascinating personal insights into the day to day pressures, joys, and frustrations of running one of Ireland's most iconic institutions.

ISBN: 978-1-904505-38-9 (2008)   €35

Interactions: Dublin Theatre Festival 1957-2007. Irish Theatrical Diaspora Series: 3

Eds. Nicholas Grene and Patrick Lonergan with Lilian Chambers

For over 50 years the Dublin Theatre Festival has been one of Ireland's most important cultural events, bringing countless new Irish plays to the world stage, while introducing Irish audiences to the most important international theatre companies and artists. Interactions explores and celebrates the achievements of the renowned Festival since 1957 and includes specially commissioned memoirs from past organizers, offering a unique perspective on the controversies and successes that have marked the event's history. An especially valuable feature of the volume, also, is a complete listing of the shows that have appeared at the Festival from 1957 to 2008.

ISBN: 978-1-904505-36-5   €25

The Informer: A play by Tom Murphy based on the novel by Liam O'Flaherty

The Informer, Tom Murphy's stage adapatation of Liam O'Flaherty's novel, was produced in the 1981 Dublin Theatre Festival, directed by the playwright himself, with Liam Neeson in the leading role. The central subject of the play is the quest of a character at the point of emotional and moral breakdown for some souce of meaning or identity. In the case of Gypo Nolan, the informer of the title, this involves a nightmarish progress through a Dublin underworld in which he changes from a Judas figure to a scapegoat surrogate for Jesus, taking upon himself the sins of the world. A cinematic style, with flash-back and intercut scenes, is used rather than a conventional theatrical structure to catch the fevered and phantasmagoric progression of Gypo's mind. The language, characteristically for Murphy, mixes graphically colloquial Dublin slang with the haunted intricacies of the central character groping for the meaning of his own actions. The dynamic rhythm of the action builds towards an inevitable but theatrically satisfying tragic catastrophe. ' [The Informer] is , in many ways closer to being an original Murphy play than it is to O'Flaherty...' Fintan O'Toole.

ISBN: 978-1-904505-37-2 (2008)   €10

Shifting Scenes: Irish theatre-going 1955-1985

Eds. Nicholas Grene and Chris Morash

Transcript of conversations with John Devitt, academic and reviewer, about his lifelong passion for the theatre. A fascinating and entertaining insight into Dublin theatre over the course of thirty years provided by Devitt's vivid reminiscences and astute observations.

ISBN: 978-1-904505-33-4 (2008)   €10

Irish Literature: Feminist Perspectives

Eds Patricia Coughlan and Tina O'Toole

The collection discusses texts from the early 18th century to the present. A central theme of the book is the need to renegotiate the relations of feminism with nationalism and to transact the potential contest of these two important narratives, each possessing powerful emancipatory force. Irish Literature: Feminist Perspectives contributes incisively to contemporary debates about Irish culture, gender and ideology.

ISBN: 978-1-904505-35-8 (2008)   €25

Silenced Voices: Hungarian Plays from Transylvania

selected and translated by Csilla Bertha and Donald E. Morse

The five plays are wonderfully theatrical, moving fluidly from absurdism to tragedy, and from satire to the darkly comic. Donald Morse and Csilla Bertha's translations capture these qualities perfectly, giving voice to the 'forgotten playwrights of Central Europe'. They also deeply enrich our understanding of the relationship between art, ethics, and politics in Europe.

ISBN: 978-1-904505-34-1 (2008)   €25

A Hazardous Melody of Being: Seóirse Bodley's Song Cycles on the poems of Micheal O'Siadhail

Ed. Lorraine Byrne Bodley

This apograph is the first publication of Bodley's O'Siadhail song cycles and is the first book to explore the composer's lyrical modernity from a number of perspectives. Lorraine Byrne Bodley's insightful introduction describes in detail the development and essence of Bodley's musical thinking, the European influences he absorbed which linger in these cycles, and the importance of his work as a composer of the Irish art song.

ISBN: 978-1-904505-31-0 (2008)   €25

Irish Theatre in England: Irish Theatrical Diaspora Series: 2

Eds. Richard Cave and Ben Levitas

Irish theatre in England has frequently illustrated the complex relations between two distinct cultures. How English reviewers and audiences interpret Irish plays is often decidedly different from how the plays were read in performance in Ireland. How certain Irish performers have chosen to be understood in Dublin is not necessarily how audiences in London have perceived their constructed stage personae. Though a collection by diverse authors, the twelve essays in this volume investigate these issues from a variety of perspectives that together chart the trajectory of Irish performance in England from the mid-nineteenth century till today.

ISBN: 978-1-904505-26-6 (2007)   €20

Goethe and Anna Amalia: A Forbidden Love?

By Ettore Ghibellino, Trans. Dan Farrelly

In this study Ghibellino sets out to show that the platonic relationship between Goethe and Charlotte von Stein – lady-in-waiting to Anna Amalia, the Dowager Duchess of Weimar – was used as part of a cover-up for Goethe's intense and prolonged love relationship with the Duchess Anna Amalia herself. The book attempts to uncover a hitherto closely-kept state secret. Readers convinced by the evidence supporting Ghibellino's hypothesis will see in it one of the very great love stories in European history – to rank with that of Dante and Beatrice, and Petrarch and Laura.

ISBN: 978-1-904505-24-2 €20

Ireland on Stage: Beckett and After

Eds. Hiroko Mikami, Minako Okamuro, Naoko Yagi

The collection focuses primarily on Irish playwrights and their work, both in text and on the stage during the latter half of the twentieth century. The central figure is Samuel Beckett, but the contributors freely draw on Beckett and his work provides a springboard to discuss contemporary playwrights such as Brian Friel, Frank McGuinness, Marina Carr and Conor McPherson amongst others. Contributors include: Anthony Roche, Hiroko Mikami, Naoko Yagi, Cathy Leeney, Joseph Long, Noreem Doody, Minako Okamuro, Christopher Murray, Futoshi Sakauchi and Declan Kiberd

ISBN: 978-1-904505-23-5 (2007) €20

'Echoes Down the Corridor': Irish Theatre - Past, Present and Future

Eds. Patrick Lonergan and Riana O'Dwyer

This collection of fourteen new essays explores Irish theatre from exciting new perspectives. How has Irish theatre been received internationally - and, as the country becomes more multicultural, how will international theatre influence the development of drama in Ireland? These and many other important questions.

ISBN: 978-1-904505-25-9 (2007) €20

Musics of Belonging: The Poetry of Micheal O'Siadhail

Eds. Marc Caball & David F. Ford

An overall account is given of O'Siadhail's life, his work and the reception of his poetry so far. There are close readings of some poems, analyses of his artistry in matching diverse content with both classical and innovative forms, and studies of recurrent themes such as love, death, language, music, and the shifts of modern life.

ISBN: 978-1-904505-22-8 (2007) €25 (Paperback)
ISBN: 978-1-904505-21-1 (2007) €50 (Casebound)

Brian Friel's Dramatic Artistry: 'The Work has Value'

Eds Donald E. Morse, Csilla Bertha and Maria Kurdi

Brian Friel's Dramatic Artistry presents a refreshingly broad range of voices: new work from some of the leading English-speaking authorities on Friel, and fascinating essays from scholars in Germany, Italy, Portugal, and Hungary. This book will deepen our knowledge and enjoyment of Friel's work.

ISBN: 978-1-904505-17-4 (2006) €30

The Theatre of Martin McDonagh: 'A World of Savage Stories'

Eds. Lilian Chambers and Eamonn Jordan

The book is a vital response to the many challenges set by McDonagh for those involved in the production and reception of his work. Critics and commentators from around the world offer a diverse range of often provocative approaches. What is not surprising is the focus and commitment of the engagement, given the controversial and stimulating nature of the work.

ISBN: 978-1-904505-19-8 (2006) €35

Edna O'Brien: New Critical Perspectives

Eds. Kathryn Laing, Sinead Mooney and Maureen O'Connor

The essays collected here illustrate some of the range, complexity, and interest of Edna O'Brien as a fiction writer and dramatist…They will contribute to a broader appreciation of her work and to an evolution of new critical approaches, as well as igniting more interest in the many unexplored areas of her considerable oeuvre.

ISBN: 978-1-904505-20-4 (2006) €20

Irish Theatre on Tour

Eds. Nicholas Grene and Chris Morash

'Touring has been at the strategic heart of Druid's artistic policy since the early eighties. Everyone has the right to see professional theatre in their own communities. Irish theatre on tour is a crucial part of Irish theatre as a whole'. Garry Hynes

ISBN 978-1-904505-13-6 (2005) €20

Poems 2000-2005 by Hugh Maxton

Poems 2000-2005 is a transitional collection written while the author – also known to be W. J. Mc Cormack, literary historian – was in the process of moving back from London to settle in rural Ireland.

ISBN 978-1-904505-12-9 (2005) €10

Synge: A Celebration

Ed. Colm Tóibín

A collection of essays by some of Ireland's most
creative writers on the work of John Millington Synge, featuring Sebastian Barry , Marina Carr,
Anthony Cronin, Roddy Doyle, Anne Enright, Hugo Hamilton, Joseph O'Connor, Mary O'Malley,
Fintan O'Toole, Colm Toibin, Vincent Woods.

ISBN 978-1-904505-14-3 (2005) €15

East of Eden: New Romanian Plays

Ed. Andrei Marinescu

Four of the most promising Romanian playwrights, young and very young, are in this
collection, each one with a specific way of seeing the Romanian reality, each one with a style
of communicating an articulated artistic vision of the society we are living in. Ion Caramitru,
General Director Romanian National Theatre Bucharest.

ISBN 978-1-904505-15-0 (2005) €10

George Fitzmaurice: 'Wild in His Own Way', Biography of an Irish Playwright

by Fiona Brennan

Fiona Brennan's...introduction to his considerable output allows us a much greater
appreciation and understanding of Fitzmaurice, the one remaining under-celebrated genius
of twentieth-century Irish drama. Conall Morrison

ISBN 978-1-904505-16-7 (2005) €20

Out of History: Essays on the Writings of Sebastian Barry

Ed. Christina Hunt Mahony

The essays address Barry's engagement with the contemporary cultural debate in Ireland and
also with issues that inform postcolonial criticial theory. The range and selection of
contributors has ensured a high level of critical expression and an insightful assessment of
Barry and his works.

ISBN: 978-1-904505-18-1 (2005) €20

Three Congregational Masses by Seoirse Bodley

'From the simpler congregational settings in the Mass of Peace and the Mass of Joy to the
richer textures of the Mass of Glory, they are immediately attractive and accessible, and with a
distinctively Irish melodic quality.' Barra Boydell

ISBN: 978-1-904505-11-2 (2005) €15

Georg Büchner's Woyzeck, A new translation

by Dan Farrelly

The most up-to-date German scholarship of Thomas Michael Mayer and Burghard Dedner has finally made it possible to establish an authentic sequence of scenes. The widespread view that this play is a prime example of loose, open theatre is no longer sustainable. Directors and teachers are challenged to "read it again".

ISBN: 978-1-904505-02-0 (2004)   €10

Playboys of the Western World: Production Histories

Ed. Adrian Frazier

'The book is remarkably well-focused: half is a series of production histories of Playboy performances through the twentieth century in the UK, Northern Ireland, the USA, and Ireland. The remainder focuses on one contemporary performance, that of Druid Theatre, as directed by Garry Hynes. The various contemporary social issues that are addressed in relation to Synge's play and this performance of it give the volume an additional interest: it shows how the arts matter.' Kevin Barry

ISBN: 978-1-904505-06-8 (2004)   €20

The Power of Laughter: Comedy and Contemporary Irish Theatre

Ed. Eric Weitz

The collection draws on a wide range of perspectives and voices including critics, playwrights, directors and performers. The result is a series of fascinating and provocative debates about the myriad functions of comedy in contemporary Irish theatre. Anna McMullan

As Stan Laurel said, it takes only an onion to cry. Peel it and weep. Comedy is harder. These essays listen to the power of laughter. They hear the tough heart of Irish theatre – hard and wicked and funny. Frank McGuinness

ISBN: 978-1-904505-05-1 (2004)   €20

Sacred Play: Soul-Journeys in contemporary Irish Theatre

by Anne F. O'Reilly

'Theatre as a space or container for sacred play allows audiences to glimpse mystery and to experience transformation. This book charts how Irish playwrights negotiate the labyrinth of the Irish soul and shows how their plays contribute to a poetics of Irish culture that enables a new imagining. Playwrights discussed are: McGuinness, Murphy, Friel, Le Marquand Hartigan, Burke Brogan, Harding, Meehan, Carr, Parker, Devlin, and Barry.'

ISBN: 978-1-904505-07-5 (2004)   €25

The Irish Harp Book

by Sheila Larchet Cuthbert

This is a facsimile of the edition originally published by Mercier Press in 1993. There is a new preface by Sheila Larchet Cuthbert, and the biographical material has been updated. It is a collection of studies and exercises for the use of teachers and pupils of the Irish harp.

ISBN: 978-1-904505-08-2 (2004)   €35

The Drunkard by Tom Murphy

'The Drunkard is a wonderfully eloquent play. Murphy's ear is finely attuned to the glories and absurdities of melodramatic exclamation, and even while he is wringing out its ludicrous overstatement, he is also making it sing.' The Irish Times

ISBN: 978-1-904505-09-9 (2004)   €10

Goethe: Musical Poet, Musical Catalyst

Ed. Lorraine Byrne

'Goethe was interested in, and acutely aware of, the place of music in human experience generally - and of its particular role in modern culture. Moreover, his own literary work - especially the poetry and Faust - inspired some of the major composers of the European tradition to produce some of their finest works.' Martin Swales

ISBN: 978-1-904505-10-5 (2004)   €40

The Theatre of Marina Carr: "Before rules was made"

Eds. Anna McMullan & Cathy Leeney

As the first published collection of articles on the theatre of Marina Carr, this volume explores the world of Carr's theatrical imagination, the place of her plays in contemporary theatre in Ireland and abroad and the significance of her highly individual voice.

ISBN: 978-0-9534257-7-8 (2003)   €20

Critical Moments: Fintan O'Toole on Modern Irish Theatre

Eds. Julia Furay & Redmond O'Hanlon

This new book on the work of Fintan O'Toole, the internationally acclaimed theatre critic and cultural commentator, offers percussive analyses and assessments of the major plays and playwrights in the canon of modern Irish theatre. Fearless and provocative in his judgements, O'Toole is essential reading for anyone interested in criticism or in the current state of Irish theatre.

ISBN: 978-1-904505-03-7 (2003)   €20

Goethe and Schubert: Across the Divide

Eds. Lorraine Byrne & Dan Farrelly

Proceedings of the International Conference, 'Goethe and Schubert in Perspective and Performance', Trinity College Dublin, 2003. This volume includes essays by leading scholars – Barkhoff, Boyle, Byrne, Canisius, Dürr, Fischer, Hill, Kramer, Lamport, Lund, Meikle, Newbould, Norman McKay, White, Whitton, Wright, Youens – on Goethe's musicality and his relationship to Schubert; Schubert's contribution to sacred music and the Lied and his setting of Goethe's Singspiel, Claudine. A companion volume of this Singspiel (with piano reduction and English translation) is also available.

ISBN: 978-1-904505-04-4 (2003)   €25

Goethe's Singspiel, 'Claudine von Villa Bella'

set by Franz Schubert

Goethe's Singspiel in three acts was set to music by Schubert in 1815. Only Act One of Schuberts's Claudine score is extant. The present volume makes Act One available for performance in English and German. It comprises both a piano reduction by Lorraine Byrne of the original Schubert orchestral score and a bilingual text translated for the modern stage by Dan Farrelly. This is a tale, wittily told, of lovers and vagabonds, romance, reconciliation, and resolution of family conflict.

ISBN: 978-0-9544290-0-3 (2002)   €20

Theatre of Sound, Radio and the Dramatic Imagination

by Dermot Rattigan

An innovative study of the challenges that radio drama poses to the creative imagination of the writer, the production team, and the listener.

"A remarkably fine study of radio drama – everywhere informed by the writer's professional experience of such drama in the making…A new theoretical and analytical approach – informative, illuminating and at all times readable." Richard Allen Cave

ISBN: 978- 0-9534-257-5-4 (2002)   €20

Talking about Tom Murphy

Ed. Nicholas Grene

Talking About Tom Murphy is shaped around the six plays in the landmark Abbey Theatre Murphy Season of 2001, assembling some of the best-known commentators on his work: Fintan O'Toole, Chris Morash, Lionel Pilkington, Alexandra Poulain, Shaun Richards, Nicholas Grene and Declan Kiberd.

ISBN: 978-0-9534-257-9-2 (2002)   €15

Hamlet: The Shakespearean Director

by Mike Wilcock

"This study of the Shakespearean director as viewed through various interpretations of HAMLET is a welcome addition to our understanding of how essential it is for a director to have a clear vision of a great play. It is an important study from which all of us who love Shakespeare and who understand the importance of continuing contemporary exploration may gain new insights."

From the Foreword, by Joe Dowling, Artistic Director, The Guthrie Theater, Minneapolis, MN

ISBN: 978-1-904505-00-6 (2002) €20

The Theatre of Frank Mc Guinness: Stages of Mutability

Ed. Helen Lojek

The first edited collection of essays about internationally renowned Irish playwright Frank McGuinness focuses on both performance and text. Interpreters come to diverse conclusions, creating a vigorous dialogue that enriches understanding and reflects a strong consensus about the value of McGuinness's complex work.

ISBN: 978-1904505-01-3. (2002) €20

Theatre Talk: Voices of Irish Theatre Practitioners

Eds Lilian Chambers and Ger Fitzgibbon

"This book is the right approach - asking practitioners what they feel." Sebastian Barry, Playwright

"... an invaluable and informative collection of interviews with those who make and shape the landscape of Irish Theatre." Ben Barnes, Artistic Director of the Abbey Theatre

ISBN: 978-0-9534-257-6-1 (2001) €20

In Search of the South African Iphigenie

by Erika von Wietersheim and Dan Farrelly

Discussions of Goethe's "Iphigenie auf Tauris" (Under the Curse) as relevant to women's issues in modern South Africa: women in family and public life; the force of women's spirituality; experience of personal relationships; attitudes to parents and ancestors; involvement with religion.

ISBN: 978-0-9534257-8-5 (2001) €10

'The Starving' and 'October Song': Two contemporary Irish plays

by Andrew Hinds

The Starving, set during and after the siege of Derry in 1689, is a moving and engrossing drama of the emotional journey of two men.

October Song, a superbly written family drama set in real time in pre-ceasefire Derry.

ISBN: 978-0-9534-257-4-7 (2001) €10

Seen and Heard: Six new plays by Irish women

Ed. Cathy Leeney

A rich and funny, moving and theatrically exciting collection of plays by Mary Elizabeth Burke-Kennedy, Síofra Campbell, Emma Donoghue, Anne Le Marquand Hartigan, Michelle Read and Dolores Walshe.

ISBN: 978-0-9534-257-3-0 (2001) €20

Theatre Stuff: Critical essays on contemporary Irish theatre

Ed. Eamonn Jordan

Best selling essays on the successes and   debates of contemporary Irish theatre at home and abroad.

Contributors include: Thomas Kilroy, Declan Hughes, Anna McMullan, Declan Kiberd, Deirdre Mulrooney, Fintan O'Toole, Christopher Murray, Caoimhe McAvinchey and Terry Eagleton.

ISBN: 978-0-9534-2571-1-6 (2000) €20

Under the Curse. Goethe's "Iphigenie Auf Tauris", A New Version

by Dan Farrelly

The Greek myth of Iphigenie grappling with the curse on the house of Atreus is brought vividly to life. This version is currently being used in Johannesburg to explore problems of ancestry, religion, and Black African women's spirituality.

ISBN: 978-09534-257-8-5 (2000) €10

Urfaust, A New Version of Goethe's early "Faust" in Brechtian Mode

by Dan Farrelly

This version is based on Brecht's irreverent and daring re-interpretation of the German classic.

"Urfaust is a kind of well-spring for German theatre... The love-story is the most daring and the most profound in German dramatic literature." Brecht

ISBN: 978-0-9534-257-0-9 (1998) €20